BEAT
BOBBY
FLAY

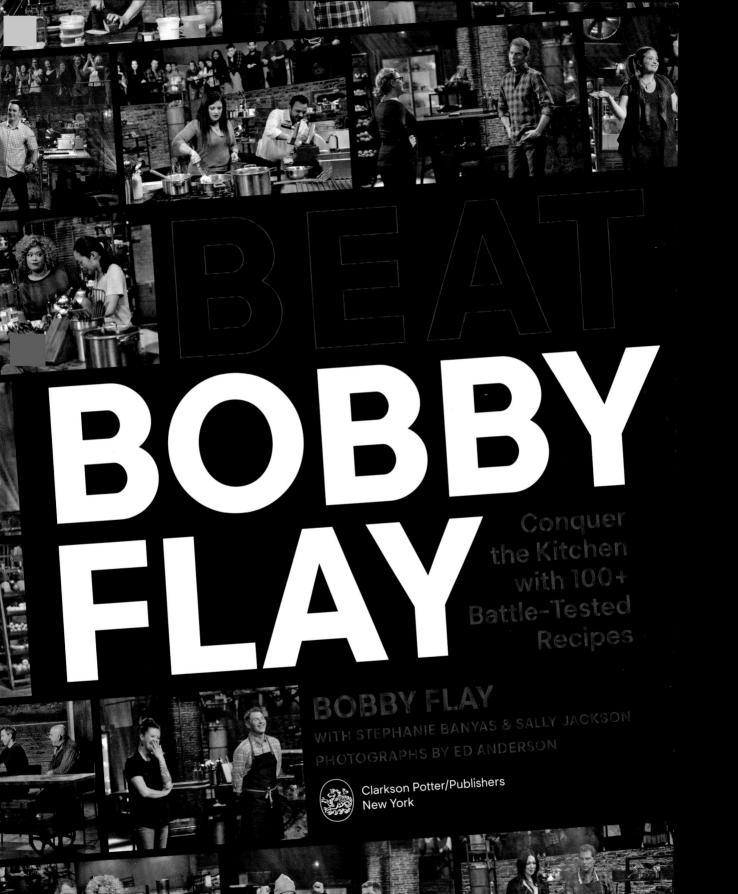

BEAT
BOBBY
FLAY

Conquer
the Kitchen
with 100+
Battle-Tested
Recipes

BOBBY FLAY

WITH STEPHANIE BANYAS & SALLY JACKSON

PHOTOGRAPHS BY ED ANDERSON

Clarkson Potter/Publishers
New York

CONTENTS

INTRODUCTION

How did *Beat Bobby Flay* come about? I get asked that question often, and there really isn't one single answer. Instead, it's a product of many factors: past events and current shows, but overwhelmingly, my desire to showcase chefs who might never otherwise get a chance at national recognition. Plus, it satisfies viewers' never-ending appetite for competitive cooking shows.

Beat also fulfills a need for me to continue my culinary evolution: from a young chef trying to get his name and food known in the city of New York, to a chef on TV who started out as the cohost of arguably one of the worst-made food television shows in history, called *Grillin' & Chillin'* (yeah, it was bad), to one who made his mark by grilling every imaginable ingredient known in the world on countless versions of outdoor cookery shows like *Boy Meets Grill* and *Grill It!* From there I jumped from the heat of the grill to a guerilla-style competition show called *Throwdown!*—a show that was more fun than hard-core competition—then finally landed on the mighty planet of *Iron Chef America*. Those iterations of the professional Bobby Flay all had one thing in common: I cooked. Cooking is the engine that wakes me every day, and always excites me for the next act of transformation to take place in my kitchen. Whether it's in one of my restaurants, at home, or on one of my shows, I need to be cooking—and if I'm not, it's never going to be my best day.

I'm a lucky guy. I get to sharpen my skills in any environment. Working the line in my restaurants has always been an amazing training course, so when I'm trying to put together dozens of dishes under the gun of the running clock on *Iron Chef*, I have the confidence to get to the finish line. It's practical experience that works both in my restaurant life and under the bright, hot lights of the competition shows.

Beat Bobby Flay is my latest stage, and it's one I'm ready and willing to share with any chef who wants it. Let's get a few things out of the way: As of 2020, we'd shot about 500 episodes, which means close to 500 chefs have come through the *Beat* arena. Like any competition show, we always face the question of whether the judging is rigged or fixed in any way. I can tell you honestly and truthfully it is 100 percent legit. If it weren't, there would be a lot of chefs who lost yelling and screaming "fixed," something you don't hear because it's not true. People point out to me all the time that I never lose. Well, those people clearly don't watch that often! The bottom line is that I win about 65 to 70 percent of the time.

Winning and losing is not the point of *Beat Bobby Flay*, but because the audience likes finality, and it is TV after all, we have to do it. If it were up to me, we'd just cook, taste each other's dishes, and share a cocktail and a high five before going home. That wouldn't rate very well, though, so we have to have a winner.

I created this show because it allows me to do the two things I love most: cooking and hanging out with my friends. (The third thing is dancing, which only happens occasionally on the show—lucky for you.) Yes, I want to win every time, but I'm actually thrilled when I lose. It's great for the show, every one of the 150-person production staff is happy (they all root against me), and, most important, it's fantastic for the chef who wins and his or her community. It creates a lot of local media for the chef, and they have giant viewing parties in their hometowns so all their family, friends, and customers can gather together to watch them slay Bobby Flay.

For me personally, the show also allows me to continue my quest to learn all I can about cultures that are not my own. I always say, if you want to learn about particular people, eat their food. It tells a story rich in history and flavor. I have my go-to cuisines that I'm most comfortable with because of my thirty-five years of experience cooking them in my restaurants, including Southwestern American, Mediterranean, and my most recent culinary passions, Spanish and Italian cuisines. Because of a show I shot twenty years ago for Food Network, called *FoodNation*, I got to travel all over America, and I'm fairly comfortable with my knowledge of regional cooking in most corners of the country as a result. I also have certain ingredients and techniques that I use to get me out of jams when I'm a little confused by what I'm supposed to be doing. You'll see these secret (or not-so-secret) weapons often: fresh and dried chiles (including Calabrian chiles from Southern Italy), anchovies, bacon, tons of butter to finish sauces, and blackberries, coconut, and caramel for desserts. I'll make any rice dish crispy and will be sure to finish dishes with enough acidity, like lemon, lime, or vinegar. Most judges love that.

My classic weaknesses are well documented: sweet dishes, desserts, or anything that has to be measured and includes butter, sugar, flour, and eggs, like pastries, cakes, and pies. I do eke out a surprising victory here and there with desserts, but it's usually because the pastry chef took it easy on me with their choice of dish or I wowed the judges with a coconut garnish or something unexpected like that.

Dishes from most Asian countries always give me trouble. I love the cuisines from places like Korea, Japan, China, and Southeast Asia, especially the Philippines, but finding the correct balance of all the flavors oftentimes proves problematic for me. That said, I'm a little better at things like wrapping dumplings and creating delicious dipping sauces than I was before this show was born.

As I said, I play to win every time and I always try my hardest. Not a single chef who's come into our arena would want me to lie down and hand them a victory just for show. They all want to see me walk out of my own kitchen a loser thanks to their hands and skills. It's an amazing moment for them to throw their arms up in victory, with sweat dripping off their forehead and a giant smile filling their face as they let America know their name and exclaim with the verve of a world heavyweight champion..."I JUST BEAT BOBBY FLAY!"

IN IT TO WIN IT!

Wanna be a winner in the kitchen? Here are my top 10 tips.

1 × Be organized. Have all of your ingredients in place.

2 × Season every step of the way with salt and pepper and taste each time.

3 × Use high heat. When you only have 45 minutes to create an entire dish, start to finish, cooking on low is not an option. Also, the only way to get great color and flavor on food is to get a great sear; you are not going to get a sear on low heat.

4 × Use cast-iron skillets for a great sear on steaks, burgers, chicken, and Crispy Rice (page 243).

5 × Use nonstick pans to cook eggs and fish.

6 × Use honey to balance flavor, not to sweeten dishes.

7 × Homemade stock makes all the difference. You control the flavor and the salt level, and the natural gelatin in the bones will create a thick sauce with body.

8 × Always make sure there is a contrast of textures— chewy, crispy, crunchy, smooth.

9 × Add a touch of acid to balance or brighten a dish—a squeeze of citrus, a splash of vinegar, or a dollop of yogurt.

10 × Whenever possible, add an egg!

BOBBY'S PANTRY & SPECIAL EQUIPMENT

PANTRY

There is a huge pantry (both dry and cold) available for my competitors and me to use during every *Beat Bobby Flay* battle. There are whole and ground spices and chiles, assorted oils and vinegars, flours, chocolates, liqueurs and liquor, and every condiment known to man- and womankind—not to mention dairy products, meats, fruits, and vegetables.

At the beginning of each season, I am allowed to submit a list of my favorite items that must be available to me (and also to my competitors, if they would like to use them) for every battle.

Though my list for the show is pages and pages long—because who knows what dish the day will hold?—I have narrowed it down here to only the items you'll need to cook from this book. While some may be new additions to your current pantry, I hope you'll keep reaching for them and they'll become staples in your cooking like they are in mine.

SPICES

Bay leaves

Black peppercorns

Fennel seeds

Garlic powder

Ground coriander

Ground cumin

Hot smoked Spanish paprika

Kosher salt

Madras mild curry powder

Onion powder

Pink peppercorns

Sweet smoked Spanish paprika

Sweet Spanish paprika

CHILES
Whole, Dried, Ground, Pastes & Sauces

Ají amarillo paste

Anchos

Calabrian chile paste

Calabrian red chile flakes

Canned chipotle peppers in adobo sauce

Cascabel chiles

Chiles de árbol

Chipotle powder

Chipotles

Frank's RedHot sauce

Gochujang

Guajillos

Habanero powder

Harissa

New Mexico chiles

Sriracha

Tabasco hot sauce

NUTS

Blanched almonds

Blanched hazelnuts

Pecans

Pine nuts

Walnuts

GRAINS & BEANS

Arborio rice

Calasparra rice

Canned black beans

Canned chickpeas

Carolina long-grain rice

Dried pasta

Instant polenta

Jasmine rice

SWEETENERS

Clover honey

Grenadine

Molasses

Pomegranate molasses

Pure maple syrup

Sorghum syrup

ALCOHOL

Bourbon

Dark rum

OIL, VINEGAR & MORE

Aged sherry vinegar

Canola oil

Cider vinegar

Dijon mustard

Extra-virgin olive oil (my fave kind)

Ketchup

Low-sodium chicken stock/broth

Maesri Thai green curry paste

Maesri Thai red curry paste

Mayonnaise

Red wine vinegar

Rice vinegar

Soy sauce

Unsweetened coconut milk

White wine vinegar

Whole-grain mustard

Yuzu juice

BAKING

All-purpose flour

Baking powder

Baking soda

Bittersweet chocolate (66% cacao)

Dark brown muscovado sugar

Dutch-process cocoa powder

Graham crackers

Light brown muscovado sugar

Milk chocolate

Powdered sugar

Pure cane sugar

Pure vanilla extract

Quinoa flour

Rice flour

Unsweetened chocolate

Vanilla beans

COLD PANTRY
Freezer & Refrigerator

Bacon (both thick-cut and thin-cut)

Chicken thighs (bone-in, skin-on or boneless)

Chorizo

Crème fraîche

Fresh chiles

Fresh herbs

Greek yogurt

Heavy cream

Lemons

Limes

Oranges

Pearl onions

Peas

Unsalted butter

Whole milk

SPECIAL EQUIPMENT

A well-stocked kitchen for someone who cooks often should be filled with several sizes of heavy-duty pots and pans, both stainless steel and nonstick. You should have measuring cups and metal spatulas, wooden spoons, ladles, sieves, rubber spatulas, a chef's knife, a paring knife, a serrated knife, and wooden and plastic cutting boards. With those basics, you can cook most things, but for some of the recipes in the book, you will also need a few specialty items listed below.

Cast-iron skillet

Deep fryer (or a Dutch oven)

Deep-fry thermometer: *It's very important to know that your oil is at the proper temperature for frying. You will also use this when making sugar syrups.*

Enamel-coated cast-iron Dutch oven: *I recommend having a 5-quart and a 7-quart.*

Food mill

Food processor

Heavy-duty stand mixer

Instant-read thermometer: *the only way to truly know the internal temperature of meat*

Large stockpot: *for stocks, soups, and pasta*

Pasta machine

Pressure cooker: *My favorite brand is Sitram. If you want to cook braised meats like I do on Beat Bobby Flay, you will need this piece of equipment.*

Sheet pans

Spider strainer

Wire racks

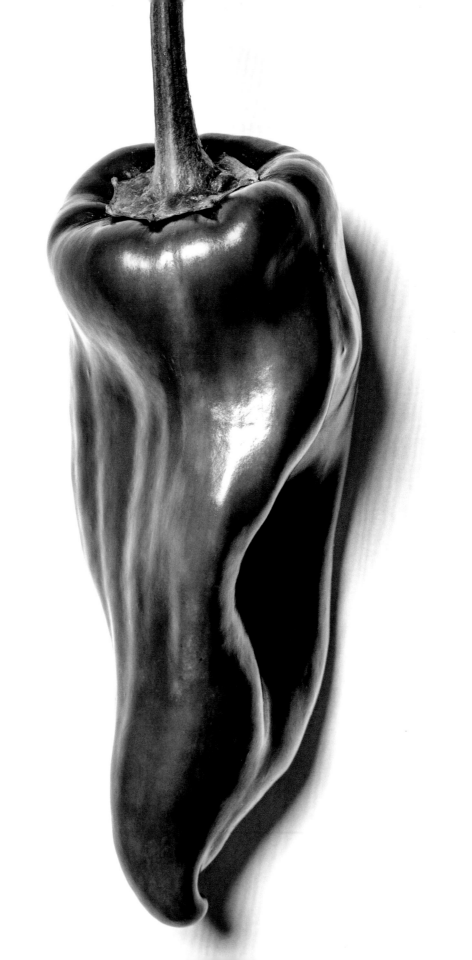

VEGETABLES

Tortelloni Filled with Sweet Potato & Mushroom with Brown Butter Sauce & Hazelnut Pecorino ✳ **17**

Ric Orlando's Luscious Lacy Latkes with Chipotle Applesauce, Chive Crema & Smoked Salmon ✳ **19**

Pumpkin Red Curry with Seafood ✳ **22**

Mushroom & Goat Cheese Chiles Rellenos with Smoked Red Pepper Sauce ✳ **25**

Carolina Veggie Burger with Smoked Gouda & Dijon-Scallion Slaw ✳ **27**

Eggplant Rollatini with Anchovy Bread Crumbs ✳ **31**

Vegetable Chili with Cumin-Lime Yogurt & Avocado-Shishito Relish ✳ **32**

Falafel with Mango-Cucumber Relish, Feta-Yogurt Dip & Spicy Red Pepper Tahini ✳ **35**

Manish Tyagi's Palak Paneer ✳ **38**

Chris Henry's Fried Green Tomato Sandwiches with Pimento Cheese ✳ **41**

EPISODE 906: *"Ladies Night"*
COMPETITOR: Jennifer Jasinski
DISH: Tortelloni
WINNER: Bobby Flay

TORTELLONI FILLED WITH SWEET POTATO & MUSHROOM

with Brown Butter Sauce & Hazelnut Pecorino

SERVES 4

¾ pound sweet potatoes (2 large or 3 medium), peeled and cubed

Kosher salt

4 tablespoons canola oil

2 tablespoons clover honey

1 large shallot, finely diced

8 ounces cremini mushrooms, stems discarded, caps thinly sliced

Freshly ground black pepper

½ cup skinless hazelnuts, toasted (see page 247) and finely chopped

⅓ cup freshly grated Pecorino Romano cheese

Pasta Dough (page 235), rested

Egg wash: 1 egg beaten with 1 tablespoon water until frothy

2 sticks (16 tablespoons) unsalted butter

2 tablespoons chopped fresh sage

2 tablespoons finely chopped fresh chives

There are some battle dishes that are especially intimidating to hear announced—this was one of them. Making homemade tortelloni is tricky, *especially* when it's something you don't do every day. I wished I had 4 hours instead of 45 minutes to make the pasta, compose the filling, and roll and form each one before saucing them in that brown butter deliciousness—let's just say I heard the tick of every second on the clock. That said, this dish has become a favorite in my house, especially in the fall. Word to the wise: Hazelnuts lose their freshness quickly. Before you use them in your recipe, give one or two a taste to make sure they're not rancid.

1. Put the sweet potatoes in a large saucepan, add cold water to cover by 2 inches, and season with 2 tablespoons salt. Bring to a boil and cook until tender, about 12 minutes. Drain well.

2. Heat 2 tablespoons of the oil in a large sauté pan over high heat until shimmering. Add the sweet potatoes and cook until golden brown and caramelized on both sides, about 2 minutes per side. Transfer to a large bowl, add the honey, and mash with a potato masher.

3. Heat the remaining 2 tablespoons oil in another large sauté pan over high heat. Add the shallot and cook until soft, about 3 minutes. Add the mushrooms and cook until golden brown and soft and their liquid has evaporated, about 9 minutes. Season with salt and pepper.

4. Add the mushrooms to the mashed sweet potato and let cool before filling the pasta. (The filling can be made 1 day in advance and stored, tightly covered, in the refrigerator. Bring to room temperature before filling the pasta.)

5. Mix together the hazelnuts and pecorino in a small bowl and season with salt and pepper. Set aside.

continued >

6. Roll out the pasta dough as directed. Cut 3-inch rounds from the pasta sheets and make sure they are lightly floured so as not to stick to the work surface. Place a heaping teaspoon of the filling in the center of each round and, using a pastry brush, brush well with egg wash around the edges. Fold in half to make a half-moon. Bring the two corners together with a little bit of egg wash and press firmly to make the traditional tortelloni shape.

7. Bring a large pot of water to a boil and add 2 tablespoons salt.

8. When the water is a few minutes away from coming to a boil, add the butter to a large deep sauté pan over high heat and cook until the butter turns a nutty brown color, 5 to 8 minutes. It is important to time this well, because if the butter has browned and the pasta is not cooked yet, it will continue to cook in the pan and become too dark and bitter. If your butter is at the perfect color but your pasta is not ready to be cooked yet, immediately transfer the brown butter to a bowl to stop the cooking.

9. When the pasta water has come to a boil, add the tortelloni and cook until they rise to the top, then cook for 20 seconds longer. Immediately remove with a slotted spoon, put directly into the butter sauce, and cook over low heat, gently stirring or tossing, for 1 minute until just heated through. Add the sage and season with salt and pepper.

10. Divide the pasta among pasta bowls and sprinkle with the hazelnut-pecorino mixture and the chives.

RIC ORLANDO'S LUSCIOUS LACY LATKES

with Chipotle Applesauce, Chive Crema & Smoked Salmon

SERVES 4 TO 6

8 medium-large russet potatoes (about 4 pounds), peeled

1 large Spanish onion

2 tablespoons grated fresh horseradish

Kosher salt and freshly ground black pepper

3 large eggs, beaten

⅔ to ¾ cup cornstarch, depending on how wet the batter is

2 cups duck fat, for frying, plus more as needed

Chive Crema (recipe follows)

Chipotle Applesauce (recipe follows)

8 ounces smoked salmon, flaked into bite-size pieces

"The Coliseum. The Cage. WWF. That is where my mind went when I was selected to compete on *Beat Bobby Flay*. Cooking competition shows are intense and the time flies by like a flash of lightning, but I really relished the experience. It brought out both the inner rock-and-roller and jock in me. I certainly wanted to entertain, to get the crowd dancing and cheering, and of course I wanted to win. During the final judging, I was calm—at first. My dish was the first the judges tasted. It first got raves, but then I received the feedback on the applesauce. Maneet Chauhan, who has an amazing palate, commented that I would have been better off if I had served only the one latke with the salmon. Suddenly, I had a sick feeling in the pit of my stomach. When Bobby's latkes were tasted, my confidence returned, as all three judges noted that the latkes themselves left something to be desired. When I was pronounced the winner, I smiled big. I expected to win, and I did." **—RIC ORLANDO**

1. Grate 6 of the potatoes on the large holes of a box grater or in a food processor fitted with the large grater disc. Grate the onion the same way and combine them with the potato in a large bowl.

2. Using a mandoline, julienne the remaining 2 potatoes into thin strips. Add to the grated potato-onion mixture. Add the horseradish and season with salt and pepper, leaning a bit toward salty. Pour the beaten eggs over the potato-onion mixture and stir to combine. Sprinkle on the cornstarch a little at time and combine until completely incorporated.

3. Fill a large heavy skillet with ½ inch of duck fat. Heat over medium heat until shimmering. (You want your duck fat hot enough to brown, but not so hot that the latkes cook too fast and burn. Test for heat by dropping a small amount of the potato mixture into the duck fat. If it sizzles, the fat is ready.)

continued >

4. Take some of the mixture—about ¼ cup packed—in your hand. Toss it gently and carefully up and down like you're a pitcher getting ready to pitch. After five or six tosses, it will begin to get rounder and rounder. When it is round and tight, place it carefully in the duck fat. Repeat to form a few more latkes, being careful not to overcrowd the pan. Allow the latkes to cook on one side (they should still be round), until they are fully golden, 4 to 5 minutes on each side, then use a spatula to flip each latke and *now* press them down until they are about ½ inch thick. Monitor your heat, making sure the duck fat is not too hot but hot enough to keep the pan-frying going. Cook until golden brown and crispy and transfer to a sheet pan. Repeat with the remaining mixture. (Latkes can be reheated in a 350°F oven for 5 minutes.)

5. To serve, place 2 lakes on each plate. Spread the top of the latkes with a little chive crema. Top one latke with a heaping tablespoon of chipotle applesauce and the other with a piece of smoked salmon.

Chive Crema

✻ MAKES ABOUT 3½ CUPS

¼ cup buttermilk

½ cup packed chopped fresh dill fronds

¼ cup chopped fresh chives, plus more for garnish

1 teaspoon grated lemon zest

3 cups sour cream

Pinch of kosher salt

Combine the buttermilk, dill, chives, and lemon zest in a blender and blend until smooth and green. Transfer the mixture to a medium bowl. Fold in the sour cream and season with the salt and garnish with more chives. Cover and refrigerate for at least 30 minutes and up to 2 days. (Use leftover crema as a dip for fresh vegetables.)

Chipotle Applesauce

✻ MAKES ABOUT 1 CUP

2 pounds sweet red apples (about 6), such as Empire, Macoun, or Red Delicious, stemmed left whole

Kosher salt

1 dried chipotle chile

Pure cane sugar or pure maple syrup, if needed

1. Put the apples in a large nonreactive saucepan and add cold water to cover by 2 inches. Add a pinch of salt and the chile and bring to a boil. Reduce the heat to simmer, cover, and cook until the apples collapse and are very soft, about 20 minutes.

2. Using a slotted spoon, remove the apples in batches and transfer to a food mill set over a large bowl. Process until smooth. Repeat with the remaining apples until all of the pulp has been run through the food mill. Discard the solids in the food mill and the cooking liquid.

3. Season the purée with a pinch of salt and cane sugar for additional sweetness, if desired. The applesauce can be made up to 3 days in advance and stored, tightly covered, in the refrigerator. Bring to room temperature before serving.

SERVES 4

Canola oil

1 large Spanish onion, coarsely chopped

2-inch piece fresh ginger, peeled and chopped

5 garlic cloves, coarsely chopped

Kosher salt and freshly ground black pepper

1 teaspoon ground allspice

1 heaping teaspoon ground cinnamon

1 teaspoon ground ginger

¼ teaspoon freshly grated nutmeg

2 tablespoons Thai red curry paste

1 cup canned unsweetened pumpkin purée

1 (13.5-ounce) can unsweetened full-fat coconut milk

2 cups Shrimp Stock (page 234) or store-bought low-sodium vegetable stock

1 large sweet potato, peeled and cut into ½-inch dice

1 small eggplant, peeled and diced (optional)

12 large shrimp, peeled and deveined

2 teaspoons sweet smoked Spanish paprika

Clover honey (optional)

Pomegranate molasses (optional)

1 cup jumbo lump crabmeat, picked over

PUMPKIN RED CURRY with Seafood

Pumpkin and Thai curry are two of my favorite things. Here, it's not just the pumpkin I love but the warm, familiar spices that transform the shrimp and crabmeat into a bowl of bold and intensely delicious flavors. Coconut milk balances that boldness with its calm, rich touch. This might be a Thanksgiving appetizer for me this year.

1. Heat 3 tablespoons of oil in a large Dutch oven over high heat until shimmering. Add the onion and fresh ginger and cook until soft, about 5 minutes. Add the garlic and cook for 1 minute longer. Season with salt and pepper.

2. Add the allspice, cinnamon, ground ginger, and nutmeg and cook, stirring constantly, for 1 minute. Add the curry paste and pumpkin purée and cook, stirring constantly, until some of the rawness is cooked out, about 5 minutes.

3. Add the coconut milk, bring to a boil, and cook until reduced by half, about 7 minutes. Stir in the stock, bring to a boil, then reduce the heat to medium and cook, stirring occasionally, until the flavors meld and the sauce reduces slightly, about 30 minutes.

4. Meanwhile, bring 4 cups water to a boil in a medium saucepan. Add 1 teaspoon salt and the sweet potato and cook until just tender, about 12 minutes. Drain well and transfer to a plate.

5. Heat 3 tablespoons of oil in a large sauté pan over high heat until shimmering. Add the eggplant in an even layer and cook until the bottom is golden brown, about 4 minutes. Turn the eggplant over and season with salt and pepper. Continue cooking until the bottom is golden brown, about 4 minutes longer. Remove the eggplant with a slotted spoon to a plate.

6. Add 2 tablespoons oil to the pan and heat until shimmering. Add the sweet potato, season with salt and pepper, and cook until lightly golden brown on both sides, about 2 minutes per side. Remove to the plate with the eggplant.

7. Wipe out the pan that you cooked the eggplant and sweet potato in. Add 2 tablespoons of oil and heat over high heat until shimmering. In a medium bowl, season the shrimp with salt, pepper, and the smoked paprika and toss well to coat. Cook the shrimp until golden brown on both sides, about 1½ minutes per side. Remove to the plate with the eggplant and sweet potato.

Finely grated zest and juice of 2 limes

¼ cup chopped fresh cilantro leaves

COCONUT RELISH

½ cup Toasted Coconut (page 247), made with sweetened shredded or flaked coconut

½ cup hulled pumpkin seeds, toasted

¼ cup coarsely crushed blue corn tortilla chips

½ cup pomegranate seeds

FOR SERVING

½ cup crema or crème fraîche

✻ **IN IT TO WIN IT:** To get the most intense flavor, the spices and spice pastes must be toasted in the oil. The spices bloom in oil and the rawness get cooked out of the paste.

8. Working in batches if needed, transfer the curry to a blender and carefully blend until smooth, then return it to the pot. Taste the curry and season with salt and pepper; if too spicy, add honey and pomegranate molasses to taste. Add the crab, shrimp, eggplant, and sweet potato and cook until just heated through, about 1 minute. Add the lime zest, lime juice, and cilantro.

9. Make the coconut relish: Combine the coconut, pumpkin seeds, and tortilla chips in a bowl. Just before serving, fold in the pomegranate seeds.

10. To serve: Ladle the curry into bowls, garnish with the coconut relish, and drizzle with the crema.

SERVES 6

SPECIAL EQUIPMENT
Six 6-inch skewers

3 tablespoons canola oil

6 large shiitake mushrooms, stems discarded, caps thinly sliced

8 ounces cremini mushrooms, stems discarded, caps thinly sliced

5 garlic cloves, mashed to a paste with ¼ teaspoon kosher salt

Kosher salt and freshly ground black pepper

4 ounces coarsely grated Monterey Jack cheese

4 ounces soft goat cheese, crumbled

¼ cup chopped fresh cilantro leaves

6 large poblano peppers, roasted (see page 240)

2 cups rice flour

1 cup ice water

2 cups white or yellow cornmeal

¼ pound Brussels sprouts

6 cups peanut oil

Smoked Red Pepper Sauce (recipe follows), for serving

MUSHROOM & GOAT CHEESE CHILES RELLENOS
with Smoked Red Pepper Sauce

I have used chile peppers in every iteration possible during my thirty years cooking in the kitchen of Mesa Grill, my contemporary Southwest American restaurant. Green chiles, particularly poblanos, are a great choice for stuffing. I've always served chiles rellenos as the dedicated vegetarian entrée for the restaurant, changing the fillings to reflect the seasons.

I was so happy to have Perrey Reeves on this episode. I played her "boyfriend" on *Entourage* in its final season on HBO. I think it's safe to say my try at acting landed me right back where I belong . . . in the kitchen!

1. Heat the canola oil in a large sauté pan over high heat until shimmering. Add the shiitakes and creminis and cook until golden brown and soft and their liquid has evaporated, about 12 minutes. Add the garlic, cook for 1 minute longer, and season with salt and pepper. Transfer to a large plate and let cool.

2. Transfer the cooled mushrooms to a large bowl and stir in the Monterey Jack, goat cheese, and cilantro. Season with salt and pepper. (The filling can be made up to 2 days in advance and stored, tightly covered, in the refrigerator.)

3. Remove the filling from the refrigerator 30 minutes before filling roasted peppers (this ensures the filling is not too cold and will cook through by the time the outside of the pepper is cooked). Divide the filling among the peppers, compressing it into the shape of each one (the roasted pepper is very delicate and may begin to tear but will be fine). Thread a skewer through the middle of the pepper, making sure not to spill the filling, to keep the whole pepper intact.

continued >

4. Place 1 cup of the rice flour on a plate and season with salt and pepper. Whisk together the remaining 1 cup rice flour and the ice water in a bowl until smooth. Put the cornmeal in a medium baking dish or plate and season with salt and pepper. Dredge the filled pepper completely in the dry flour and tap off any excess. Dip the pepper into the rice batter and allow the excess to drain off. Dredge the pepper in the cornmeal. Set aside and repeat with the remaining peppers.

5. Cut off the stem ends of the Brussels sprouts and peel off the leaves until you get to the hard part and can't peel off any more.

6. Line a sheet pan with paper towels. Pour 4 inches of peanut oil into a deep fryer or large Dutch oven and heat over medium heat to 365°F on a deep-fry thermometer.

7. Working in batches, fry the Brussels sprout leaves until crispy and golden brown, about 15 seconds. Drain on the paper towels and season with salt.

8. Working in batches, add the peppers to the oil and fry, turning gently, until lightly browned, about 4 minutes. Drain on the paper towels and season with a bit of salt while hot.

9. To serve, ladle sauce into the center of each plate and place a chile relleno on top. Garnish with the Brussels sprout leaves. Serve immediately.

Smoked Red Pepper Sauce

✖ MAKES ABOUT 1¼ CUPS

1 (12-ounce) can or jar piquillo peppers, drained

2 tablespoons red wine vinegar

1 canned chipotle pepper in adobo sauce, plus 1 teaspoon of the adobo

1 teaspoon sweet smoked Spanish paprika

2 teaspoons clover honey

Kosher salt and freshly ground black pepper

¼ cup canola oil

Combine the peppers, vinegar, chipotle pepper, adobo sauce, smoked paprika, honey, and salt and black pepper to taste in a blender and blend until combined. With the machine running, slowly add the oil and blend until emulsified. Taste for seasoning and add more salt and pepper as desired. The sauce will keep, tightly covered, in the refrigerator for up to 3 days.

EPISODE 1105:
"You Won't Like Him When He's Angry"
COMPETITOR: Daniel Angerer
DISH: Veggie burgers
WINNER: Bobby Flay

CAROLINA VEGGIE BURGER
with Smoked Gouda & Dijon-Scallion Slaw

This veggie burger is part of Bobby's Burger Palace lore. Despite cries from my loyal customers, our early menus never included a veggie burger. To be honest, I didn't like the idea because I had never found one I thought was great. Well, leave it to the *Beat Bobby Flay* contenders to force me out of my comfort zone! I want to thank Chef Angerer for pushing my limits . . . and my doubts, because guess what? As it turned out, I made a pretty good one. Good enough, in fact, for this veggie burger to become a happy part of BBP's everyday menu.

SERVES 6

1 (15.5-ounce) can chickpeas, rinsed and drained

Kosher salt

1 cup white or tricolor (red, black, and white) quinoa

2 tablespoons canola oil, plus more for frying

1 pound cremini mushrooms, stems discarded, caps sliced about ¼ inch thick

Freshly ground black pepper

Scant ½ cup Bobby's Barbecue Sauce (page 239) or your favorite BBQ sauce

½ cup chopped fresh cilantro leaves

3 large eggs

2 cups quinoa flour

6 slices smoked cheese, such as Gouda, American, or cheddar

6 soft sesame seed burger buns, insides scooped out, lightly toasted

Dijon-Scallion Slaw (recipe follows)

1. Preheat the oven to 200°F.

2. Line a sheet pan with paper towels, spread the chickpeas on the towels, and let dry for at least 15 minutes. Remove the paper towels and discard. Transfer the sheet pan to the oven and allow the chickpeas to dry out for 15 minutes. Let cool at room temperature for 10 minutes. Transfer to a food processor and pulse until just coarsely chopped; do not purée them.

3. Combine 2 cups cold water and 1 teaspoon salt in a medium saucepan and bring to a boil over high heat. Stir in the quinoa and bring to a boil again. Reduce the heat to medium-low, cover, and cook until the quinoa is tender and the water is absorbed, about 18 minutes. Remove from the heat and let rest, covered, for 5 minutes before fluffing with a fork.

4. Spread the quinoa in a single layer on a small sheet pan. Fluff with a fork to separate the grains and let cool to room temperature. (The quinoa can be made a day ahead and stored, tightly covered, in the refrigerator.)

5. While the quinoa is cooking, heat the oil in a large sauté pan over high heat until the oil begins to shimmer. Add the mushrooms and cook until golden brown and dry, about 9 minutes; season with salt and pepper to taste. Add the barbecue sauce and a splash of water to deglaze the pan and cook until the mushrooms are glazed, about 2 minutes. Transfer to a large plate and let cool to room temperature.

6. Combine the mushrooms, quinoa, and chopped chickpeas in a large bowl. Add the cilantro and taste for seasoning, adding more

continued >

salt and pepper if needed. (Remember that all the components have been seasoned and the breading will be seasoned, too.) Cover the mixture and refrigerate until chilled, at least 2 hours and up to 24 hours.

7. Line a plate with paper towels and set it near the stove. Pour 2 inches oil into a deep cast-iron skillet or sauté pan and heat over medium heat to 375°F on a deep-fry thermometer.

8. Using a 3-inch ring mold, form the quinoa mixture into 6 burgers (about 6 ounces each). Whisk the eggs with a splash of water in a shallow baking dish and season with salt and pepper. Put the quinoa flour into another shallow baking dish and season with salt and pepper.

9. Using a fish spatula, dip a burger patty into the egg mixture to coat, then gently remove and let any excess egg drip off. Dredge the patty in the flour mixture and tap off any excess. Working in batches, transfer the coated patties to the hot oil and fry until golden brown and crispy on the bottom, about 4 minutes. Flip over and fry until the bottoms are golden brown, about 4 minutes longer. Transfer to the paper towels to drain and immediately top each with a slice of cheese. Repeat with the remaining patties.

10. Place each burger on the bottom of a toasted bun. Top each with a heaping spoonful of the slaw, some of the slaw dressing, and the top half of the bun. Serve immediately, with the remaining slaw on the side.

Dijon-Scallion Slaw

✖ **MAKES ABOUT 2 CUPS**

Whisk both mustards, the honey, vinegar, onion, salt, and pepper in a large bowl until smooth. Add the cabbage and scallions and toss well to coat. Cover and refrigerate for least 30 minutes and up to 8 hours to allow the cabbage to soften and the flavors to meld.

¼ cup Dijon mustard

¼ cup whole-grain mustard

2 tablespoons clover honey

1 tablespoon red wine vinegar

2 tablespoons finely grated Spanish onion (use the next-to-finest holes on a box grater)

¼ teaspoon kosher salt

¼ teaspoon freshly ground black pepper

¼ head red cabbage, finely shredded

¾ cup thinly sliced scallions, green tops and pale-green parts only

EPISODE 1802: *"Knighted Sir Loin"*
COMPETITOR: *Tracey Shepos Cenami*
DISH: *Eggplant rollatini*
WINNER: *Bobby Flay*

SERVES 4

3 medium eggplants, cut lengthwise into twelve ½-inch-thick slices

8 tablespoons extra-virgin olive oil

Kosher salt and freshly ground black pepper

1 medium Spanish onion, finely diced

5 garlic cloves, mashed to a paste with ¼ teaspoon kosher salt

1 (28-ounce) can peeled whole tomatoes, undrained

1 to 2 tablespoons Calabrian chile paste, to taste

12 fresh basil leaves, torn into pieces, plus more (optional) for serving

16 ounces whole-milk ricotta cheese

1 large egg, lightly beaten

4 ounces fresh mozzarella cheese, cut into small dice

¾ cup freshly grated Pecorino Romano cheese

3 tablespoons finely chopped fresh flat-leaf parsley

1 tablespoon finely chopped fresh oregano

4 ounces low-moisture whole-milk mozzarella, coarsely grated

Anchovy Bread Crumbs (page 245), for serving

EGGPLANT ROLLATINI
with Anchovy Bread Crumbs

This is a terrific Sunday-night, dished-out-from-the-center-of-the-dinner-table, friends-who-are-family kind of meal. Eggplant rollatini is vegetarian but doesn't feel that way. I always utilize eggplant for my non-meat-eating friends; it's so hearty and savory, and it works so well in this case. You'll have to leave off the bread crumb topping if you're cooking for strict vegetarians, but if not, you have to go for it. Anchovies have become a theme in my cooking—their salty, savory touch does all the right things. In this case, they meet up with their crunchy friend—panko bread crumbs—to create a punch of salty, delicious texture.

1. Preheat the oven to 400°F.

2. Arrange the eggplant in an even layer on two sheet pans. Brush both sides with 6 tablespoons of the oil and season with salt and pepper. Roast until lightly golden brown and very tender, about 25 minutes. Remove from the oven and let cool. (The eggplant can be cooked up to 1 day in advance, cooled, and stored, covered, in the refrigerator.) Reduce the oven temperature to 375°F.

3. Meanwhile, make the sauce: Heat the remaining 2 tablespoons oil in a large Dutch oven over high heat until shimmering. Add the onion and cook until soft, about 4 minutes. Add the garlic and cook for 1 minute longer. Add the tomatoes with their juices and season with salt and pepper. Bring to a boil and cook until the tomatoes begin to soften, about 10 minutes. Crush the tomatoes with a potato masher. Add the chile paste and basil and cook the sauce until it thickens, stirring occasionally, about 25 minutes. Season with salt and pepper.

4. Make the filling: Mix together the ricotta, egg, diced mozzarella, and ¼ cup of the pecorino in a medium bowl until combined. Season with salt and pepper and fold in the parsley and oregano.

5. Ladle 1 cup of the sauce into the bottom of a 9 × 13-inch baking dish. Spread 2 tablespoons of the cheese filling over each eggplant slice. Carefully roll up and place them, seam-side down, in the baking dish. Once all the eggplant rolls are in the dish, ladle another cup of the sauce evenly over them and sprinkle the grated mozzarella and remaining ½ cup pecorino over the top.

6. Bake until the sauce is bubbling and the cheese has melted and turned lightly golden brown, about 20 minutes. Sprinkle the bread crumbs over the top and garnish with torn basil, if desired.

SERVES 4 TO 6

8 tablespoons canola oil

1 large Spanish onion, finely diced

6 garlic cloves, mashed to a paste with ¼ teaspoon kosher salt

2 teaspoons ancho chile powder

2 teaspoons New Mexico chile powder

1 teaspoon guajillo chile powder

1 teaspoon chipotle powder

1 teaspoon ground coriander

1 teaspoon ground cumin

2 tablespoons tomato paste

1 (12-ounce) bottle dark beer

1 (35-ounce) can peeled whole plum tomatoes, undrained

Kosher salt and freshly ground black pepper

1 tablespoon finely chopped fresh oregano leaves

3 large portobello mushrooms, stems discarded, caps cut into ½-inch dice

6 cups ½-inch-diced peeled eggplant (1 large or 2 medium)

1 (15.5-ounce) can black beans, rinsed and drained

¼ cup chopped fresh cilantro leaves

2 scallions, green tops and pale-green parts only, thinly sliced

1 tablespoon clover honey

Cumin-Lime Yogurt (recipe follows)

Avocado-Shishito Relish (recipe follows)

ingredients continued >

VEGETABLE CHILI
with Cumin-Lime Yogurt & Avocado-Shishito Relish

I'm going to be honest; I wasn't excited when I heard "vegetarian chili" announced as the secret dish. I mean, if you're gonna make chili, let's get some meat in the pot, right? Well, I stand corrected. I substituted eggplant and mushrooms, both meaty vegetables, for the beef or lamb I normally would have reached for, and it worked—and I mean *really* worked. The vegetables held up in texture while truly absorbing the other flavors. Call me convinced and converted: Vegetable chili is a winner.

1. Heat 3 tablespoons of the oil in a large Dutch oven over high heat until shimmering. Add the onion and cook until soft, about 4 minutes. Add the garlic and cook for 1 minute longer. Add all of the chile powders, the coriander, and cumin. Cook, stirring constantly, until the spices are fragrant and deepen in color, about 2 minutes. Stir in the tomato paste and cook for 1 minute. Add the beer and cook until the mixture is reduced by about half, about 5 minutes.

2. Add the tomatoes and their juices and cook until the tomatoes begin to soften and break down, about 15 minutes. Using a potato masher or wooden spoon, coarsely mash the tomatoes. Season with salt and pepper and stir in the oregano. Cook until the sauce starts to thicken, about 20 minutes.

3. While the sauce is cooking, heat 2 tablespoons of the oil in a large cast-iron skillet over high heat. Add the mushrooms and cook, stirring a few times, until golden brown and their liquid has evaporated, about 10 minutes. Season with salt and pepper and transfer to a large bowl.

4. Return the skillet to the heat and add the remaining 3 tablespoons oil. Working in batches, add the eggplant in a single layer, season with salt and pepper, and cook, stirring a few times, until golden brown and soft, about 10 minutes. Add the eggplant, mushrooms, and black beans to the tomato sauce and stir to combine. Cook for 15 minutes to meld the flavors and thicken the mixture. Stir in the cilantro and scallions and season with the honey, salt, and pepper.

continued >

½ cup coarsely grated queso blanco

¼ cup finely grated Cotija cheese

Fried tortillas strips or crumbled tortilla chips, for garnish (optional)

1 cup 2% Greek yogurt

Finely grated zest and juice of 1 lime

½ teaspoon ground cumin

Kosher salt and freshly ground black pepper

1 tablespoon canola oil

7 shishito peppers

Kosher salt and freshly ground black pepper

Avocado Relish (page 240; omit the chiles)

✳ **IN IT TO WIN IT:** Whether it's vegetarian or meat-based, great chili is all about layers of flavor and good texture. I hit the texture point with meaty veggies and layered in flavor with all the same ingredients I add to my meat chilis: chiles, beer, onions, and garlic.

5. Ladle the chili into bowls, top with a dollop of the cumin-lime yogurt and avocado-shishito relish, a sprinkle of the queso blanco and Cotija cheeses, and some tortilla chips, if desired.

Cumin-Lime Yogurt

✳ MAKES 1 CUP

Whisk together the yogurt, lime zest, lime juice, and cumin in a small bowl. Season with salt and pepper. Cover and refrigerate for at least 30 minutes and up to 24 hours before serving.

Avocado–Shishito Relish

✳ MAKES ABOUT 1 QUART

1. Heat the oil in a large cast-iron or nonstick skillet over high heat until shimmering. Add the shishitos, season with salt and pepper, and cook until charred on both sides, about 2 minutes per side. Transfer to a cutting board, let cool for a few minutes, then finely dice.

2. Make the avocado relish in a large bowl, then gently fold in the diced shishitos to combine. The relish can be made up to 4 hours in advance, tightly covered, and refrigerated.

SERVES 6

2 cups dried chickpeas, soaked overnight

½ cup packed fresh parsley leaves

½ cup packed fresh cilantro leaves

¼ cup packed chopped fresh dill fronds

2 small scallions, green tops and pale-green parts only, coarsely chopped

1 jalapeño or serrano chile, coarsely chopped

½ small Spanish onion, coarsely chopped

6 garlic cloves, coarsely chopped

Finely grated zest and juice of 1 lemon

2 teaspoons baking powder

Kosher salt

2 teaspoons ground coriander

2 teaspoons ground cumin

½ teaspoon chile de árbol powder

Canola oil, for deep-frying

Spicy Red Pepper Tahini (recipe follows)

Mango-Cucumber Relish (recipe follows)

Feta-Yogurt Dip (recipe follows)

Pita chips, for serving

Pickled Red Onions (page 248, optional)

Fresh herbs, for garnish (optional)

FALAFEL
with Mango-Cucumber Relish, Feta-Yogurt Dip & Spicy Red Pepper Tahini

I had so much fun losing this one. Anne Burrell, the most competitive member of my family of cohosts, and supermodel and super lady Gigi Hadid really took me down in this battle. Anne never lets me breathe when she's in the house, and Gigi has apparently been a falafel-making expert since her childhood—an exhausting if thoroughly amusing combination. I don't remember much about the cooking part except that my falafel were a little misshapen, but all the flavors were delicious together. I stand by the flavor, and think with a little more time on the clock and less noise from the peanut gallery, the form will follow suit. I'll get you one day, Burrell!

1. Drain the chickpeas, then rinse and drain again. Transfer to a sheet pan lined with paper towels and let sit until dry, about 15 minutes.

2. Combine the parsley, cilantro, dill, scallions, and jalapeño in a food processor and pulse until the herbs are coarsely chopped. Add the chickpeas, onion, garlic, lemon zest, lemon juice, baking powder, 2 teaspoons salt, the coriander, cumin, and chile de árbol. Process until the mixture just comes together and is green but not overly smooth or puréed; it should have some texture. Cover and refrigerate for at least 30 minutes and up to 24 hours to allow the flavors to meld. (You can fry the falafel balls immediately, but allowing the chickpea mixture to rest improves the flavor and helps keep them together when frying.)

3. When ready to fry, line a sheet pan with parchment paper. Use a medium 2-tablespoon ice cream scoop or a spoon to scoop out a portion of the chickpea mixture, then use your hands to shape it into a ball. Put the ball on the lined pan. Repeat with the remaining mixture.

4. Line another sheet pan with a few layers of paper towels. Pour 4 inches of oil into a large Dutch oven and heat over medium heat to 365°F on a deep-fry thermometer.

5. Working in batches, fry the balls until deep golden brown and crispy, about 3 minutes. Transfer with a slotted spoon to the paper towels to drain and season with salt.

continued >

6. To serve, spread some of the spicy red pepper tahini on dinner plates. Put some of the mango-cucumber relish off to one side. Place the feta-yogurt dip, sprinkled with pomegranate seeds, on another side. Place 3 falafel in the center. Arrange pita chips in the feta dip and garnish with pickled red onions and fresh herbs, if desired.

Spicy Red Pepper Tahini

✖ MAKES ABOUT 1½ CUPS

1 (12-ounce) jar piquillo peppers, drained well

½ cup tahini

Juice of 1 lemon

2 tablespoons harissa

½ teaspoon sweet smoked Spanish paprika

1 tablespoon clover honey

Kosher salt and freshly ground black pepper

Combine the piquillos, tahini, lemon juice, harissa, smoked paprika, and honey in a food processor and process until smooth. Add a few splashes of water to thin out (it should be the texture of heavy cream) and season with salt and pepper. The sauce will keep, tightly covered, in the refrigerator for up to 2 days.

Mango-Cucumber Relish

✖ MAKES ABOUT 3 CUPS

1 small mango, finely diced

½ English cucumber, finely diced

Juice of ½ lemon

¼ cup Pickled Shallots (page 248), drained and chopped, plus more for garnish

¼ cup chopped fresh mint leaves

Kosher salt and freshly ground black pepper

Combine the mango, cucumber, lemon juice, pickled shallots, and mint in a medium bowl and season with salt and pepper and garnish with more picked shallots. Let sit at room temperature for at least 15 minutes before serving. The relish can be made up to 8 hours in advance and stored, tightly covered; do not add the mint until just before serving.

Feta-Yogurt Dip

✖ MAKES ABOUT 2 CUPS

1 cup 2% Greek yogurt

½ cup crumbled feta cheese

Kosher salt and freshly ground black pepper

2 tablespoons pomegranate molasses

½ cup pomegranate seeds, for garnish

Stir together the yogurt and feta in a small bowl and season with salt and pepper. Swirl the pomegranate molasses into the dip. Refrigerate, tightly covered, for at least 30 minutes and up to 1 day before serving. Garnish with the pomegranate seeds just before serving.

SERVES 6

Kosher salt

16 ounces baby spinach

6 tablespoons ghee or neutral oil

1 tablespoon cumin seeds

9 garlic cloves, chopped

½ small Spanish onion, finely diced

2 fresh Thai green chiles, finely chopped, or 2 teaspoons finely chopped jalapeño or serrano chile

1-inch piece fresh ginger, peeled and chopped

2 tablespoons ground fenugreek

1 tablespoon pav bhaji masala (see Note)

2 teaspoons turmeric

¼ cup chopped fresh tomato

18 slices (⅛ inch thick) paneer cheese (each slice should be 3 × 2 inches)

⅓ cup grated white cheddar cheese

Spiced Tomato Sauce (recipe follows)

Roti (recipe follows)

✖ **NOTE:** Pav bhaji masala is a blend of dry-roasted Kashmiri chiles, coriander, cumin, fennel seeds, cloves, cinnamon, cardamom, mango powder, and black sea salt—it can be found in specialty shops or online.

MANISH TYAGI'S PALAK PANEER

"I chose this method—a layered version of palak paneer, almost like a spinach lasagna—because it is a very unique way of making the classic Indian dish. Paneer does not have much flavor compared to other cheeses, so to make it more interesting, I cut it into thin slices and layered it with sautéed spinach. The spiced tomato sauce gives it another winning dimension, loading flavor into each bite. The judges agreed!"
—MANISH TYAGI

1. Fill a large bowl with ice and water. Bring a large pot of water to a boil and add 2 tablespoons salt. Add the spinach, in batches, and blanch for 1 minute. Transfer with tongs to the ice bath and let cool, about 5 minutes. Drain well and squeeze to remove excess water. Finely chop and set aside.

2. Heat the ghee in a large, deep, heavy-bottomed sauté pan over medium heat until shimmering. Add the cumin seeds and cook until they begin to pop, 1 to 2 minutes. Add the garlic and cook until lightly golden brown, about 1 minute. Add the onion, chiles, and ginger and cook until soft, about 4 minutes. Stir in the fenugreek, masala, and turmeric and cook for 1 minute longer. Add the chopped tomato and cook until the mixture thickens, about 5 minutes. Add the cooked spinach and cook for 3 minutes longer. Season with salt.

3. Preheat the oven to 450°F. Line a sheet pan with parchment paper or foil.

4. Arrange 6 slices of the paneer on the prepared sheet pan, leaving a few inches between the slices. Top each slice with some of the spinach mixture, then top with another slice of the paneer and more of the spinach mixture. Place the remaining slices of paneer on top to make 6 three-layer pieces. Top with the cheddar. Bake until the paneer is slightly puffed and heated through and the cheddar is golden brown and bubbling, about 25 minutes.

5. To serve, ladle some of the spiced tomato sauce onto a dinner plate and top with one serving of the spinach paneer. Serve with more sauce and roti on the side.

continued >

3 tablespoons ghee
or neutral oil

2 tablespoons finely grated
fresh ginger

3 garlic cloves, mashed to a
paste with ¼ teaspoon
kosher salt

1 tablespoon deggi mirch
(see Note)

4 cups chopped fresh tomatoes

Scant ¼ cup chopped unsalted
roasted cashews

1 tablespoon crushed
fenugreek leaves

2 tablespoons clover honey

3 tablespoons unsalted butter

3 tablespoons heavy cream

Kosher salt

✱ **NOTE:** Deggi mirch, a distinctive Indian spice made from a blend of colorful red peppers and Kashmiri red chiles, adds a mild heat and a deep red-orange color to soups, tandoori chicken, and other traditional dishes. You can find it in specialty shops or online.

1 cup whole wheat flour,
plus more for rolling

½ teaspoon salt

1 teaspoon neutral oil

Ghee, for brushing

Spiced Tomato Sauce

✱ **MAKES ABOUT 3 CUPS**

1. Heat the ghee in a large, deep heavy-bottomed sauté pan over medium-high heat until shimmering. Add the ginger and garlic and cook, stirring constantly, until softened and the moisture cooks out, about 2 minutes.

2. Add the deggi mirch and cook for 1 minute. Add the tomatoes and cashews and cook until the tomatoes begin to break down and the mixture thickens slightly, about 10 minutes. Transfer the mixture to a blender and blend until a smooth paste forms, adding a few splashes of water if needed.

3. Wipe the pan out and strain the mixture through a fine-mesh sieve into the pan. Return to medium heat, add the fenugreek and honey, and cook for 1 minute. Stir in the butter and cream and season with salt to taste.

Roti

✱ **MAKES 6 (8-INCH) ROUNDS**

1. Combine the flour, salt, and about ½ cup lukewarm water and knead until a soft, pliable dough is formed. Add the oil and knead again until a smooth dough forms. Let rest for 10 minutes, then divide into 6 equal portions and roll into balls. Roll out each ball on a lightly floured surface into an 8-inch round.

2. Heat a large cast-iron skillet or nonstick griddle over medium heat. Add a round of dough and cook for 1 minute. Flip and cook for another minute until the bottom becomes golden brown. Turn over once again and cook until the bottom is golden brown, about 1 minute longer. Brush the top with ghee and serve warm.

EPISODE 1808: *"Cream of the Crop"*
COMPETITOR: Chris Henry
DISH: Fried green tomato sandwiches
WINNER: Chris Henry

CHRIS HENRY'S FRIED GREEN TOMATO SANDWICHES

with Pimento Cheese

SERVES 6

PIMENTO CHEESE

8 ounces Velveeta cheese, cut into pieces

8 ounces coarsely grated sharp cheddar cheese

½ cup mayonnaise

1 tablespoon hot sauce, such as Crystal or Frank's RedHot

1½ teaspoons kosher salt

1 teaspoon freshly ground black pepper

½ cup jarred diced pimentos, drained

Pinch of garlic powder

Pinch of onion powder

Pinch of sweet Spanish paprika

Pinch of cayenne pepper

FRIED GREEN TOMATO SANDWICHES

12 slices (¼ inch thick) green tomatoes (from 2 to 4 large green tomatoes)

2 cups well-shaken buttermilk

4 cups coarse cornmeal

2 cups corn flour or rice flour

1 cup long-grain rice, ground to a fine powder in a blender

2 tablespoons kosher salt

2 tablespoons freshly ground black pepper

1 teaspoon garlic powder

1 teaspoon onion powder

1 tablespoon mustard powder

1 tablespoon Old Bay seasoning

ingredients continued >

"Being on *Beat Bobby Flay* would have been a whirlwind experience on its own, but eleven days before the show, my daughter was born! I thought that coming from such an emotional event would hurt my performance, but I think it made me even more motivated to win, knowing my wife and son were cheering me on from afar with our newest family member. Since this was a dish I've done hundreds of times, I was able to really focus on precision. The minutes still flew by, and when it came time for the judges' comments and I saw Bobby's final dish for the first time, my heart dropped. His was the opposite of mine: big, full of color, and with lots of fresh veggies. My three-ingredient sandwich was going to have to be perfect to go up against his and have a chance. Fortunately, the judges preferred mine and it was all a blur from there. It felt great beating Bobby Flay, but after my daughter's birth so soon before, it was still only the second-best thing to happen to me that month!" —**CHRIS HENRY**

1. Prepare the pimento cheese: In the bowl of a stand mixer fitted with the paddle, combine the cheeses, mayonnaise, hot sauce, salt, black pepper, and pimentos and mix until combined. Season to taste with a pinch each of garlic powder, onion powder, paprika, cayenne, and more salt and black pepper. The cheese can be made 1 day in advance and stored, tightly covered, in the refrigerator. Let soften at room temperature for 20 minutes before using.

2. Prepare the fried green tomato sandwiches: Put the tomato slices in a large baking dish, cover completely with the buttermilk, and let sit for 5 minutes. Combine the cornmeal, flour, ground rice, salt, black pepper, garlic powder, onion powder, mustard powder, and Old Bay in a large baking dish.

continued >

12 slices bacon

2 tablespoons light brown sugar

Canola oil, for frying

12 tablespoons mayonnaise

12 slices (¼ inch thick) best-quality sourdough bread

6 tablespoons unsalted butter, at room temperature

3. Preheat the oven to 350°F.

4. Lay the bacon on a sheet pan, leaving a bit of space between the slices. Bake until almost crispy, about 20 minutes. Sprinkle the brown sugar over each slice. Return to the oven and bake until the sugar has melted and the bacon is crispy, about 6 minutes longer. Remove from the oven, let rest for 5 minutes, then transfer to a sheet pan lined with paper towels to drain.

5. Pour 2 inches of oil into a cast-iron skillet and heat over medium heat to 400°F on a deep-fry thermometer.

6. Set a wire rack over a sheet pan. Remove the tomatoes from the buttermilk one at a time and dredge on both sides in the seasoned flour mixture. Transfer to the wire rack. Working in batches, fry the tomatoes until golden brown on both sides and crispy, about 3 minutes. Return the fried tomatoes to the rack and season the top with a bit of salt.

7. Spread 1 tablespoon mayonnaise on each slice of bread. Heat the butter in a large nonstick skillet over medium heat until shimmering. Working in batches, put the bread in the pan, mayonnaise-side down, and cook until lightly golden brown on the bottom, 4 to 5 minutes. Spread the other side of each slice of bread with a few tablespoons of the soft pimento cheese. Cover half of the bread slices with 2 fried green tomatoes and 2 slices of bacon each and top with the remaining bread, pimento-side down. Slice on the diagonal and serve immediately.

SEAFOOD

Pierogis with Lobster, Shiitakes & Bacon ✖ **47**

Lobster Bisque with Garlic Croutons & Crispy Lobster Claws ✖ **49**

Lobster Risotto with Basil, Parsley & Anchovy Bread Crumbs ✖ **53**

Shrimp Pad Thai with Peanuts & Tofu ✖ **54**

Spice-Crusted Shrimp with Cheesy Grits & Pickled Chiles ✖ **57**

Seafood Fra Diavolo with Saffron Fettuccine & Anchovy Bread Crumbs ✖ **58**

Shrimp Scampi with Toasted Polenta & Basil Pesto ✖ **61**

Crispy Soft-Shell Crab Sandwiches with Avocado Aioli & BBQ Potato Salad ✖ **63**

Fried Clam Belly Roll with Tangerine–Fresno Chile Tartar Sauce ✖ **67**

Cal-Ital Crab Cakes with Salsa Verde & Citrus Tartar Sauce ✖ **68**

Fish Curry with Scallion & Cashew Rice ✖ **71**

Beer-Battered Fish & Chips with Salsa Verde Tartar Sauce ✖ **74**

New Orleans–Style Sole Meunière with Crawfish Butter Sauce ✖ **77**

Yellowtail Poke with Spicy Pineapple Sauce & Taro Chips ✖ **78**

Alex Guarnaschelli's Lobster Newberg ✖ **81**

Jamarius Banks's Creole Shrimp & Grits ✖ **83**

Damaris Phillips's Tuna Noodle Casserole ✖ **87**

Darren Sayphraraj's Lobster Tom Yum Soup with Vermicelli Noodles ✖ **88**

SERVES 6

PIEROGI DOUGH

2 large egg yolks

¾ cup sour cream

1 stick (8 tablespoons) unsalted butter, at room temperature

1 teaspoon kosher salt

2 cups all-purpose flour, sifted

LOBSTER REDUCTION

4 cups Lobster Stock (page 234) or store-bought stock from your local fishmonger

½ cup dry white wine

½ small Spanish onion, chopped

1 head garlic, halved horizontally

FILLING

2 large russet potatoes, peeled and cut into 2-inch cubes

Kosher salt

2 tablespoons canola oil

2 large shiitake mushrooms, stems discarded, caps finely chopped

1 large shallot, finely chopped

3 large garlic cloves, chopped

2 teaspoons finely chopped fresh thyme

Freshly ground black pepper

1 pound cooked lobster meat, chopped

4 thick-cut slices bacon, cut crosswise into ¼-inch-wide lardons

ingredients continued >

PIEROGIS
with Lobster, Shiitakes & Bacon

These are Eastern Europe's version of a boiled, then pan-fried dumpling. Usually, they are filled with humble ingredients like ground meats or vegetables and served with sour cream. While my friend Michael Symon (the self-proclaimed pierogi master!) uses short ribs of beef in his signature pierogi dish, I went all out with succulent lobster and wild mushrooms. For this battle, I knew I needed a filling that would knock the judges' socks off, but the real key to success is in the rich yet tender dough.

1. Make the pierogi dough: Whisk together the egg yolks, sour cream, butter, and salt. Gently mix in the flour until the mixture forms a dough; be careful not to overmix. Form into a disc, wrap in plastic, and refrigerate for at least 2 hours and up to 3 days.

2. Make the lobster reduction: Combine the stock, wine, onion, and garlic in a large pot. Bring to a boil and cook until reduced by half, about 20 minutes. Strain into a small saucepan (discard the solids) and cook over high heat, until reduced to 1 cup, about 10 minutes longer. Keep warm while you form and cook the pierogi.

3. Make the filling: Put the potatoes in a medium pot, add cold water to cover by 2 inches, and season with 2 tablespoons salt. Bring to a boil and cook until tender, about 12 minutes. Drain well, return to the pot, turn to high heat, and cook for a minute longer to dry out the potatoes. Transfer to a bowl and mash the potatoes with a potato masher until almost smooth.

4. Meanwhile, heat the oil in a large sauté pan over high heat until shimmering. Add the mushrooms and cook until golden brown and their liquid has evaporated, about 9 minutes. Add the shallot and garlic and cook 2 minutes longer. Stir in the thyme and season with salt and pepper to taste. Transfer to the bowl with the potatoes and combine using the masher. Fold in the lobster.

5. Put the bacon in the pan and turn the heat to medium. Cook, stirring occasionally, until the bacon is golden brown and crispy, about 8 minutes. Remove with a slotted spoon to a plate lined with paper towels and let drain.

continued >

FOR ASSEMBLY

All-purpose flour, for the work surface

Egg wash: 2 eggs, beaten

Kosher salt

Unsalted butter

Freshly ground black pepper

2 tablespoons chopped fresh parsley leaves, for garnish

1 tablespoon finely chopped fresh tarragon, for garnish

✖ **IN IT TO WIN IT:** Ensuring the dough is chilled and rested will make it easier to handle and yield a more tender pierogi. Half of my pierogi fell apart during the cooking process because my dough wasn't chilled enough and the water was boiling too hard. Don't make those mistakes! Chill the dough and keep your water at a hard simmer.

6. Assemble the pierogi: Line a sheet pan with parchment paper. Divide the dough in half. Place one half on a lightly floured surface and return the other half to the refrigerator. Roll the dough to a ⅛-inch thickness. Use a 3-inch biscuit cutter to cut out rounds. Spoon a scant tablespoon of the filling in the center of each round. Lightly brush the bottom half with egg wash, fold the top half over to form a half-moon, and press the edges with a fork to seal. Place the pierogi on the prepared sheet pan and refrigerate for at least 15 minutes. Repeat with the remaining dough and filling.

7. Bring a large pot of salted water to a boil over high heat. Working in batches, add the pierogi to the boiling water. Once they float, reduce the heat to medium and cook for exactly 4 minutes. Drain well in a colander.

8. Heat a few tablespoons of butter in a sauté pan over medium heat until it is melted and sizzling. Add the pierogi, in batches, and sauté on both sides to lightly crisp the exterior, 2 minutes per side. Season with salt and pepper and repeat with the remaining butter and pierogies.

9. To serve, spoon some of the lobster reduction into bowls, top with pierogis, and drizzle with more of the reduction. Garnish with the parsley and tarragon.

SERVES 4

STEAMED LOBSTERS

2 live lobsters (2 pounds each)

Kosher salt

LOBSTER BISQUE

2 tablespoons extra-virgin olive oil

2 large shallots, coarsely chopped

1 small fennel bulb, coarsely chopped

1 medium carrot, coarsely chopped

1 medium celery stalk, chopped

4 garlic cloves, smashed and peeled

½ cup Pernod

3 tablespoons all-purpose flour

1 quart Lobster Stock (page 234) or store-bought stock from your local fishmonger

1 cup canned peeled whole tomatoes, drained and chopped

½ cup crème fraîche

2 tablespoons chopped fresh tarragon

2 tablespoons chopped fresh chives

TO FINISH

Crispy Lobster Claws (recipe follows)

Garlic Croutons (recipe follows)

Chopped fresh tarragon, for garnish (optional)

Chopped fresh chives, for garnish (optional)

LOBSTER BISQUE
with Garlic Croutons & Crispy Lobster Claws

Lobster bisque reminds me of my dad, Bill Flay. He loves soup and he loves lobster, so when a menu presents him with the opportunity, lobster bisque is his go-to. The key for this dish's success is twofold: Great lobster flavor is critical, as is the perfect, silky-smooth texture—with just the right amount of body. The crispy lobster claws and crispy, garlicky croutons served on top are *Beat Bobby Flay* signatures!

1. Steam the lobsters: Fill a large bowl (big enough to hold both lobsters) with ice and water. Bring a large pot of water to a boil, then add 2 tablespoons salt and the lobsters. Put the lid on, and cook until the lobsters are just cooked through, about 12 minutes. Remove the lobsters with tongs and immediately plunge them into the ice bath. Let sit until cool enough to handle, about 3 minutes. Remove the meat and claws from the shell. Coarsely chop the meat and reserve the claws for Crispy Lobster Claws. Coarsely chop the shells and reserve them for the bisque base.

2. Make the lobster bisque: Heat the oil in a large Dutch oven over high heat until shimmering. Add the shallots, fennel, carrot, and celery and cook until soft, about 5 minutes. Add the garlic and cook for 2 minutes longer. Add the Pernod and cook until completely reduced, 3 minutes.

3. Add the flour and cook, stirring constantly, until pale blonde in color, about 2 minutes. Whisk in the stock, tomatoes, and reserved lobster shells and bring to a boil. Reduce the heat to medium and cook, stirring occasionally, until reduced and thickened and the flour taste is cooked out, about 30 minutes. Strain the soup into a large bowl.

4. Rinse out the Dutch oven and return the soup to the pot. Set it over high heat and cook until reduced to a bisque consistency (it should coat the back of a spoon), about 12 minutes. Whisk in the crème fraîche, tarragon, and chives and cook until thickened, about 5 minutes longer. Keep warm until ready to serve.

5. To finish: Stir the reserved chopped lobster meat into the bisque and cook for 1 minute to heat through. Ladle the bisque into bowls, garnish each with a crispy lobster claw, a few garlic croutons, and more tarragon and chives, if desired.

continued >

1¼ cups rice flour

Kosher salt and freshly ground black pepper

Canola oil, for frying

4 cooked lobster claws reserved (from steamed lobster, page 49)

Crispy Lobster Claws

✖ MAKES 4

1. Whisk together 1 cup of the flour and 1 cup cold water in a medium bowl and season with salt and pepper. Refrigerate for 15 minutes.

2. Line a plate with paper towels. Pour 2 inches of oil into a medium saucepan and heat over medium heat to 375°F on a deep-fry thermometer.

3. Put the remaining ¼ cup flour on a plate and season with salt and pepper. Season the lobster claws with salt and pepper, dredge in the flour, and tap off the excess. Dip in the rice flour batter and let the excess run off. Fry the claws two at a time in the oil until crispy and lightly golden brown, about 2 minutes. Remove with a slotted spoon to the paper towels to drain and season with a bit more salt.

½ cup extra-virgin olive oil

3 garlic cloves, mashed to a paste with ¼ teaspoon kosher salt

4 slices (½ inch thick) good-quality pain de mie, crusts removed, cut into ⅓-inch dice

Kosher salt and freshly ground black pepper

2 tablespoons finely chopped fresh flat-leaf parsley

Garlic Croutons

✖ MAKES ABOUT 3 CUPS

1. Preheat the oven to 375°F.

2. Heat the oil in a small sauté pan over low heat. Add the garlic and cook until soft and fragrant, about 2 minutes.

3. Put the bread in a medium bowl, add the garlic oil, and toss to coat. Season the croutons with salt and pepper and spread onto a sheet pan in an even layer.

4. Bake, turning once, until lightly golden brown, about 10 minutes. Remove from the oven, stir in the parsley, and season with a bit more salt. Serve immediately or let cool and store in a container with a tight-fitting lid at room temperature for 3 days.

EPISODE 2303:
"America's Funniest Food Show"
COMPETITOR: Sam Diminich
DISH: Lobster risotto
WINNER: Sam Diminich

SERVES 4 TO 6

Kosher salt

2 live lobsters (2 pounds each)

1 stick (8 tablespoons) unsalted butter, at room temperature

2 oil-packed anchovy fillets

9 garlic cloves

Freshly ground black pepper

6 to 7 cups Lobster Stock (page 234) or store-bought stock from your local fishmonger

3 tablespoons extra-virgin olive oil

2 large shallots, finely diced

2 heaping tablespoons tomato paste

2 cups Arborio rice

1 cup dry white wine

2 teaspoons Calabrian chile paste

Finely grated zest of 1 lemon

¼ cup chopped fresh basil leaves, plus more (optional) for garnish

¼ cup chopped fresh parsley leaves, plus more (optional) for garnish

½ cup Anchovy Bread Crumbs (page 245)

LOBSTER RISOTTO
with Basil, Parsley & Anchovy Bread Crumbs

Anne Burrell always gives me a hard time no matter what I'm cooking, and never more so than when I'm making risotto or pasta, two things she is very adept at. I really thought I was in a good pace to win this one: Creamy rice! Decadent lobster! Herbaceous parsley and basil! And those crispy, savory, and oh-so-flavorful bread crumbs! But lo and behold, Chef Diminich bested me with his own gorgeous version of lobster risotto.

1. Fill a large bowl (big enough to hold both lobsters) with ice and water. Bring a large pot of water to a boil and add 2 tablespoons salt and the lobsters. Put the lid on and cook until the lobsters are just cooked through, about 12 minutes. Remove the lobsters with tongs, immediately plunge them into the ice bath, and let sit until just cool enough to handle, about 3 minutes. Transfer to a sheet pan. Remove and discard the shells and cut the meat into 1-inch chunks. Set aside until the risotto is finished.

2. Combine 4 tablespoons of the butter and the anchovies in a food processor. Chop 2 of the garlic cloves, add to the food processor, and process until smooth. Season with salt and pepper and scrape the mixture into a bowl. Finely chop the remaining 7 garlic cloves and set aside.

3. Put the stock in a large saucepan and bring to a simmer over low heat. Keep warm while you make the risotto.

4. Heat the oil in a large Dutch oven over medium heat. Add the shallots and chopped garlic and cook, stirring occasionally, until the shallots are soft and the garlic is lightly toasted, about 6 minutes. Stir in the tomato paste and cook until it is fragrant and it deepens in color, about 2 minutes. Stir in the rice and cook, stirring constantly, for 2 minutes.

5. Add the wine, increase the heat to high, and cook until completely reduced, about 5 minutes. Add 2 cups of the warm stock and cook, stirring constantly. When the rice appears almost dry, add another ladle of stock and repeat the process until the rice is al dente, about 25 minutes.

6. Stir in the anchovy butter, chile paste, lemon zest, basil, and parsley and season with salt and pepper. Fold in the lobster meat just before serving. Ladle into bowls and top with the anchovy bread crumbs and more basil and parsley, if desired.

COMPETITOR: Tim Freeman

DISH: Pad Thai

WINNER: Tim Freeman

SERVES 4

1 (8-ounce) package pad Thai noodles, soaked in warm water for 20 minutes and drained well

1 cup tamarind paste

¼ cup good-quality fish sauce, such as Red Boat

¼ cup finely grated palm sugar

¼ cup light brown sugar

Juice of 2 limes

1 to 2 teaspoons Calabrian chile paste (for authenticity, use Sriracha)

3 tablespoons pork fat or canola oil

20 large shrimp, peeled and deveined

Kosher salt

2 large shallots, thinly sliced lengthwise

2 large eggs, lightly beaten

4 ounces firm tofu, pressed and patted dry, halved lengthwise, and cut crosswise into ¼-inch-thick slices

1 cup bean sprouts

2 tablespoons finely chopped Thai preserved radish

½ cup chopped fresh cilantro leaves

½ cup unsalted roasted peanuts, coarsely chopped

Lime wedges, for serving

✖ **BEAT THE CLOCK:** Asian cooking is all about mise en place—things in place. Have your noodles soaked and your ingredients measured out in bowls, ready to go. The cooking happens fast and there isn't time to stop and measure or chop ingredients.

SHRIMP PAD THAI
with Peanuts & Tofu

Truth be told, I've only made pad Thai a handful of times, and while it usually turns out pretty good, I don't always get the balance of flavors exactly right. The key here is striking the right notes of sweet, sour, and spicy. When it comes to the spicy part, classically, you would use Sriracha, but any chance I get to sneak in a bit of Calabrian chile paste (even if the dish is not Italian), I will. If you can make that happen, you'll be victorious in your own kitchen! Tamarind paste and Thai preserved radishes can be found online at Import Foods or in specialty Asian markets.

1. Place the noodles in a large bowl. Whisk together the tamarind paste, fish sauce, palm sugar, brown sugar, lime juice, and chile paste in a medium bowl until smooth. Set the tamarind sauce aside.

2. Heat the pork fat in a wok or large nonstick sauté pan over high heat until shimmering. Add the shrimp, season with salt, and cook on one side until lightly golden brown, about 2 minutes. Remove with a slotted spoon to a plate (they will continue cooking in the sauce).

3. Add the shallots to the pan and cook, stirring constantly, until soft, about 2 minutes. Add the eggs and cook, stirring constantly, until just cooked through, about 2 minutes. Add ¼ cup of the tamarind sauce to the pan and stir to deglaze the pan.

4. Add the noodles, shrimp, tofu, bean sprouts, preserved radish, and remaining tamarind sauce to the pan and toss well to combine and coat the noodles. Continue cooking for 2 minutes longer. Remove from the heat and stir in the cilantro and peanuts.

5. Divide among four bowls and serve with lime wedges on the side.

EPISODE 1302: *"Fancy Versus Rustic"*
COMPETITOR: Angie Berry
DISH: Shrimp and grits
WINNER: Bobby Flay

SPICE-CRUSTED SHRIMP
with Cheesy Grits & Pickled Chiles

This recipe sounds fancier than it is, but dressed up or not, we're still talking about one of America's great dishes: shrimp and grits. My first encounter with a bowl of classic shrimp and grits occurred over twenty years ago in Savannah, Georgia, during a stint on a show I used to do called *FoodNation*. It's been a part of my repertoire ever since. In this case, I just pull out a few extra touches like a spice rub for the shrimp and some pickled chiles to finish with a flourish. Homemade shrimp stock ensures the grits get an extra dose of shrimpy flavor.

SERVES 6

GRITS

2 tablespoons canola oil

8 thick-cut slices bacon, cut crosswise into ¼-inch-wide lardons

5 garlic cloves, finely chopped

1 medium Spanish onion, finely diced

4 cups Shrimp Stock (page 234) or store-bought low-sodium vegetable broth or chicken stock, plus more as needed

1 cup instant polenta

Kosher salt and freshly ground black pepper

SPICE-CRUSTED SHRIMP

30 large Gulf shrimp, peeled and deveined

Kosher salt and freshly ground black pepper

3 tablespoons Bobby's Spice Rub (page 243)

¼ cup canola oil

TO FINISH

6 ounces sharp white cheddar cheese, coarsely grated

4 tablespoons unsalted butter, cut into pieces

¼ cup crème fraîche

¼ cup Pickled Chiles (page 248)

✖ **BEAT THE CLOCK:** I used instant polenta instead of grits because they cook in 10 minutes, plus polenta is finer in texture and creates a creamier result.

1. Make the grits: Heat the oil in a large Dutch oven over medium heat until shimmering. Add the bacon and cook, stirring occasionally, until the fat is rendered and the bacon is golden brown and crispy, about 8 minutes. Add the garlic and cook for 1 minute. Leaving 2 tablespoons of fat behind in the pan, put the bacon and garlic into a small bowl and keep warm.

2. Increase the heat to high. Add the onion to the rendered fat and cook until soft, about 4 minutes. Add the stock and bring to a boil. Slowly whisk in the polenta and continue whisking until combined and starting to thicken. Reduce the heat to low, cover, and cook, stirring occasionally, until soft and thickened, about 10 minutes longer, adding more stock or water if needed. Season with salt and pepper to taste.

3. When the polenta is almost done, prepare the shrimp: Season the shrimp with salt, pepper, and the spice rub and toss well to coat. Heat the oil in a large nonstick sauté pan over high heat until shimmering. Working in batches if necessary, add the shrimp in a single layer and cook until golden brown on both sides and just cooked through, about 1½ minutes per side. Remove to a plate.

4. To finish: Once the polenta is soft and thickened, add the cheddar, butter, and crème fraîche and whisk until smooth; if too thick, add a few splashes of stock or water to loosen. Spoon the grits into a bowl, top with the shrimp, and garnish with the bacon-garlic mixture and pickled chiles.

SERVES 6

FRA DIAVOLO SAUCE

3 tablespoons extra-virgin olive oil

1 large Spanish onion, finely chopped

5 garlic cloves, chopped

2 tablespoons Calabrian chile paste

1 (35-ounce) can peeled whole tomatoes, undrained

SEAFOOD

Kosher salt

2 (8-ounce) lobster tails

1 cup dry white wine

20 littleneck clams, scrubbed

20 mussels, scrubbed (and debearded, if needed)

4 tablespoons canola oil

12 large shrimp, peeled and deveined

Freshly ground black pepper

1 pound squid, cleaned and bodies sliced crosswise into ¼-inch-thick rings

TO FINISH

Saffron Pasta Dough (page 235), cut into fettuccine

2 tablespoons unsalted butter

¼ cup chopped fresh flat-leaf parsley

¼ cup chopped fresh basil leaves

Anchovy Bread Crumbs (page 245)

SEAFOOD FRA DIAVOLO
with Saffron Fettuccine & Anchovy Bread Crumbs

These are the flavors I really love to cook at home. A tomato-based sauce is laced with garlic, chiles, lots of fresh herbs, and fresh seafood—whatever you can get from the fish department will work. You don't have to make the saffron fettuccine from scratch; you can use a pound of store-bought fresh or dried fettuccine, but if you're feeling it in the kitchen, go for it. Extra points!

1. Make the fra diavolo sauce: Heat the olive oil in a large Dutch oven over high heat until shimmering. Add the onion and cook until soft, about 4 minutes. Add the garlic and cook for 1 minute longer. Stir in the chile paste and cook for 30 seconds. Add the tomatoes and their juices, bring to a boil, and cook until the tomatoes begin to break down, about 10 minutes. Coarsely mash with a potato masher. Reduce the heat to medium and cook the sauce, stirring occasionally, until thickened, about 20 minutes longer.

2. Meanwhile, prepare the seafood: Fill a large bowl with ice and water. Bring 6 cups of water to a boil in a large saucepan and season with 2 tablespoons salt. Add the lobster tails and cook until just tender, 8 to 10 minutes. Reserving the boiling water for cooking the pasta, remove the lobster tails with tongs, immediately plunge them into the ice bath, and let sit until cool enough to handle, about 2 minutes. Remove the shells, halve the tails lengthwise, and cut crosswise into ½-inch pieces. Set aside on a large plate.

3. Meanwhile, bring the wine to a boil in a large saucepan over high heat. Add the clams, cover, and cook until all of them open (discard any that do not), about 8 minutes. Remove the clams with a slotted spoon to a large bowl. Bring the liquid back to a boil, add the mussels, cover, and cook until all the mussels open (discard any that do not), about 4 minutes. Remove with a slotted spoon to the bowl with the clams.

4. Cook the mussel/clam cooking liquid over high heat until reduced by half, about 5 minutes. Add the cooking liquid to the fra diavolo sauce and cook over high heat until thickened to sauce consistency, about 15 minutes longer.

5. Heat 2 tablespoons of the canola oil in a large sauté pan over high heat until shimmering. Season the shrimp with salt and pepper and cook until golden brown on both sides and just cooked through, about 1 minute per side. Remove to a plate. Heat

✖ IN IT TO WIN IT: My strategy was to cook the seafood separately to make sure that none of it was overcooked. A bit more work and a lot more dishes to wash, but the worst thing that you can do to beautiful fresh seafood is overcook it.

the remaining 2 tablespoons oil in the pan over high heat until shimmering. Season the squid with salt and pepper and cook, stirring occasionally, until lightly golden brown and just cooked through, about 3 minutes. Remove to the plate with the shrimp.

6. To finish: While the sauce is thickening, bring the pot of water back to a boil and add the pasta. Cook until it rises to the top, then cook for 1 minute longer, about 4 minutes total. Reserve a cup of the cooking water and drain the pasta well.

7. Add all the seafood to the fra diavolo sauce, along with the pasta, butter, and some of the reserved pasta cooking liquid, if needed. Toss to coat the pasta in the sauce, then stir in the parsley and basil. Divide among six bowls, sprinkle with the bread crumbs, and serve.

SERVES 6

TOASTED POLENTA

1½ cups instant polenta

5 cups Shrimp Stock
(page 234), store-bought
low-sodium vegetable broth,
or water

Kosher salt and freshly
ground black pepper

¼ cup crème fraîche

¼ cup mascarpone cheese

SHRIMP SCAMPI

30 extra-large shrimp, peeled
and deveined

Kosher salt and freshly
ground black pepper

2 teaspoons sweet Spanish
paprika

5 tablespoons canola oil

8 garlic cloves, mashed
to a paste with ½ teaspoon
kosher salt

1 cup dry white wine

1 stick (8 tablespoons) unsalted
butter, cut into pieces

Finely grated zest and juice
of 2 lemons

¼ teaspoon crushed red
pepper flakes

¼ cup chopped fresh flat-leaf
parsley

FOR SERVING

½ cup Basil Pesto
(recipe follows)

½ cup Anchovy Bread Crumbs
(page 245)

Chopped fresh flat-leaf parsley
(optional)

SHRIMP SCAMPI
with Toasted Polenta & Basil Pesto

Okay, I lost this battle, but I'm still always happy to make this dish! An old-school favorite in Italian American restaurants, shrimp scampi is a very simple dish that combines the big flavors of garlic, lemon, butter, and crushed red pepper with sweet shrimp. We all know shrimp scampi is a natural over pasta, but I was inclined to substitute polenta during this particular battle. Toasting the grains before cooking gives the polenta a deeper, almost nutty flavor, and crème fraîche and mascarpone make it smooth and creamy. Perhaps I went a little overboard on the pesto, but I know I got it right with those crispy bread crumbs. It may not have been a winner in the *Beat* arena, but it's still great for a Friday-night dinner.

1. Make the toasted polenta: Pour the polenta into a large sauté pan in an even layer and cook over medium heat, stirring occasionally, until lightly toasted and fragrant, about 5 minutes.

2. Bring the stock to a boil in a large saucepan over high heat and season with 1 tablespoon salt and ¼ teaspoon black pepper. Slowly whisk in the polenta and continue whisking until the mixture is smooth and begins to thicken. Reduce the heat to medium and cook until thick, about 10 minutes longer. Remove from the heat and whisk in the crème fraîche and mascarpone until smooth. Season with salt and black pepper. Cover and keep warm while you make the scampi.

3. Make the shrimp scampi: Put the shrimp in a large bowl, season with salt, black pepper, and the paprika, and toss to coat. Heat 2 tablespoons of the oil in a large sauté pan over high heat until shimmering. Add half of the shrimp in an even layer and cook until golden brown on both sides, about 1 minute per side. Remove to a large plate. Add 2 more tablespoons oil and repeat with the remaining shrimp.

4. Wipe out the pan with a paper towel and return to high heat. Add the remaining 1 tablespoon oil and the garlic and cook until soft and lightly golden brown, about 2 minutes. Carefully add the wine and cook until reduced by half, 5 minutes. Whisk in the butter, a tablespoon at a time, then add the lemon zest, lemon juice, and pepper flakes and cook until the butter is melted. Season with salt and black pepper.

continued >

5. Return the shrimp and their juices to the pan and cook to just heat through, about 1 minute. Stir in the parsley.

6. To serve: Spoon the polenta into bowls and stir in the pesto as desired. Top with some of the shrimp and garnish with the anchovy bread crumbs and some parsley, if desired. Serve immediately.

Basil Pesto

✖ MAKES ABOUT ½ CUP

2 cups packed fresh basil leaves

1 garlic clove, smashed and peeled

¼ cup pine nuts

½ cup extra-virgin olive oil

¼ cup freshly grated Parmigiano Reggiano cheese

Kosher salt and freshly ground black pepper

Combine the basil, garlic, and pine nuts in a food processor and process until coarsely chopped. With the motor running, add the oil and process until emulsified. Remove the lid, add the Parmigiano, salt, and pepper, and process until the pesto is completely smooth. Scrape into a bowl. The pesto can be stored, tightly covered, in the refrigerator for up to 1 week or in the freezer for up to 1 month.

EPISODE 912: *"Get in the Zone"*
COMPETITOR: Todd Gray
DISH: Soft shell crab sandwich
WINNER: Bobby Flay

CRISPY SOFT-SHELL CRAB SANDWICHES
with Avocado Aioli & BBQ Potato Salad

SERVES 4

BBQ POTATO SALAD

1½ pounds fingerling potatoes, scrubbed

Kosher salt and freshly ground black pepper

1 tablespoon onion powder

1 tablespoon garlic powder

1 tablespoon sweet smoked Spanish paprika

1 tablespoon light brown sugar

¼ cup white wine vinegar

2 tablespoons Dijon mustard

2 tablespoons whole-grain mustard

1 tablespoon mayonnaise

½ cup canola oil

2 tablespoons finely chopped fresh tarragon

¼ head red cabbage, finely shredded

SOFT-SHELL CRABS

1½ cups rice flour

Kosher salt and freshly ground black pepper

Canola oil, for frying

4 medium soft-shell crabs, cleaned, rinsed, and patted dry

SANDWICHES

Avocado Aioli (recipe follows)

4 soft rolls, such as kaiser rolls, insides scooped out, lightly toasted

4 thick-cut slices Oven-Roasted Crispy Bacon (page 246), halved crosswise

This is my business partner and best friend Laurence Kretchmer's favorite poolside lunch. Soft-shell crabs are one of the coolest ingredients. I mean, you eat the *whole thing*—rich, buttery meat, (soft) shell, and all. Coated with a stealth-like coating of rice flour batter, the crabs' soft shells are crisped, not battered, as the key is creating crunch while still being able to taste the crab.

1. Make the BBQ potato salad: Put the potatoes in a large saucepan, add cold water to cover by 2 inches, and season with 2 tablespoons salt. Bring to a boil and cook until tender, about 25 minutes, depending on the size of the potatoes.

2. Meanwhile, to make the BBQ spice mixture, mix together 2 teaspoons salt, 1 teaspoon pepper, the onion powder, garlic powder, smoked paprika, and brown sugar in a medium bowl until combined. To make the vinaigrette, in a separate medium bowl, whisk together the vinegar, both mustards, the mayonnaise, 1 teaspoon salt, and ¼ teaspoon pepper until combined. Slowly whisk in the oil until emulsified and stir in the tarragon.

3. Drain the potatoes in a colander and let sit just until cool enough to handle, about 5 minutes. Slice the potatoes crosswise into 1-inch-thick slices and put in a large bowl. Add the BBQ spice mixture and mix well to combine. Add half of the vinaigrette and gently mix to coat. Let sit at room temperature.

4. Put the shredded cabbage in a large bowl, add the remaining vinaigrette, and toss well to coat. Let the slaw sit at room temperature to wilt.

5. Prepare the soft-shell crabs: Whisk together 1 cup of the rice flour and 1 cup very cold water in a large bowl until smooth. Season with salt and pepper and refrigerate for at least 30 minutes and up to 4 hours.

6. Line a sheet pan with paper towels. Pour 6 cups of oil into a deep fryer or a large Dutch oven and heat over medium heat to 360°F on a deep-fry thermometer.

continued >

2 large egg yolks

½ teaspoon fresh lemon juice

1 cup canola oil

2 teaspoons Calabrian chile paste

½ small avocado, mashed

Kosher salt and freshly ground black pepper

7. Spread the remaining ½ cup rice flour on a large plate and season with salt and pepper. Season the crabs on both sides with salt and pepper and dredge them, one at a time, in the flour, tapping off the excess. Dip the crab in the batter and let the excess run off. Working in batches (one or two at a time, depending on how big your fryer or pot is), add the crabs, top-side down, and fry until lightly golden brown and just cooked through, about 3 minutes per side. Remove with a spider to the lined sheet pan to drain and season with salt.

8. Assemble the sandwiches: Spread some aioli on both sides of the rolls and put a crab on the bottom of each roll. Top with a spoonful of slaw, then the bacon, and finally the top of the roll. Serve with the potato salad on the side.

Avocado Aioli

✖ **MAKES ABOUT 2 CUPS**

Whisk the yolks and lemon juice in a large bowl until pale and smooth, 2 minutes. Slowly, drop by drop, begin whisking in the oil and continue adding the oil and whisking until the mayonnaise is emulsified. Stir in the chile paste and avocado and season with salt and pepper. The aioli will keep, tightly covered, in the refrigerator for 24 hours.

SERVES 6

FRIED CLAM BELLIES

Canola oil, for deep-frying

2 cups cracker meal

1 cup panko bread crumbs

¼ cup cornstarch

Kosher salt and freshly ground black pepper

1 cup buttermilk

36 whole belly clams in their shells (aka steamers, Maine clams, or Ipswich clams), shucked

SANDWICHES

Tangerine–Fresno Chile Tartar Sauce (recipe follows)

6 brioche buns, halved, insides scooped out, and lightly toasted

1 small head radicchio or ¼ head iceberg lettuce (or a combination of both), finely shredded

Pickled Chiles (page 248), for garnish

2 cups tangerine juice

1 teaspoon finely grated tangerine or orange zest

1 tablespoon clover honey

Kosher salt and freshly ground black pepper

1 cup mayonnaise

¼ cup Homemade Hot Sauce (page 249)

¼ cup finely diced cornichons

2 tablespoons chopped capers

2 tablespoons finely chopped fresh chives

FRIED CLAM BELLY ROLL
with Tangerine–Fresno Chile Tartar Sauce

I was excited when I heard the challenger Nick Williams tell me we were cooking fried clams. They remind me of summers in the Hamptons and my years as a kid on the Jersey shore. Great fish shacks always have a killer fried clam roll. That said, they never served it with a tangerine–Fresno chile tartar sauce. Hmm, maybe that's why I lost? It's good, though—I promise.

1. Prepare the fried clam bellies: Line a sheet pan with several layers of paper towels. Pour 4 inches of oil into a deep-fryer or a large Dutch oven and heat over medium heat to 375°F on a deep-fry thermometer.

2. While the oil is heating, combine the cracker meal, panko, and cornstarch in a large bowl and season with salt and pepper. Pour the buttermilk into a large bowl and season with salt and pepper.

3. Put the clam meats in the buttermilk. Working in batches, remove them with a slotted spoon, transfer to the breading mixture, and toss to coat. Fry until golden brown, about 2 minutes. Remove with a slotted spoon to the paper towels to drain and season with salt.

4. Assemble the sandwiches: Spread some of the tartar sauce on the top and bottom of each bun and arrange radicchio on the bottom half of each bun. Divide the clams among the buns and top with some of the pickled chiles and the remaining half of the bun.

Tangerine–Fresno Chile Tartar Sauce
✖ **MAKES ABOUT 1½ CUPS**

1. Put the tangerine juice and zest in a medium saucepan, bring to a boil over high heat, and cook until reduced to about ¼ cup, about 20 minutes. Whisk in the honey and season with salt and pepper to taste. Let cool completely. The reduction can be made up to 3 days in advance and stored, tightly covered, in the refrigerator.

2. Whisk together the tangerine reduction, mayonnaise, and hot sauce in a medium bowl. Stir in the cornichons, capers, and chives and season with salt and pepper to taste. Cover and refrigerate for at least 30 minutes and up to 1 day before serving.

MAKES 8 CRAB CAKES/SERVES 4

CRAB CAKES

3 tablespoons extra-virgin olive oil

3 large shallots, finely diced

½ cup mayonnaise

2 tablespoons whole-grain mustard

2 tablespoons prepared horseradish, drained

1 to 2 tablespoons Calabrian chile paste, to taste

Finely grated zest of 1 lemon

Finely grated zest of ½ orange

Kosher salt and freshly ground black pepper

2 pounds jumbo lump crabmeat, picked over

¼ cup Wondra flour, plus more for frying

Canola oil, for frying

FOR SERVING

Salsa Verde (recipe follows)

Orange-Lemon Tartar Sauce (recipe follows)

✖ **BEAT THE CLOCK:** The salsa verde and the tartar sauce can be made up to a day in advance and stored, tightly covered, in the refrigerator. In fact, both sauces will be more flavorful if they are allowed to sit for at least 4 hours.

CAL-ITAL CRAB CAKES
with Salsa Verde & Citrus Tartar Sauce

Any version of a crab cake is a big seller on all of my menus. The key is to make sure that it's all about the crab! In this case, I chose to flavor the crab with some favorite Italian touches: Calabrian chiles and a basil-heavy *salsa verde*. The orange- and lemon-flecked tartar sauce gives the dish the brightness it needs.

1. Make the crab cakes: Heat the olive oil in a medium sauté pan over high heat until shimmering. Add the shallots and cook until soft, about 4 minutes. Transfer to a large bowl and stir in the mayonnaise, mustard, horseradish, chile paste, and both citrus zests. Season with salt and pepper and gently mix until combined.

2. Add the crabmeat, sprinkle the flour over the top, and gently mix until just combined. Divide the mixture into 8 equal portions and form into cakes. Transfer to a sheet pan lined with parchment paper, loosely cover with plastic wrap, and refrigerate until chilled, at least 1 hour and up to 12 hours.

3. Line a sheet pan with several layers of paper towels. Pour 2 inches canola oil into a deep cast-iron skillet and heat over medium heat to 350°F on a deep-fry thermometer.

4. Spread some flour on a plate. Carefully dredge the crab cakes in the flour and tap off the excess. Working in batches, fry the cakes on both sides until golden brown, about 3 minutes per side. Transfer to the paper towels to drain and season with a bit of salt.

5. To serve: Divide the crab cakes among four plates (2 crab cakes per plate) and serve topped with the salsa verde and tartar sauce.

continued >

Salsa Verde

✖ MAKES ABOUT 1½ CUPS

½ cup extra-virgin olive oil

3 garlic cloves, mashed
to a paste with ¼ teaspoon
kosher salt

2 oil-packed anchovy fillets,
finely chopped to a paste

6 cornichons, finely diced

1 cup chopped fresh parsley
leaves

¼ cup chopped fresh basil
leaves

Kosher salt and freshly
ground black pepper

Whisk together the oil, garlic, anchovies, and cornichons in a large bowl. Add the parsley and basil and mix until combined. Season with salt and pepper. Let sit at room temperature for at least 15 minutes or up to 1 day in the refrigerator before serving. Bring to room temperature before using.

Citrus Tartar Sauce

✖ MAKES ABOUT 1½ CUPS

1 cup mayonnaise

1 teaspoon finely grated
orange zest

1 teaspoon finely grated
lemon zest

1 tablespoon freshly
squeezed orange juice

1 tablespoon freshly
squeezed lemon juice

5 cornichons, finely diced

1 tablespoon capers,
drained and chopped

Kosher salt and freshly
ground black pepper

Combine the mayonnaise, both citrus zests, both citrus juices, the cornichons, and the capers in a medium bowl and season with salt and pepper. Cover and refrigerate for at least 30 minutes and up to 24 hours before serving to allow the flavors to meld.

SERVES 6

RICE

2 cups Light Chicken Stock (page 233) or store-bought low-sodium chicken stock or broth

Kosher salt and freshly ground black pepper

2 cups long-grain white rice

CURRY SAUCE

3 tablespoons canola oil

4 large shallots, coarsely chopped

3-inch piece fresh ginger, sliced, not peeled

2 jalapeños, coarsely chopped

3 heaping tablespoons mild Madras curry powder

1 (13.5-ounce) can unsweetened full-fat coconut milk, stirred well

4 cups Light Chicken Stock (page 233), Shrimp Stock (page 234), or store-bought low-sodium chicken stock or vegetable broth

1 head garlic, halved horizontally

1 cup fresh coconut water (don't kill yourself opening the coconut) or store-bought

Kosher salt and freshly ground black pepper

ingredients continued >

FISH CURRY
with Scallion & Cashew Rice

I love all curries and I especially love them served with rice to soak up the excess broth. In this dish I reached for one of my winning weapons—texture—and made the cashew rice *crispy*. When the audience at *Beat* sees me crisping up the rice, they know I'm going for the win. For me, the key for a well-balanced dish is to mellow the assertive curry flavors with the addition of coconut milk and to finish the dish with something sweet like ripe fruits, honey, cane sugar, or, as I do here, a sweet and savory chutney of ripe mangoes and charred shishito peppers.

1. Cook the rice: At least 4 hours and up to 48 hours before you are ready to serve, combine the stock, 2 cups cold water, 1 teaspoon salt, and ¼ teaspoon pepper in a medium saucepan. Bring to a boil over high heat. Stir in the rice, bring back to a boil, cover, reduce the heat to low, and cook until the water is absorbed and the rice is tender, about 17 minutes.

2. Remove the pot from the heat and let it sit, covered, for 5 minutes. Remove the lid, fluff the rice with a fork, spread it on a sheet pan in an even layer, and let cool to room temperature. Cover and refrigerate until the rice is cold and the grains are separate, for at least 2 hours and up to 48 hours.

3. Make the curry sauce: Heat the oil in a large Dutch oven over high heat until shimmering. Add the shallots, ginger, and jalapeños and cook until soft, about 4 minutes. Stir in the curry powder and cook, stirring constantly, until fragrant and deepened in color, about 2 minutes. Add the coconut milk and cook, stirring constantly, until reduced, 10 minutes.

4. Add the stock, garlic, and coconut water and bring to a boil. Reduce the heat to a simmer and cook, stirring occasionally, until the mixture thickens slightly and the curry powder rawness starts to cook out, about 30 minutes. Remove the garlic and working in batches, carefully transfer the mixture to a blender and blend until smooth. Return the sauce to the pot, bring to a simmer over low heat, and season with salt and pepper.

continued >

2 scallions, green tops and pale-green parts only, thinly sliced

Kosher salt and freshly ground black pepper

¼ cup plus 2 tablespoons canola oil

½ cup cashews, toasted (see page 247) and coarsely chopped

2 pounds halibut fillets, cut into 2-inch pieces

¼ cup crème fraîche

¼ cup chopped fresh cilantro leaves

Finely grated zest and juice of 2 fresh limes

Mango Chutney (recipe follows)

½ cup rice vinegar

½ cup pure cane sugar

4 large mangoes, diced

6 shishito peppers

¼ cup chopped fresh cilantro leaves

✖ **BEAT THE CLOCK:** There are great mango chutneys on the market, so feel free to use one of those as your base and then follow the rest of the chutney recipe for the charred shishito peppers. Also, for the rice, you can buy a quart of white rice from your local Chinese restaurant. Just be sure to get it the day before you make this dish: Day-old rice makes a crispier crispy rice.

5. To finish: Combine the cold rice and the scallions in a large bowl and season with salt and pepper. Heat ¼ cup of the oil in a large cast-iron skillet or nonstick sauté pan over high heat until shimmering. Put the rice into the pan, press it down into an even layer with a metal spatula, and cook, without stirring, until the bottom is golden brown, about 5 minutes. Turn the rice over, press down again into an even layer, and cook until the bottom is golden brown, about 5 minutes longer. Stir in the cashews and transfer to a bowl.

6. Heat the remaining 2 tablespoons oil in the same pan over high heat until shimmering. In batches, if necessary, season with salt and pepper and cook the fish in a single layer until golden brown on both sides, about 2 minutes per side. (It will finish cooking in the curry sauce.)

7. Transfer the fish to the curry sauce and cook until just cooked through, about 5 minutes longer. Remove the fish to a large shallow bowl. Whisk the crème fraîch, cilantro, lime zest, and lime juice into the curry sauce and pour it over the fish. Serve with the crispy rice and mango chutney.

Mango Chutney

✖ **MAKES ABOUT 2 CUPS**

1. Combine the vinegar and sugar in a deep medium sauté pan over high heat and cook until the sugar dissolves, about 1 minute. Add the mangoes and cook until they begin to break down and the mixture thickens, about 20 minutes.

2. Meanwhile, heat a cast-iron skillet or nonstick sauté pan over high heat until smoking. Add the shishitos and cook until charred on both sides, about 3 minutes per side. Remove to a cutting board, let cool slightly, and cut into thin slices.

3. Remove the chutney from the heat and stir in the shishitos and cilantro. Let the chutney cool to room temperature and serve or cover and refrigerate for up to 3 days.

BEER-BATTERED FISH & CHIPS

with Salsa Verde Tartar Sauce

SERVES 4

1½ cups all-purpose flour

½ cup rice flour

¼ cup cornstarch

1 to 1½ cups very cold dark beer

Kosher salt and freshly ground black pepper

Canola oil, for frying

8 (3- to 4-ounce) cod fillets

Yukon Gold Chips (recipe follows)

Salsa Verde Tartar Sauce (recipe follows)

Lemon wedges, for serving

The best fish and chips I've ever had was at a take-away place called FISH! in Borough Market in London. It was light and crispy and the fish was just perfectly cooked and luscious. Maybe I need to work there for a summer to improve my fried fish cookery, because I seem to stumble when the dish is announced on game day. Since I haven't gotten the job offer yet, I'm stuck with perfecting my fish and chips stateside—good thing I love it!

1. Whisk together ½ cup of the all-purpose flour, the rice flour, and the cornstarch in a large bowl until combined. Slowly whisk in the beer until the mixture reaches the consistency of a pancake batter. Season with salt and pepper and refrigerate for 15 minutes.

2. Set a wire rack over a sheet pan. Pour 6 inches of oil into a deep fryer or large Dutch oven and heat over medium heat to 375°F on a deep-fry thermometer.

3. Put the remaining 1 cup all-purpose flour on a large plate and season with salt and pepper. Season the fish fillets on both sides with salt and pepper. Dredge the fillets in the flour and tap off the excess, then dip them in the batter and let the excess run off. Working in batches, fry the fish until golden brown and cooked through, about 5 minutes. Drain on the prepared rack and immediately season with a sprinkling of salt.

4. Serve with the chips, tartar sauce, and a lemon wedge on the side.

Yukon Gold Chips ✳ SERVES 4

Kosher salt

6 large Yukon Gold potatoes, scrubbed and cut lengthwise into eighths

Canola oil, for frying

1. Bring a large pot of water to a boil and add 2 tablespoons salt. Add the potatoes and cook until just tender, about 8 minutes. Remove the potatoes with a slotted spoon, drain well, spread on a sheet pan to cool, and then refrigerate until cold, 30 minutes (see Beat the Clock, opposite).

2. Line a sheet pan with several layers of paper towels. Fill a deep fryer or large Dutch oven halfway with oil and heat over medium heat to 350°F on a deep-fry thermometer.

3. Working in batches, fry the potatoes until golden brown and crisp, about 4 minutes. Remove with a slotted spoon to the paper towels to drain and season liberally with salt.

1 cup mayonnaise

2 garlic cloves, mashed
to a paste with ¼ teaspoon
kosher salt

3 oil-packed anchovy fillets,
finely chopped

Finely grated zest of 1 large
lemon

¼ cup finely diced cornichons

2 tablespoons capers, drained

1 cup finely chopped fresh
flat-leaf parsley

¼ cup fresh tarragon leaves,
finely chopped

Kosher salt and freshly
ground black pepper

Salsa Verde Tartar Sauce

✖ MAKES ABOUT 2 CUPS

Whisk together the mayonnaise, garlic, anchovies, lemon zest, cornichons, and capers in a large bowl until combined. Add the parsley and tarragon and mix until incorporated. Season with salt and pepper to taste. Cover and refrigerate for at least 30 minutes and up to 8 hours before serving to allow the flavors to meld.

✖ **BEAT THE CLOCK:** Fries (or chips) are hard to get crispy under the clock—I had to first blanch the potatoes, then dry them out in the refrigerator to amp their crisp factor on the show. It's a technique to use when you HAVE to, but otherwise not one I'd recommend. You should soak your potatoes in cold water in the refrigerator for at least 8 hours and up to 24 hours before frying, making sure to change the water once or twice during that time.

EPISODE 2108: *"Clear the Deck"*
COMPETITOR: Matthew Ridgway
DISH: Sole meunière
WINNER: Bobby Flay

NEW ORLEANS–STYLE SOLE MEUNIÈRE

with Crawfish Butter Sauce

People who know me well know that I'm an old-school guy at heart—music, clothes, and even food. Talk about old-school, this dish—perfectly sautéed fillet of sole and a white pan sauce scattered with briny crawfish tails—is a New Orleans classic. Make me a Sazerac cocktail to start and I'm ready for Louisiana cuisine and spirit to follow.

SERVES 4

CRAWFISH BUTTER SAUCE

2 tablespoons canola oil

2 large shallots, diced

5 large garlic cloves, chopped

3 cups Shrimp Stock (page 234)

3 tablespoons crème fraîche

4 tablespoons cold unsalted butter, cut into pieces

1 pound crawfish tails, fresh or thawed frozen

Finely grated zest and juice of 1 lemon

1 tablespoon finely chopped fresh tarragon

Kosher salt and freshly ground black pepper

PAN-FRIED SOLE

1 cup all-purpose flour

1 teaspoon garlic powder

½ teaspoon sweet Spanish paprika

⅛ teaspoon cayenne pepper

Kosher salt and freshly ground black pepper

8 (3- to 4-ounce) sole fillets

1 stick (8 tablespoons) unsalted butter, cut into pieces

¼ cup chopped fresh flat-leaf parsley, for garnish (optional)

1. Prepare the crawfish butter sauce: Heat the oil in a large deep sauté pan over medium heat. Add the shallots and garlic and cook until soft, about 2 minutes. Add the stock and cook until slightly thickened and reduced to about 1 cup, about 25 minutes.

2. Strain the sauce into a small saucepan set over low heat and whisk in the crème fraîche and butter until thickened. Remove from the heat and stir in the crawfish, lemon zest, lemon juice, and tarragon and season with salt and black pepper. Cover and keep warm.

3. Prepare the pan-fried sole: Stir together the flour, garlic powder, paprika, and cayenne in a medium bowl and season with salt and black pepper. Season the fillets on both sides with salt and black pepper.

4. Melt half of the butter in a large nonstick sauté pan over high heat. Dredge the skin sides of half of the fillets in the seasoned flour and tap off any excess. Put the fish into the pan, floured-side down, and cook until golden brown, about 3 minutes. Flip and cook for 30 seconds longer. Transfer to a plate. Repeat with the remaining butter and fish.

5. Transfer the fish to serving plates. Spoon some of the crawfish butter sauce over the top and garnish with fresh parsley leaves, if desired.

✖ **IN IT TO WIN IT:** If you can't find crawfish in your area or they just aren't to your liking, you can substitute cooked crab or lobster meat.

EPISODE 1403: *"Ain't That Dandy"*
COMPETITOR: Jason Dady
DISH: Poke
WINNER: Bobby Flay

YELLOWTAIL POKE
with Spicy Pineapple Sauce & Taro Chips

Poke (rhymes with "okay") is a dish with deep roots in Hawaiian cuisine. It commonly consists of diced raw fish (usually tuna) seasoned with ingredients like soy sauce (shoyu) and sesame oil and tossed with seaweed and sliced onions and scallions—the result is big flavor in a super-fresh bite. Scooped up with crunchy taro chips and dusted with *shichimi tōgarashi* (a Japanese spice blend made with sesame seeds, nori, orange peel, chile, and more), my version is so delicious and hard to resist.

SERVES 6

SPICY PINEAPPLE SAUCE

3 cups fresh pineapple juice

3-inch piece fresh ginger, peeled and chopped

2 garlic cloves, chopped

1 fresh red Thai chile, finely chopped

Juice of 1 lime

2 tablespoons reduced-sodium soy sauce

1 teaspoon toasted sesame oil

TARO CHIPS

1 small taro root (about 1 pound), peeled and thinly sliced on a mandoline

Canola oil, for frying

Kosher salt

Shichimi tōgarashi

POKE

1½ pounds yellowtail fillet, cleaned, cut into ½-inch dice, and kept cold

¼ cup chopped fresh cilantro leaves

2 scallions, green tops and pale-green parts only, thinly sliced

Microgreens (optional)

Crispy Shallots (page 246, optional)

1. Make the spicy pineapple sauce: Combine the pineapple juice, ginger, garlic, and chile in a medium saucepan. Bring to a boil over high heat and cook, stirring occasionally, until reduced to 1 cup, about 20 minutes. Transfer to a bowl. Stir in the lime juice, soy sauce, and sesame oil. Taste for seasoning, adding more lime, soy, or sesame oil if needed.

2. Meanwhile, make the taro chips: Soak the taro slices in cold water for at least 5 minutes to remove excess starch.

3. Line a sheet pan with several layers of paper towel. Fill a large Dutch oven halfway with canola oil and heat over medium heat to 325°F on a deep-fry thermometer.

4. Drain and pat the taro dry between sheets of paper towels. Working in batches, fry the taro until crispy, about 2 minutes. Remove with a spider strainer to the paper towels to drain and season with salt and some shichimi tōgarashi.

5. Assemble the poke: To the bowl of spicy pineapple sauce, add the fish, cilantro, and scallions and stir to combine. Divide among six shallow bowls. If desired, garnish with microgreens and crispy shallots. Serve with some of the taro chips on the side.

✖ **BEAT THE CLOCK:** I made homemade taro chips for the competition, but there are really great prepared versions at the grocery store. To make them taste like homemade, freshen them up in the oven: Preheat the oven to 300°F. Spread the chips on a sheet pan in an even layer, sprinkle some shichimi tōgarashi over the top, and bake until just heated through, about 5 minutes.

ALEX GUARNASCHELLI'S LOBSTER NEWBERG

SERVES 6

12 ounces maitake (hen of the woods) mushrooms

½ pound sunchokes, cut into 1-inch-thick rounds

6 tablespoons extra-virgin olive oil

Kosher salt

3 live lobsters (2 pounds each)

1 tablespoon chopped fresh or canned truffles, plus some slices for garnish

4 tablespoons unsalted butter

3 large shallots, thinly sliced

1 large garlic clove, thinly sliced

¾ cup dry vermouth

1 cup Light Chicken Stock (page 233) or store-bought low-sodium chicken stock or broth

1 cup heavy cream

Lemon juice

✖ **IN IT TO WIN IT:** Normally, this dish has cheese and truffle oil and is served with spinach. I decided to abandon those classic aspects and make some truffle toast on the side. Hey—if you want to beat Bobby, it's go big or go home! If you want to do the same, gently spread 2 or 3 tablespoons of chopped truffles (fresh or canned), with some butter, on toasted slices of brioche bread. Serve on the side for dragging through the sauce and for added texture. —A. G.

"I knew Bobby would try to get super cheffy and fancy. And he did. I couldn't see exactly what he was doing, but I think he batter-dipped and fried some lobster and added tons of technique to this simple dish. To be honest, I went into it with two thoughts in mind: One, this man is my friend, a mentor, and someone whom I admire so much. Two, there's really no beating him at his own game. He's a technically perfect cook with tons of instinct, imagination, and speed. And you know what else? For all his Southwestern and Italian influences, he has a lot of French training in his DNA. That's what makes him a culinary threat on all fronts. One of the judges said he almost didn't pick my dish because of the sunchokes and the lack of Gruyère cheese (a classic taste in the dish), so I won by a hair! The most important thing: Bobby and I admire one another. He makes me always want to be a better cook and a better person. Lobster dishes come and go. So do competitions. True friendship is forever. For me, there really is no 'beating' Bobby." **—ALEX GUARNASCHELLI**

1. Preheat the oven to 350°F.

2. Break the mushrooms into smaller pieces and spread them on one half of a sheet pan. On the other half, arrange the sunchoke slices in a single layer. Drizzle with 4 tablespoons of the oil and a sprinkle of salt. Roast until the sunchokes are tender and the mushrooms are browned, 15 to 20 minutes. Remove from the oven and keep warm.

3. While the vegetables are roasting, bring a large stockpot of water to a rolling boil and salt it. Plunge the lobsters into the water, taking care that they are completely submerged, and adjust the heat to medium. Cook until cooked through, 9 minutes. Use a large slotted spoon to transfer the lobsters to a flat surface in a single layer to drain and cool.

4. Once the lobsters are cool enough to handle, extract the meat gingerly from the tails, claws, and legs. Take care that the claw meat

continued >

does not have any cartilage. Slice the tail meat into bite-size chunks. Leave the claws and other pieces whole.

5. In a medium bowl, gently mix the lobster meat with the chopped truffles. Cover with plastic and refrigerate.

6. Clean the lobster bodies: Remove the spongy lungs running alongside both sides of the inner layer of the lobster heads, split them in half lengthwise, and reserve.

7. Melt the butter in a large skillet over medium heat. Stir in the shallots and garlic with a pinch of salt and cook until translucent and tender, 2 to 3 minutes. Add the lobster heads in a single layer in the pan. Cook over medium-low heat, tossing to make sure any excess moisture cooks out but the mixture does not burn, 8 to 10 minutes.

8. Remove the pan from the heat and add the vermouth. Return the pan to medium heat and cook until all of the vermouth has evaporated, about 5 minutes. Add the stock and a pinch of salt and cook until the liquid is flavorful, 3 to 5 minutes. You should have about 1 cup total. You do not need a lot of broth, but you do need as much flavor as possible. Stir in the cream and simmer gently until the sauce thickens, 3 to 5 minutes.

9. Strain the sauce, pressing down on the shells to extract the maximum flavor. Discard the shells and let the sauce cool. Taste for seasoning. Season with lemon juice to taste. Sauces, like meat, need a few minutes to "rest" before serving.

10. Heat the remaining 2 tablespoons oil in a medium skillet over medium heat until it begins to smoke lightly. Add the cooked mushrooms and brown and "crisp" them in the oil, 3 to 5 minutes. Season with salt and drain on a kitchen towel.

11. When ready to serve, warm the sauce over low heat. Add the lobster pieces and gently warm them in the sauce. Arrange some of the sunchokes on the bottom of six plates (or a large platter, if serving family-style). Top each with half a lobster's worth of meat. Top with the crisped mushrooms (and truffle toast, if desired; see In It to Win It, page 81). Serve immediately.

JAMARIUS BANKS'S CREOLE SHRIMP & GRITS

SERVES 4 TO 6

Canola oil

1 pound andouille sausage, sliced on the diagonal into ¼-inch-thick slices

1 stick (8 tablespoons) unsalted butter

1 large Spanish onion, finely diced

3 bell peppers (1 each green, red, and orange), finely diced

½ celery stalk, finely diced

1 pound fresh okra, ½ pound cut on the diagonal into ¼-inch-thick slices and ½ pound halved lengthwise

5 garlic cloves, finely chopped

Creole Seasoning (recipe follows)

¾ cup all-purpose flour

4 to 6 cups Shrimp Stock (page 234) or store-bought low-sodium chicken stock or broth

1 teaspoon filé powder

3 sprigs thyme

1 bay leaf

1 cup buttermilk

2 cups yellow cornmeal

Kosher salt and freshly ground black pepper

2 pounds U10 shrimp, peeled and deveined

Juice of 1 lemon

¼ cup chopped fresh flat-leaf parsley

4 scallions, green tops and pale-green parts only, thinly sliced

1 pound jumbo lump crabmeat, picked over

Grits (recipe follows)

"I can honestly say I truly enjoyed competing on the show. Going into the experience, I did not know what to expect. But once the gates closed and the cameras started rolling, it all came so naturally. After winning the first round, I was extremely excited that I would now be competing against my idol, Bobby Flay. I gave it my all and ultimately was defeated, but I wouldn't trade the opportunity for anything." —JAMARIUS BANKS

1. Heat 2 tablespoons oil in a large Dutch oven over high heat until shimmering. Add the sausage and cook until golden brown on both sides, about 7 minutes. Remove with a slotted spoon to a plate lined with paper towels.

2. Melt the butter in the same pan. Add the onion, bell peppers, celery, and thinly sliced okra and cook until soft, about 5 minutes. Stir in the garlic and cook for 1 minute longer. Add 2 tablespoons Creole seasoning and cook, stirring constantly, for 1 minute.

3. Sprinkle ½ cup of the flour over the mixture and mix until smooth. Reduce the heat to medium-low and cook, stirring occasionally, until the roux becomes a deep reddish-brown color, about 12 minutes. Stir in the stock, filé, thyme, and bay leaf. Bring to a boil, then reduce to a simmer and cook, stirring occasionally, until the okra is tender, the sauce thickens, and the flour taste is cooked out, about 30 minutes.

4. While the sauce is cooking, put the buttermilk in a medium bowl. Add the okra and let sit for 10 minutes. Combine the remaining ¼ cup flour and the cornmeal in a medium bowl and season with salt and pepper.

5. Line a sheet pan with paper towels. Fill a deep fryer or large Dutch oven halfway with oil and heat over medium heat to 350°F on a deep-fry thermometer.

6. Working in batches, remove the okra from the buttermilk with a slotted spoon and let the excess run off. Dredge in the cornmeal mixture. Add to the hot oil and fry until golden brown and crispy, about 2 minutes. Remove with a slotted spoon to the paper towels to drain and season with salt.

continued >

7. Put the shrimp in a large bowl, add 3 tablespoons Creole seasoning, and stir well to combine. Heat 3 tablespoons oil in a large cast-iron skillet over high heat until shimmering. Working in batches, add the shrimp and cook until golden brown on both sides and just cooked through, about 5 minutes total. Remove to a plate. Add more oil if needed for the remaining shrimp.

8. To serve, stir the lemon juice, parsley, scallions, and crab into the gumbo sauce. Spoon some of the grits into each bowl and ladle some of the gumbo sauce over the grits. Top with 3 of the shrimp and garnish with some of the fried okra.

Creole Seasoning

✖ MAKES ABOUT 6 TABLESPOONS

2 teaspoons dried oregano

2 teaspoons garlic powder

2 teaspoons onion powder

2 teaspoons mustard powder

2 teaspoons kosher salt

2 teaspoons freshly ground black pepper

2 teaspoons freshly ground white pepper

2 teaspoons cayenne pepper

2 teaspoons sweet Spanish paprika

2 teaspoons pure cane sugar

Stir together all the ingredients in a bowl until combined. Keep tightly covered in the pantry for up to 6 months.

Grits

✖ MAKES 1½ QUARTS

4 to 5 cups Shrimp Stock (page 234), Light Chicken Stock (page 233), or store-bought low-sodium chicken stock (or a combination)

4 cups heavy cream

2 teaspoons kosher salt

2 cups stone-ground white or yellow grits

1. Combine 4 cups of the stock, the cream, and salt in a large saucepan and bring to a boil over high heat. Slowly whisk in the grits and continue whisking until the mixture begins to thicken.

2. Reduce the heat to medium and cook, stirring frequently, until the grits are very thick, 40 to 50 minutes. Depending on the grind, cooking may take longer. As the grits thicken, they can scorch easily, so be sure to stir often. If the grits absorb all of the cooking liquid before they are done, add more hot stock or hot water.

EPISODE 1208:
"The Next Food Network Star Is"
COMPETITOR: Damaris Phillips
DISH: Tuna noodle casserole
WINNER: Damaris Phillips

DAMARIS PHILLIPS'S TUNA NOODLE CASSEROLE

SERVES 4 TO 6

Kosher salt

12 ounces campanelle pasta

3 cloves Roasted Garlic (page 240), mashed to a paste

2½ cups mushroom stock, Light Chicken Stock (page 233), or store-bought low-sodium chicken stock or broth

2 cups heavy cream

2 tablespoons sherry vinegar

1 tablespoon soy sauce

7 tablespoons unsalted butter

1 cup medium-diced Spanish onion (about 1 medium)

½ cup medium-diced celery (about 2 stalks)

12 ounces wild mushrooms, stems discarded, caps coarsely chopped

¼ to ½ teaspoon crushed red pepper flakes

¼ cup all-purpose flour

8 ounces smoked Gruyère cheese, grated

1 cup sour cream

10 ounces frozen peas

¼ cup chopped fresh parsley

1 pound smoked tuna fillets in oil, flaked

Freshly ground black pepper

½ cup plain fresh bread crumbs

½ cup crushed potato chips

½ cup coarsely grated smoked cheddar cheese

"I will be completely honest: It felt great to beat Bobby and it really had everything to do with the dish I chose. Eighty-nine times out of one hundred, I think Bobby would destroy me in the kitchen. So I knew that if I wanted to win, I had to dig deeper than 'What doesn't Bobby cook?' Instead, my strategy was 'What wouldn't Bobby eat?' The answer I came up with was tuna noodle casserole. I thought there was exactly a zero percent chance that this debonair chef has ever or will ever eat a casserole famous for using canned tuna and soup. Plus, the idea of Bobby pulling a bubbling-hot 1950s casserole out of his oven made me giggle. On all of these accounts, I was right. Bobby Flay makes a terrible tuna noodle casserole, but this winning recipe is delicious!" —DAMARIS PHILLIPS

1. Preheat the oven to 375°F.

2. Bring a large pot of water to a boil and add 2 tablespoons salt. Add the noodles and cook for 6 minutes. Drain well, rinse with cold water, and drain well again. The noodles will be very al dente but will continue to cook as the casserole bakes.

3. Whisk together the garlic paste, mushroom stock, cream, vinegar, and soy sauce in a large bowl.

4. Melt 3 tablespoons of the butter in a large (14-inch) cast-iron skillet over medium heat. Add the onion, celery, and mushrooms and cook until tender, 4 to 5 minutes. Add the pepper flakes and cook for 15 seconds. Stir in the flour and cook for 2 to 3 minutes. Slowly whisk in the mushroom stock mixture and cook, whisking constantly, until the mixture thickens and coats the back of a spoon, about 7 minutes.

5. Remove the pan from the heat and whisk in the Gruyère, sour cream, peas, and half of the parsley. Add the cooked noodles and the tuna and stir well. Season with salt and black pepper.

6. Melt the remaining 4 tablespoons butter. Combine the melted butter, bread crumbs, potato chips, and cheddar in a medium bowl. Sprinkle over the casserole.

7. Bake until the center is hot and the top is golden brown, about 17 minutes. Remove from the oven and top with the remaining parsley. Let cool for 5 minutes before serving.

DARREN SAYPHRARAJ'S LOBSTER TOM YUM SOUP with Vermicelli Noodles

SERVES 6

PICKLED BEECH MUSHROOMS

½ **cup distilled white vinegar**

½ **cup pure cane sugar**

1 **tablespoon kosher salt**

1 **package (about 8 ounces) beech mushrooms or enoki**

1 **jalapeño or Fresno chile, thinly sliced**

TOM YUM BROTH

Kosher salt

2 **live lobsters (2 to 3 pounds each)**

2 **lemongrass stalks, trimmed and thinly sliced**

2 **large shallots, chopped**

4 **Thai bird's eye chiles, chopped**

2-**inch piece fresh ginger, peeled and sliced**

2-**inch piece galangal, peeled and sliced**

10 **makrut lime leaves**

3 **tablespoons canola oil**

3 **plum tomatoes, quartered**

2 **quarts Lobster Stock (page 234), Light Chicken Stock (page 233), or store-bought low-sodium chicken stock or broth**

2 **tablespoons palm sugar, jaggery, or light brown sugar, plus more to taste**

2 **teaspoons fish sauce, plus more to taste**

"Being on *Beat Bobby Flay* was one of the most fun experiences I have had as a chef. At the time I was opening a new restaurant and going through all the countless responsibilities that come with it. Competing on *BBF* allowed me to have some fun, show people a glimpse of my personality, and let loose a little. It was a blast to cook against one of the most recognizable chefs on the planet—a man who has cooked and won thousands of cooking competitions against chefs from all over the world. I will point out that there is no TV magic to what Bobby does day in and day out on this show. He really does not know what dish he is cooking, and he and the producers have to make up everything on the fly. The challengers have a dish picked out and the ingredients all laid out for them, so Bobby is at a real disadvantage. Much respect to you, Bobby, and I hope you'll have me again for a rematch. I'll even let you choose the dish." —**DARREN SAYPHRARAJ**

1. Pickle the beech mushrooms: Bring 1 cup water, the vinegar, cane sugar, and salt to a boil in a medium saucepan over high heat. Cut the stems off the mushrooms, making sure that they are all separated, and place them in a large bowl. Add the chile. Pour the hot pickling liquid over the mushrooms and chile. Let cool to room temperature, then cover and refrigerate. The mushrooms can be made up to 3 days in advance.

2. Make the tom yum broth: Fill a large bowl (large enough to hold both lobsters) with ice and water. Bring a large pot of water to a boil over high heat and add 2 tablespoons salt. Add the lobsters to the boiling water and cook for 6 minutes. Immediately plunge the lobsters into the ice bath. Let sit until cool enough to handle, 3 minutes. Remove the tail and claw meat from the shells. Clean and reserve the head and shells to be used for the broth. Cut the tail meat into chunks, but leave the claws and knuckles whole.

3. Combine the lemongrass, shallots, chiles, ginger, galangal, and lime leaves in a food processor or mortar and pestle and pulverize into a paste.

Juice of 8 limes

Kosher salt

Boiling water

12 ounces mung bean vermicelli noodles or rice noodles

Cilantro, for garnish

4. Heat the oil in a large Dutch oven or saucepan over high heat until shimmering. Add the paste and cook, stirring constantly, until softened and fragrant, about 4 minutes. Add the reserved lobster heads and shells and tomatoes and cook until the tomatoes have softened, about 5 minutes. Add the stock and simmer for at least 30 minutes and up to 60 minutes.

5. Stir in the palm sugar, fish sauce, lime juice, and salt, to taste. Depending on preference, add more palm sugar and/or fish sauce, if desired. The soup should be sour and slightly sweet. Do not boil the broth after you add the lime juice to keep the freshness of the lime.

6. In a heatproof bowl, pour boiling hot water over the vermicelli noodles. Let steep until softened, 5 minutes, then drain.

7. To serve, divide the lobster meat and noodles among six bowls and pour the hot broth over the top. Garnish with the pickled mushrooms and cilantro.

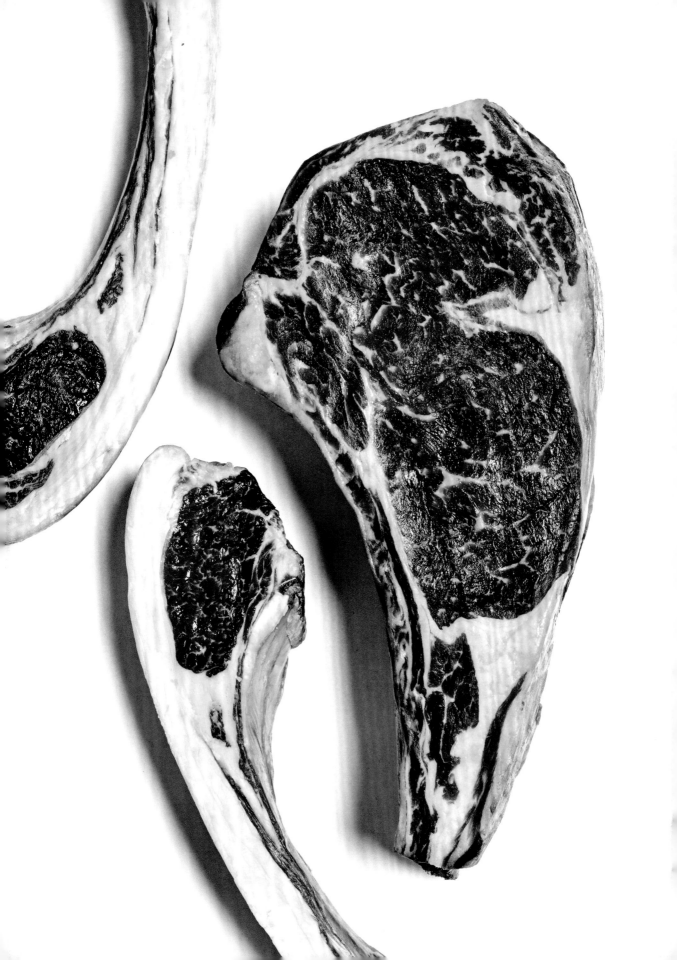

BEEF & LAMB

EPISODE 701: "A Cut Above"
COMPETITOR: John Tesar
DISH: Beef Wellington
WINNER: Bobby Flay

BEEF WELLINGTON
with Cherry-Chile Port Sauce

Truth: I was genuinely surprised I won this one. To start, I don't think I had made this Old World dish since I was a student in culinary school, and to have John Tesar as my opponent!? He is such an accomplished chef—especially when it comes to meat—that I knew I had to bring my A++++ game. If I could point to anything that possibly helped me get the win, it would have to be the sauce of red chiles, port, and cherries. They all work so well together and elevate the classic dish.

SERVES 6

12 ounces cremini mushrooms, stems discarded

7 tablespoons canola oil

3 shallots, finely diced

2 teaspoons finely chopped fresh thyme

Kosher salt and freshly ground black pepper

2 tablespoons unsalted butter

12 ounces duck livers, rinsed with cold water, drained, and patted dry

½ cup Cognac

1 sheet frozen puff pastry (half a 17.3-ounce package), thawed

All-purpose flour, for rolling out the dough

6 (6-ounce) filets mignons, at least 2 inches thick, patted dry

¼ cup Bobby's Spice Rub (page 243)

Egg wash: 2 large eggs beaten with 2 tablespoons water

Cherry-Chile Port Sauce (recipe follows)

1. Pulse the mushrooms in a food processor until finely chopped (or chop by hand with a large chef's knife). Heat 2 tablespoons of the oil in a large sauté pan over high heat until shimmering. Add the mushrooms to the pan along with half of the shallots and cook, stirring occasionally, until the mushrooms are golden brown and their liquid has evaporated, about 8 minutes. Stir in 1 teaspoon of the thyme and season with salt and pepper.

2. In another large sauté pan, heat 2 tablespoons of the oil and the butter over high heat until the butter has melted and the mixture is shimmering. Add the livers and cook until golden brown on both sides, about 4 minutes per side. Add the remaining shallots and thyme and cook for 1 minute longer. Remove the pan from the heat, slowly add the Cognac, and stand back, as it could ignite quickly. Return pan to heat and cook until completely reduced, about 3 minutes. Season with salt and pepper.

3. Combine the duck livers and mushrooms in a food processor and process until smooth. Taste for seasoning, adding more salt and pepper if needed. Transfer to a plate and let cool.

4. Preheat the oven to 450°F. Line a sheet pan with parchment paper.

5. Roll out the puff pastry on a lightly floured surface into a 16-inch square. Place on the prepared sheet pan and chill in the freezer while you prepare the beef.

6. Line a plate with paper towels. Heat the remaining 3 tablespoons oil in a large sauté pan over high heat until shimmering. Season the beef on both sides with salt and pepper and the spice rub. Sear until golden brown, about 2 minutes per side (it will keep cooking in the oven). Remove to the plate and place in the freezer for 5 minutes. Remove the beef from the freezer. Evenly top the filets with the mushroom mixture, pressing to make sure it sticks.

continued >

7. Remove the puff pastry from the freezer. Cut it into 6 squares. Roll each of those squares out to a 7-inch square. Brush the surface with some of the egg wash and season with salt and pepper. Put a filet in the center of each square. Fold the pastry over the filet as though wrapping a package and press the edges to seal. Place the packages seam-side down on the prepared sheet pan. Brush the egg wash over the tops and sides of each package.

8. Bake until the pastry is golden brown and an instant-read thermometer registers 140°F for medium-rare, 18 to 20 minutes.

9. To serve, ladle some of the sauce into the center of six dinner plates. Slice the Wellingtons in half on the diagonal and set on top of the sauce.

Cherry-Chile Port Sauce

✖ **MAKES ABOUT 1½ CUPS**

2 tablespoons canola oil

2 large shallots, chopped

Kosher salt and freshly ground black pepper

3 garlic cloves, chopped

1 cup port wine

3 cups Light Chicken Stock (page 233) or store-bought low-sodium chicken stock or broth

2 tablespoons demi-glace (optional)

2 ancho chiles, seeded

½ cup dried cherries

Clover honey (optional)

1. Heat the oil in a Dutch oven over high heat until shimmering. Add the shallots, season with salt and pepper, and cook until soft, about 3 minutes. Add the garlic and cook for 1 minute longer. Add the port and cook until reduced by half, about 5 minutes. Add ½ cup water, the stock, demi-glace (if using), the chiles, and the cherries. Season with salt and pepper and bring to a boil. Cook until reduced by half and the cherries and chiles are soft, about 15 minutes.

2. Transfer the sauce to a food processor or blender and process until smooth. Strain back into the pot and bring to a boil over high heat. Taste for seasoning and add more salt and pepper and some honey, if desired. Keep warm until ready to serve.

SERVES 6

6 New York strip steaks,
1½ to 2 inches thick

PINK PEPPERCORN SAUCE

3 tablespoons beef fat (or
2 tablespoons unsalted butter
plus 1 tablespoon canola oil)

2 large shallots, chopped

3 garlic cloves, smashed and
peeled

1 cup Cognac

3 cups veal stock, Beef Stock
(page 232), or Rich Chicken
Stock (page 233)

2 tablespoons crème fraîche

1 tablespoon pink peppercorns,
coarsely crushed

Kosher salt and freshly
ground black pepper

TO FINISH

Kosher salt

2 tablespoons coarsely ground
black peppercorns

2 tablespoons canola oil

Crispy Smashed Duck Fat
Potatoes (recipe follows)

✱ **IN IT TO WIN IT:** I rarely use veal stock
or demi-glace in my cooking, as it
takes forever to make and its flavor
can overpower a dish very quickly.
However, when making a classic
French dish such as this, it is pretty
much mandatory. If you don't eat or
use veal in your cooking, a good-
quality beef stock or rich chicken
stock will work nicely, too.

STEAK AU POIVRE
with Crispy Smashed Duck Fat Potatoes

A lusty beefsteak crusted with peppercorns and sitting
in a sauce of Cognac and crème fraîche—this is a
French bistro classic that will never get old. Be sure
your pan is smokin' hot to ensure you make that crust
happen—it's key to the ultimate steak cookery. The
crispy potatoes may be the supporting cast, but they
round out the entire meal. Fire up the fireplace and save
a sip of Cognac for after dinner.

1. Remove the steaks from the refrigerator 30 minutes before
cooking them to take the chill off.

2. Prepare the pink peppercorn sauce: Heat the fat in a deep
medium sauté pan over high heat until shimmering. Add the shallots
and garlic and cook until soft, about 4 minutes. Remove the pan
from the heat, slowly add the Cognac, and stand back, as it could
ignite quickly. Return the pan to the heat, reduce the heat to
medium, and cook until the Cognac is completely reduced, about
5 minutes.

3. Add the stock, increase the heat to high, and cook until reduced
by half, about 15 minutes. Whisk in the crème fraîche and pink
peppercorns, and season with salt and black pepper. Keep warm
while you cook the steaks.

4. Preheat the oven to 425°F.

5. To finish: Liberally season the steaks on both sides with salt
and let sit for 5 minutes. Season the top sides with the black
peppercorns, pressing them down to adhere to the meat.

6. Heat the oil in a large cast-iron sauté pan over high heat until
shimmering. Add the steaks, peppercorn-side down, and cook until
golden brown and a crust has formed, about 4 minutes. Turn the
steaks over and cook until the bottoms are golden brown, about
4 minutes longer. Transfer to the oven and cook to medium-rare,
until an instant-read thermometer registers 140°F, about 5 minutes
longer.

7. Remove the steaks from the oven and let rest on a cutting board
for 5 minutes. Transfer the steaks to plates and ladle some of the
pink peppercorn sauce over them. Serve the potatoes on the side.

continued >

1½ pounds Yukon Gold potatoes, scrubbed

Kosher salt

½ cup duck fat or chicken fat (or ¼ cup canola oil mixed with 4 tablespoons unsalted butter)

Freshly ground black pepper

2 large scallions, green tops and pale-green parts only, thinly sliced

3 Pickled Chiles (page 248), thinly sliced

Crispy Smashed Duck Fat Potatoes

✖ SERVES 6

1. Put the potatoes in a large saucepan, add cold water to cover by 2 inches, and season with 2 tablespoons salt. Bring to a boil and cook until fork-tender, about 25 minutes. Drain well and let cool for 5 minutes. Cut into large dice, leaving the skins on.

2. Heat the fat in a large cast-iron skillet over high heat until shimmering. Add the potatoes and, using a heavy-duty metal spatula, press down on them to make an even layer and smash them slightly. Cook, undisturbed, until the bottoms are golden brown, about 5 minutes. Season liberally with salt and pepper and flip over. Press down again with the spatula to form a single layer and cook until the bottoms are golden brown, 5 minutes longer. Stir in the scallions and pickled chiles and transfer to a shallow serving bowl.

EPISODE 1101: *"All at Stake"*
COMPETITOR: Todd Erickson
DISH: Salisbury steak
WINNER: Todd Erickson

CHIPOTLE SALISBURY STEAK
with Mashed Potatoes & Mushroom-Bacon Gravy

SERVES 4

4 tablespoons canola oil

8 thick-cut slices bacon, cut crosswise into ¼-inch-wide lardons

1 medium Spanish onion, finely diced

3 garlic cloves, mashed to a paste with ¼ teaspoon kosher salt

1 large egg, lightly whisked

1 or 2 chipotle chiles, depending on heat preference, finely chopped

1½ pounds ground chuck (80/20)

½ cup panko bread crumbs

Kosher salt and freshly ground black pepper

2 tablespoons unsalted butter

1 pound shiitake or cremini mushrooms (or a combination), stems discarded, caps cut into ¼-inch-thick slices

3 tablespoons all-purpose flour

1 cup dry red wine

3 cups Light Chicken Stock (page 233) or store-bought low-sodium chicken stock or broth

3 sprigs thyme

Mashed Potatoes (recipe follows)

✖ **IN IT TO WIN IT:** It is really important that the Salisbury steaks have time to braise in the gravy. Mine were not tender enough and that was one of the reasons I lost the battle. Give yourself at least 30 minutes of braising before serving.

My mom, Dorothy Flay, would have been disappointed that I lost this one—Salisbury steak TV dinners were one of her "specialties!" Unlike the ones she used to pop in the toaster oven, though, my Salisbury steak gets extra flavor from smoky chipotle, and its rich mushroom gravy is studded with thick lardons of bacon. I made a miscalculation and didn't get my steaks into the gravy soon enough in this battle—you need to give the gravy sufficient time to soak into and tenderize the steak while the flavors meld. This was something my opponent got right; chef Todd Erickson brought the Salisbury "noise" to beat me! The proof is in his winning recipe on page 101.

1. Line a plate with paper towels. Heat 1 tablespoon of the oil in a large cast-iron skillet over medium heat. Add the bacon and cook until golden brown and crispy and the fat has rendered, about 8 minutes. Leaving behind the fat, use a slotted spoon to remove the bacon to the paper towels to drain.

2. Heat the rendered bacon fat over high heat until shimmering. Add the onion and cook until soft, about 4 minutes. Add the garlic and cook for 1 minute longer. Transfer the mixture, along with the fat, to a large bowl and let cool slightly.

3. Line a sheet pan with parchment paper. Add the egg and chipotle to the cooled onion-garlic mixture and mix until combined. Add the meat and the panko, season with salt and pepper, and gently mix to combine. Divide the meat mixture into 4 equal portions and form each portion into an oval patty about 1 inch thick. Place the patties on the prepared sheet pan, cover, and refrigerate for at least 30 minutes and up to 12 hours.

4. While the meat is chilling, heat 1 tablespoon of the oil and the butter in a large high-sided sauté pan over high heat until shimmering. Add the mushrooms and cook until golden brown and their liquid has evaporated, about 8 minutes. Sprinkle the flour over the mushrooms and cook, stirring constantly, until the flour turns a light golden brown, about 2 minutes. Stir in the wine and cook until

continued >

reduced by half, about 5 minutes. Stir in the stock, thyme, and bacon and bring to a boil. Reduce the heat to medium and cook until the mushroom gravy begins to thicken and the flour taste cooks out, about 8 minutes.

5. When ready to cook the Salisbury steaks, heat the remaining 2 tablespoons oil in a large cast-iron skillet over high heat until shimmering. Add the patties and cook until golden brown on both sides, about 4 minutes per side. Carefully transfer the patties to the gravy and cook, spooning the gravy over them occasionally, until the meat is cooked through and tender, about 30 minutes.

6. Serve the Salisbury steaks with mashed potatoes and spoon the gravy over both.

Mashed Potatoes

2½ pounds russet potatoes, peeled and cut into 2-inch chunks

Kosher salt

½ cup heavy cream, plus more as needed

½ cup whole milk, plus more as needed

1 stick (8 tablespoons) unsalted butter, cut into pieces

Freshly ground black pepper

1. Put the potatoes in a large pot, add cold water to cover by 2 inches, and season with 2 tablespoons salt. Bring to a boil over high heat and cook until fork-tender, about 25 minutes. Drain well and return to the pot over high heat for 1 minute to dry out the potatoes a bit. Pass them through a food mill or potato ricer into a large bowl.

2. Heat the cream, milk, and butter in a large saucepan over medium heat until the butter melts and the liquid is warm, about 5 minutes. Add the mixture to the potatoes and mix until combined. Add more cream and milk, as needed, if the mashed potatoes seem too dry. Season with salt and pepper.

SERVES 6

SALISBURY STEAKS

2 tablespoons (1 ounce) unsalted Irish butter

1 small Spanish onion, finely diced

1 garlic clove, finely chopped

¼ cup packed fresh parsley leaves, coarsely chopped

3 tablespoons grapeseed oil

1 small red onion, halved and thinly sliced

1 pound cremini mushrooms, stems discarded, caps sliced

1½ pounds ground chuck (80/20)

3 thick-cut slices bacon, finely diced

2 large eggs

¼ cup heavy cream

3 tablespoons Worcestershire sauce

½ cup panko bread crumbs

Kosher salt and freshly ground black pepper

3 to 4 tablespoons all-purpose flour

ROASTED MUSHROOMS

½ pound wild mushrooms, such as oyster, blue foot, nameko, and chanterelles, stems discarded

¼ cup grapeseed oil

Kosher salt and freshly ground black pepper

ingredients continued >

TODD ERICKSON'S SALISBURY STEAK
with Root Vegetable Purée

"Years ago, while I was still in school at the Culinary Institute of America, Bobby's alma mater, I saw him compete on the original Japanese version of *Iron Chef*. When he completed his round, he jumped up on his workstation and raised his arms victoriously. I thought, Wow, what a cocky dude! I have always remembered that TV moment, and when I was invited to compete, I figured this was my opportunity to take him down a notch, all in good sport, of course. As the clock ran out on the shortest forty minutes of my life, I was proud of what I'd done. Bobby looked over at my plates, patted me on the back, and said, 'Very nice job.' The judges agreed, and I was unanimously named that episode's *Beat Bobby Flay* champion. The whole experience was wonderful from start to finish. Bobby is definitely one to look up to, as he's mastered his work in the kitchen and the very difficult business end of operating multiple restaurants, as well as owning a production company that produces shows that he is the star of. That type of versatility is rare. Even more rare is that, in person, he's humble about it all. I went in to bring Bobby down a notch, but instead, he lifted me up a few."
—TODD ERICKSON

1. Prepare the Salisbury steaks: Melt the butter in a large sauté pan over medium heat. Add the Spanish onion and cook until lightly caramelized, about 10 minutes. Stir in the garlic and parsley, then transfer to a bowl and refrigerate until cooled, about 15 minutes.

2. Clean out the pan with a paper towel and return it to high heat. Add the oil and heat until shimmering. Add the red onion and cook until charred on one side, about 3 minutes. Add the mushrooms and cook until golden brown and softened and their liquid has evaporated, about 12 minutes. Transfer to a plate and set aside. Wipe out the pan once more with a paper towel.

continued >

TO FINISH

3 tablespoons grapeseed oil

½ cup red wine, such as Cabernet Sauvignon

4 cups Fortified Beef Stock (recipe follows)

2 tablespoons Worcestershire sauce

All-purpose flour, if needed

4 tablespoons (2 ounces) unsalted Irish butter

2 tablespoons packed fresh parsley leaves, coarsely chopped

2 tablespoons fresh tarragon, chopped, plus sprigs for garnish

Kosher salt and freshly ground black pepper

Root Vegetable Purée (recipe follows)

2 tablespoons pink peppercorns, crushed

3. Line a sheet pan with parchment paper. Combine the ground chuck, bacon, eggs, cream, Worcestershire, panko, ½ teaspoon pepper, and the cooled onion mixture in a large bowl. Season with salt. Form the mixture into 6 equal oval-shaped patties and place on the prepared sheet pan. Dust the tops with the flour.

4. Roast the mushrooms: Preheat the oven to 450°F. Line a sheet pan with parchment paper.

5. Toss the mushrooms with the oil, salt, and pepper. Arrange on the prepared sheet pan and roast until golden brown and soft, stirring once, about 25 minutes.

6. To finish: Heat the oil in the large sauté pan over high heat until shimmering. Add the beef patties and cook until golden brown on both sides, about 4 minutes per side. Add the wine and cook until reduced by half, about 3 minutes. Spoon the red reserved onion mixture over the beef patties, followed by the stock and the Worcestershire. Cover and bring to an aggressive simmer over medium heat. Check the doneness of the beef patties after 10 minutes; they should be fully cooked through and tender. Remove the patties to a large plate and loosely tent with foil.

7. If the sauce is too runny, sprinkle in a little flour; if it is too thick, add more stock. Finish the sauce by whisking in the butter, parsley, and tarragon. Season with salt and pepper.

8. To assemble, spoon some of the vegetable purée onto six dinner plates and top with a beef patty and a generous amount of the sauce. Garnish with the roasted mushrooms, tarragon sprigs, and the crushed pink peppercorns.

Fortified Beef Stock

✖ MAKES 1 QUART

3 pounds beef neck bones

6 tablespoons grapeseed oil

1 large Spanish onion, cut into medium dice

1 cup medium-diced carrots

1 cup medium-diced celery

⅓ cup tomato paste

2 quarts Beef Stock (page 232) or store-bought low-sodium beef broth

3 bay leaves

1 teaspoon black peppercorns

7 sprigs thyme

1. Preheat the oven to 450°F.

2. Toss the beef bones with 3 tablespoons of the oil in a large bowl and arrange them on a sheet pan. Roast until deep golden brown, about 20 minutes.

3. Heat the remaining 3 tablespoons oil in a stockpot over high heat until shimmering. Add the onion and carrots and cook until well caramelized, about 6 minutes. Add the celery and cook until translucent, about 4 minutes. Add the tomato paste, mix thoroughly, and cook for 2 minutes longer.

4. Add the browned bones, stock, bay leaves, peppercorns, and thyme. Stir and scrape the tomato paste from the bottom of the pan. Partially cover the pot and reduce the heat to medium-low. Simmer until the liquid is reduced by half, about 2 hours. Strain through a fine-mesh sieve and discard the solids.

Root Vegetable Purée

✖ MAKES ABOUT 4 CUPS

1 large sweet potato, peeled and cut into medium dice

2 parsnips, peeled and cut into medium dice

2 cups heavy cream

Kosher salt

6 sprigs thyme

2 tablespoons (1 ounce) Irish butter

1. Combine the sweet potato and parsnips in a medium saucepan. Add the cream, 1 tablespoon salt, and the thyme. Bring to a simmer over medium heat and cook until the vegetables are fork-tender, about 25 minutes.

2. Remove from the heat and use a slotted spoon to transfer the vegetables to a blender or food processor. Discard the thyme sprigs. Add enough of the hot cream mixture to reach halfway up the vegetables. Purée until velvety smooth. Add the butter and purée a few seconds longer to incorporate. Season with salt to taste.

EPISODE 1206: *"Open Grill Season"*
COMPETITOR: *Brandon Byrd*
DISH: *Carne asada*
WINNER: *Bobby Flay*

CARNE ASADA VERDE
with a Fried Egg & Tomato-Avocado Salad

A delicious beefsteak bathed in green chiles and cilantro and served with a chopped salad of California and Southwestern ingredients—this dish is right in my flavor wheelhouse. The show only gives us 45 minutes, but this is the kind of food I could cook all day long. Instead of the classic skirt steak, I prefer to use the rib-cap steak for its excellent marbling, and in this battle, I was guessing that Brandon would use the skirt steak anyway.

SERVES 6

STEAK

3 cups packed chopped fresh cilantro leaves

2 or 3 large jalapeños, roasted (see page 240) and chopped

7 large garlic cloves, chopped

⅔ cup olive oil

Kosher salt and freshly ground black pepper

2-pound rib-cap steak, fat trimmed, halved crosswise

TOMATO-AVOCADO SALAD

¼ cup red wine vinegar

1 or 2 chipotle chiles, to taste, finely chopped

1 teaspoon clover honey

Kosher salt and freshly ground black pepper

½ cup canola oil

4 plum tomatoes, halved, seeded, and diced

1 Hass avocado, chopped

¼ cup Pickled Red Onions (page 248)

¼ cup chopped fresh cilantro leaves

TO FINISH

Kosher salt and freshly ground black pepper

¼ cup hulled pumpkin seeds, toasted (optional)

¼ cup pomegranate seeds (optional)

6 Fried Eggs (page 242)

4 ounces store-bought tortilla strips

1. Prepare the steaks: Combine the cilantro, jalapeños, garlic, and olive oil in a food processor and process until smooth. Season with salt and pepper. Measure out ½ cup of the salsa verde and set aside for garnishing.

2. Put the steak in a baking dish, pour the remaining salsa verde over it, and turn to coat well. Cover and refrigerate for at least 30 minutes and up to 24 hours. (The longer this steak can marinate, the better.)

3. Make the tomato-avocado salad: Whisk together the vinegar, chipotle peppers, honey, and salt and pepper in a large bowl. While whisking, slowly drizzle in the canola oil until emulsified. Add the tomatoes, avocado, pickled onions, and cilantro.

4. To finish: Remove the steak from the refrigerator 30 minutes before cooking. Heat a grill to high or a grill pan over high heat.

5. Season the steak on both sides with salt and pepper and grill until golden brown on both sides and an instant-read thermometer inserted into the center of the meat registers 135°F for medium-rare, about 5 minutes per side. Remove to a cutting board and let rest for 10 minutes.

6. Add the pumpkin seeds and pomegranate seeds, if desired, to the salad and mix until combined. Slice the steak in half lengthwise and then crosswise into ¼-inch-thick slices.

7. To serve, spread some of the reserved salsa verde on each dinner plate, top with several slices of the steak, an egg, the salad, and the tortilla strips.

JUICY LUCY PIMENTO CHEESEBURGERS

with Black Pepper–Honey Glazed Bacon & Smoked Chile Special Sauce

Juicy Lucy burgers were invented and made famous in Minneapolis, Minnesota. Sounds like it was a late-night moment of inspiration after a cocktail or two—and if it wasn't, it should have been! Think of a burger stuffed with cheese that melts *inside* the burger instead of on top. Mine has green chiles running through it, of course, and the peppery honey-glazed bacon came through as a favorite for the judges.

SERVES 4

PIMENTO CHEESE

½ cup mayonnaise

½ cup finely diced jarred piquillo peppers

½ cup finely diced roasted poblano chile (see page 240)

Pinch of chile de árbol powder

Kosher salt and freshly ground black pepper

4 ounces white cheddar cheese, coarsely grated

4 ounces yellow American cheese, coarsely grated

BURGERS

1½ pounds ground chuck (80/20)

Kosher salt and freshly ground black pepper

2 tablespoons canola oil

Smoked Chile Special Sauce (recipe follows)

4 soft sesame seed burger buns, insides scooped out, lightly toasted

8 slices Oven-Roasted Crispy Bacon (page 246)

Poblano Pickle Relish (recipe follows)

¾ cup mayonnaise

2 tablespoons ketchup

1 canned chipotle pepper in adobo sauce, finely diced

Kosher salt and freshly ground black pepper

1. Make the pimento cheese: Mix together the mayonnaise, piquillo peppers, poblano, chile de árbol, and salt and black pepper to taste in a large bowl. Add both cheeses and mix well to combine.

2. Make the burgers: Divide the meat into 8 portions (3 ounces each) and pat each portion into a 4-inch-wide patty. Place a few tablespoons of the pimento cheese in the center of 4 of the patties. Top with the remaining patties and seal the edges to enclose the cheese in the burger. Season the burgers on both sides with salt and black pepper.

3. Heat the oil in a large cast-iron or nonstick skillet over high heat until shimmering. Cook the burgers until golden brown and charred on both sides and cooked to medium doneness, about 3 minutes per side.

4. Spread the smoked chile special sauce on both sides of the buns, then top each burger with 2 slices of bacon and a few tablespoons of relish.

Smoked Chile Special Sauce

✖ **MAKES A GENEROUS ¼ CUP**

Whisk together the mayonnaise, ketchup, and chipotle until smooth. Season with salt and pepper. Cover and refrigerate for at least 30 minutes and up to 24 hours to allow the flavors to meld.

Poblano Pickle Relish

✖ MAKES ABOUT 1 CUP

1 large poblano chile, roasted (see page 240) and finely diced

½ cup finely diced dill pickles

¼ cup finely chopped Pickled Red Onions (page 248)

2 tablespoons red wine vinegar

2 teaspoons clover honey

2 tablespoons finely chopped fresh cilantro leaves

Kosher salt and freshly ground black pepper

Mix together the poblano, dill pickles, pickled onions, vinegar, and honey in a small bowl. Fold in the cilantro and season with salt and pepper. Let sit at room temperature for at least 15 minutes before using. The relish can be made up to 2 days in advance and stored, tightly covered, in the refrigerator. If making in advance, don't add the cilantro until just before serving.

SERVES 4 TO 6

3 tablespoons canola oil

8 ounces slab bacon, cut crosswise into ¼-inch-thick lardons

3 pounds boneless beef short ribs, excess fat removed, cut into 1-inch pieces

Kosher salt and freshly ground black pepper

½ pound cremini mushrooms, stems discarded, caps sliced

1 pound oyster mushrooms, stems discarded, caps chopped

1 stick (8 tablespoons) unsalted butter

1 large Spanish onion, finely chopped

4 garlic cloves, mashed to a paste with ¼ teaspoon kosher salt

2 tablespoons tomato paste

2 cups red wine, such as Pinot Noir

2 cups Beef Stock (page 232) or store-bought low-sodium beef stock

2 cups Light Chicken Stock (page 233) or store-bought low-sodium chicken stock

1 bay leaf

5 sprigs thyme

2 carrots, cut into ½-inch-thick coins

2 teaspoons pure cane sugar

1 pound cipollini onions, peeled

¼ cup chopped fresh flat-leaf parsley

Goat Cheese Butter Croutons (recipe follows)

BEEF BOURGUIGNON
with Caramelized Cipollini Onions & Goat Cheese Butter Croutons

All you need is a blustery Sunday night and some beef, red wine, and mushrooms to get you started on this old-school French bistro classic. Serve this beef and red wine stew over rice or with egg noodles. Either way, this dish spells comfort. The pressure cooker is a sure-fire way to braise meats quickly, so I use that on the show, but the recipe here is the longer version to be prepared in a Dutch oven—perfect for a Sunday.

1. Preheat the oven to 350°F.

2. Add 1 tablespoon of the oil and the bacon to a large Dutch oven and cook over medium heat until the bacon is crisp and its fat rendered, about 8 minutes. Use a slotted spoon to transfer the bacon to a plate lined with paper towels, leaving the fat in the pan.

3. Heat the bacon fat over high heat until shimmering. Season the beef liberally with salt and pepper. Working in batches, cook the beef until golden brown on both sides, about 7 minutes. Remove with a slotted spoon to a large bowl.

4. Heat the fat left in the pan over high heat until shimmering. Add both mushrooms and cook until golden brown and their liquid has evaporated, about 12 minutes. Season with salt and pepper and remove with a slotted spoon to the bowl with the beef.

5. Add 1 tablespoon of the oil and 1 tablespoon of the butter to the pan and heat over high heat until shimmering. Add the Spanish onion and cook until soft, about 4 minutes. Add the garlic and cook for 1 minute. Add the tomato paste and cook, stirring constantly, until fragrant and deepened in color, about 2 minutes. Add the wine and cook until reduced by half, about 10 minutes. Add both stocks, the bay leaf, and thyme and bring to a boil. Return the bacon, beef, and mushrooms to the pan and season with salt and pepper. Return to a boil. Cover, carefully transfer to the oven, and cook until the beef is tender, about 2 hours.

6. Remove the beef, mushrooms, and bacon from the pot using a slotted spoon and transfer to a large bowl. Discard the bay leaf and blend the sauce using an immersion blender until smooth. (Alternatively, blend in a stand blender in batches and return the sauce to the pot.) Cook the sauce over medium-high heat until reduced and thickened, about 20 minutes.

continued >

7. While the sauce is reducing, melt 3 tablespoons of the butter in a large nonstick sauté pan over high heat. Stir in the carrots, 1 teaspoon of the sugar, and ¼ cup water and cook until the water has evaporated and the carrots are tender and caramelized, about 10 minutes. Season with salt and pepper and arrange in an even layer on a sheet pan.

8. Wipe out the sauté pan and return to the stove over high heat. Add the remaining 1 tablespoon oil and 4 tablespoons butter and heat until shimmering. Stir in the whole cipollini, remaining 1 teaspoon sugar, ½ cup water, and salt and pepper to taste. Bring to a boil, cover, and cook for 5 minutes. Uncover and cook, stirring occasionally, until golden brown and caramelized, about 10 minutes. Arrange in an even layer with the carrots on the sheet pan.

9. Return the beef, bacon, and mushrooms to the Dutch oven. Add the carrots and cipollini and stir to combine. Cook over high heat for 2 minutes to heat through. Stir in the parsley and serve in bowls, with a goat cheese butter crouton on the side.

Goat Cheese Butter Croutons

✖ MAKES 12 CROUTONS

1 tablespoon canola oil

2 garlic cloves, finely chopped

1 stick (8 tablespoons) unsalted butter, at room temperature

¼ cup goat cheese, at room temperature

Kosher salt and freshly ground black pepper

1 French baguette, cut on the diagonal into twelve ¼-inch-thick slices

3 tablespoons extra-virgin olive oil

1. Preheat the broiler.

2. Heat the canola oil in a small sauté pan over low heat. Add the garlic and cook until soft, 30 seconds. Remove from the heat.

3. Scrape the garlic and oil into a mini food processor, add the butter and goat cheese, and process until smooth. Season with salt and pepper.

4. Put the bread on a sheet pan in an even layer. Brush the tops with the olive oil and season with salt and pepper. Put under the broiler until lightly golden brown, 1 to 4 minutes, depending on your broiler.

5. Slather a heaping tablespoon of the goat cheese butter over each slice of bread before serving.

SERVES 6

3 pounds certified Black Angus ground chuck (80/20)

Kosher salt and freshly ground black pepper

1 stick (8 tablespoons) unsalted butter

12 slices smoked cheddar cheese

6 sandwich-size English muffins, split

12 tablespoons Bacon Aioli (recipe follows)

2 cups finely shredded romaine lettuce

Lemon Vinaigrette (recipe follows)

6 slices beefsteak tomato

6 Fried Eggs (page 242)

12 thin-cut slices Oven-Roasted Crispy Bacon (page 246)

LEIA GACCIONE'S BRUNCH BURGERS

"When I found out I was going to be on a second episode of *Beat Bobby Flay*, I wanted to make sure I went in with a really solid dish so that I could take him down. I am fortunate to have learned a thing or two about cooking burgers from the man himself, since I worked for him for almost eight years. I created this burger when I opened my first restaurant, South + Pine American Eatery. Some people thought I was crazy for going up against someone who has made a living off of making burgers, but I never back down from a challenge, something that I am grateful to Bobby for teaching me. When it was time for the judges to give us their feedback, I had my fingers crossed behind my back, but thought for sure I had this one in the bag. When the judges said, 'And the winner is Bobby Flay,' I turned to Bobby, gave him a big hug, and whispered in his ear, 'This is rigged.' Win or lose on *BBF*, it's always a win. I'm so grateful to have had that opportunity. And you know what they say: third time's the charm, so if they call, I'll be ready." —LEIA GACCIONE

1. Form the ground chuck into 6 burgers (8 ounces each). Season liberally on both sides with salt and pepper.

2. Melt the butter in a large sauté pan over high heat. Working in batches, add the burgers and cook until golden brown on both sides and cooked to medium doneness, basting with the fat a few times during the cooking, about 5 minutes per side. During the last minute of cooking, put 2 slices of cheddar on each burger, cover the pan with a lid, and cook until the cheese is completely melted.

3. While the burgers are cooking, toast the English muffins. Spread each half with 1 tablespoon of the aioli, and season with salt and pepper. Put the lettuce in a large bowl, add 6 tablespoons of the lemon vinaigrette, and toss to coat. Season with salt and pepper.

4. Divide the lettuce among the 6 English muffin bottoms and top each with a slice of tomato, a cheeseburger, a fried egg, and 2 slices of the bacon. Spoon some of the remaining vinaigrette on top of the egg and finish with the English muffin tops. Serve immediately.

continued >

1 large egg yolk

2 teaspoons red wine vinegar

¼ cup bacon fat

¾ cup neutral oil

Kosher salt and freshly ground black pepper

½ cup finely chopped Oven-Roasted Crispy Bacon (page 246)

1 shallot, finely diced

1 garlic clove, mashed to a paste with ¼ teaspoon kosher salt

3 tablespoons fresh lemon juice

1 tablespoon white wine vinegar

1 teaspoon kosher salt

¼ teaspoon freshly ground black pepper

1 tablespoon Dijon mustard

2 tablespoons clover honey

¼ cup extra-virgin olive oil

¼ cup canola oil

Bacon Aioli

✖ MAKES ABOUT 1 CUP

Whisk the egg yolk and vinegar in a large bowl until pale. Slowly whisk in the bacon fat, drop by drop at first, and continue whisking until it begins to emulsify and thicken. Gradually add the oil in a very slow, thin stream, whisking constantly, until the aioli is thick and lighter in color, about 8 minutes. Season with salt and pepper. Fold in the bacon, cover, and refrigerate. The aioli can be made up to 2 days ahead and stored, tightly covered, in the refrigerator.

Lemon Vinaigrette

✖ MAKES ¾ CUP

Whisk together the shallot, garlic, lemon juice, vinegar, salt, and pepper in a medium bowl. Whisk in the mustard and honey until smooth. Slowly whisk in the oils until emulsified. The dressing can be made 3 days in advance and stored, tightly covered, in the refrigerator.

EPISODE 2205: "All in the Family"
COMPETITOR: Mika Leon
DISH: Cuban picadillo
WINNER: Bobby Flay

BEEF & CHORIZO CUBAN PICADILLO
with Yellow Crispy Rice & Green Olive Relish

Picadillo is a traditional dish found across Latin America and in the Philippines, with as many variations as there are towns where it is served and as there are families who love it. This battle was specifically for Cuban picadillo, and I got things rolling with a combination of beef and chorizo. When I see this dish in Cuban restaurants, most of the time the olives and peppers are mixed into the meat. I love those flavors, so in an attempt to make this dish my own, I made a relish out of those classic ingredients. The relish lends some fresh texture to the dish as well as acid to cut its richness. Crusting the yellow rice has become a technique/trick I use to curry favor with the judges. Who doesn't like crispy rice?

SERVES 6

YELLOW CRISPY RICE

2 tablespoons canola oil

1 medium Spanish onion, finely chopped

1 teaspoon ground cumin

½ teaspoon ground turmeric

1½ cups long-grain rice

3 cups Light Chicken Stock (page 233) or store-bought low-sodium chicken stock or broth

2 teaspoons kosher salt

¼ teaspoon freshly ground black pepper

PICADILLO

4 tablespoons canola oil

1 pound ground chuck (80/20)

8 ounces Mexican chorizo (see Note)

Kosher salt and freshly ground black pepper

2 medium Spanish onions, chopped

5 garlic cloves, chopped

2 tablespoons ancho chile powder

1 teaspoon ground cumin

½ teaspoon ground cinnamon

1 (12-ounce) bottle dark beer

✖ **NOTE:** This type of chorizo is my favorite. It is a cross between a fresh Mexican chorizo and a slightly drier, firmer Spanish chorizo and is fully cooked and flavored with lots of smoked paprika.

ingredients continued >

1. Start the yellow crispy rice: Heat the canola oil in a medium saucepan over high heat until shimmering. Add the onion and cook until soft, about 4 minutes. Stir in the cumin and turmeric and cook for 1 minute, stirring constantly. Stir in the rice and cook for 1 minute. Add the stock, salt, and pepper and bring to a boil. Stir, cover, reduce the heat to low, and cook until the liquid is absorbed and the rice is tender, about 16 minutes.

2. Transfer the rice to a sheet pan in an even layer and fluff with a fork to separate the grains. Let cool, then refrigerate for at least 30 minutes and up to 24 hours.

3. Meanwhile, make the picadillo: Heat 2 tablespoons of the canola oil over high heat in a large Dutch oven until shimmering. Crumble the ground chuck and the chorizo into the pan, season with salt and pepper, and cook, breaking up the meat into small pieces with a wooden spoon, until golden brown, about 8 minutes. Remove with a slotted spoon to a plate lined with paper towels.

4. Drain the fat from the pot (let cool, then discard). Add the remaining 2 tablespoons canola oil to the Dutch oven and heat over high heat until shimmering. Add the onions and cook until soft, about 4 minutes. Add the garlic and cook for 1 minute. Stir in the ancho powder, cumin, and cinnamon and cook for 2 minutes. Add the beer and cook until reduced by half, about 5 minutes.

continued >

1 (28-ounce) can peeled whole tomatoes, puréed in a blender

½ cup golden raisins

2 tablespoons capers, drained

GREEN OLIVE RELISH

4 jarred piquillo peppers, finely diced

1 cup pitted green olives, sliced

2 scallions, green tops and pale-green parts only, thinly sliced

1 tablespoon chopped fresh oregano

1 tablespoon red wine vinegar

¼ cup extra-virgin olive oil

TO FINISH

⅓ cup canola oil

6 Fried Eggs (page 242) or Poached Eggs (page 241)

Chopped fresh parsley leaves, for garnish

5. Add the puréed tomatoes and bring to a boil. Return the meat to the pot along with the raisins and cook until thickened and the meat is tender, about 30 minutes. Stir in the capers and season with salt and pepper to taste.

6. Meanwhile, prepare the green olive relish: Combine the piquillo peppers, olives, scallions, oregano, vinegar, and olive oil in a medium bowl and let sit at room temperature for at least 30 minutes and up to 4 hours.

7. To finish: Heat the canola oil in a large cast-iron or nonstick skillet over medium heat until shimmering. Add the rice in an even layer, press down on it with a metal spatula, and cook until the bottom is golden brown and crispy, about 5 minutes. Turn the rice over, press down on it again, and cook until the bottom is crispy, 5 minutes longer.

8. Divide the rice among six shallow bowls and top with a few spoonfuls of the picadillo and an egg. Spoon some of the relish around the perimeter of each bowl and garnish with the parsley.

EPISODE 802: *"Pie in the Sky"*
COMPETITOR: *Branden Levine*
DISH: *Shepherd's pie*
WINNER: *Bobby Flay*

SERVES 6 TO 8

LAMB & BEEF FILLING

2 pounds boneless lamb shoulder, excess fat trimmed, cut into 2-inch pieces

Kosher salt and freshly ground black pepper

5 tablespoons canola oil

1 cup coarsely chopped canned peeled whole tomatoes

1 large Spanish onion, coarsely chopped

4 garlic cloves, smashed

2 cups Light Chicken Stock (page 233) or store-bought low-sodium chicken stock or broth

1 cup dry red wine

6 sprigs thyme

½ pound ground chuck (80/20)

1 pound cremini mushrooms, stems discarded, caps coarsely chopped

MASHED POTATOES

2 pounds Yukon Gold potatoes, peeled and cut into 1-inch cubes

Kosher salt

1 cup crème fraîche

2 tablespoons unsalted butter

¼ cup grated Parmigiano Reggiano cheese

Freshly ground black pepper

¼ cup finely chopped fresh chives

FOR ASSEMBLY

Minted Smashed Peas (recipe follows)

2 tablespoons unsalted butter

SHEPHERD'S PIE
with Minted Smashed Peas

This dish reminds me of my teenage years. During my first cooking job at Joe Allen's, the staff would go to a place in Hell's Kitchen in NYC called Landmark Tavern. They had the best shepherd's pie in the city. To me, the slow-cooked lamb shoulder is the key to this dish, but I also use some ground chuck to balance out the gamey flavor of the lamb. This really is the best all-in-one "meat and potatoes" dinner. Make sure you brown the top of the potatoes so they have a slightly crusty texture. Save this one for a chilly Sunday evening; it's a warm and comforting dish, through and through.

1. Start the lamb and beef filling: Preheat the oven to 350°F.

2. Pat the lamb dry with paper towels, put it in a bowl, and season liberally with salt and pepper. Heat 3 tablespoons of the oil in a large Dutch oven over high heat until shimmering. Add half of the lamb and sear on both sides until golden brown, about 10 minutes. Remove to a plate lined with paper towels to blot some of the extra fat. Repeat with the remaining lamb.

3. Return all the lamb to the pot and add the tomatoes, onion, garlic, stock, wine, and thyme. Season with salt and pepper and stir to combine. Cover tightly with a lid and place in the oven. Cook until fork-tender, 1½ to 2 hours.

4. While the lamb is cooking, heat the remaining 2 tablespoons oil in a large sauté pan over high heat. Add the ground chuck and cook until golden brown, about 7 minutes. Season with salt and pepper and remove with a slotted spoon to a bowl. Add the mushrooms to the pan and cook until golden brown and their liquid has evaporated, about 10 minutes. Add the mushrooms to the bowl with the beef. Cover and keep warm until the lamb is done cooking.

5. Prepare the mashed potatoes: Put the potatoes in a large saucepan, add cold water to cover by 2 inches , and season with 2 tablespoons salt. Bring to a boil and cook until fork-tender, about 25 minutes. Drain well, return them to the hot pan over low heat, and stir a few times to remove the excess moisture.

6. Pass the potatoes through a ricer or food mill into a large bowl. Add the crème fraîche, butter, and Parmigiano and mix until combined. Season with salt and pepper to taste and stir in the chives. Keep warm while you finish the filling.

continued >

Kosher salt

12 ounces frozen green peas

3 tablespoons extra-virgin olive oil

2 tablespoons finely chopped fresh mint leaves

Freshly ground black pepper

7. When the lamb is finished cooking, remove it with a slotted spoon to a large bowl. Strain the cooking liquid into a bowl and skim off and discard the excess fat. Return the liquid to the pot and cook until reduced to a sauce consistency, about 10 minutes. Chop the lamb into bite-size pieces and add it to the sauce. Stir in the ground chuck and mushrooms and taste for seasoning.

8. Assemble the pie: Preheat the broiler and adjust the rack to the top position. Spoon the meat filling into a 2-quart baking dish (a soufflé dish works well). Top the meat with the peas and press down to make an even layer. Top the peas with the hot mashed potatoes. Smooth the top with a fork, leaving ridges in the mashed potatoes (which will add texture). Dot with the butter and broil until golden brown, about 2 minutes. Serve immediately.

Minted Smashed Peas

✖ **MAKES ABOUT 2 CUPS**

Bring a large pot of water to a boil and add 1 tablespoon salt and the peas. Cook until just soft, about 4 minutes. Drain well and transfer to a bowl. Coarsely mash the peas with a potato masher or large fork and stir in the oil and mint. Season with salt and pepper to taste.

SERVES 6

1 tablespoon Annatto Oil
(recipe follows)

1½ pounds ground chuck
(80/20)

Kosher salt

1 small Spanish onion,
finely diced

4 garlic cloves, mashed to
a paste with ¼ teaspoon
kosher salt

1 cup finely diced russet potato
(about 1 medium)

½ cup chopped Manzanilla
olives

¼ cup capers, drained

1 tablespoon Adobo Seasoning
(recipe follows)

½ cup red wine

1½ cups tomato sauce

Empanada Rounds
(recipe follows)

Canola oil, for frying

ROSANA RIVERA'S BEEF EMPANADAS

"Competing on the show was an incredible experience from the get-go. The dynamic is amazing—all high energy mixed with an adrenaline rush. I loved having the opportunity to share my culture and the flavors that define me as a chef. Facing Bobby Flay with a recipe I grew up making with my mom and my grandmother was a true honor, and I could not be any happier to share this staple of Puerto Rican cuisine. It was incredible to see Bobby in action, although you definitely don't have too much time to focus on that, as you have to bring your best every step of the way to beat him. When I was announced the winner, I was super proud, not only as a chef but as a woman, a Latina, and, most important, as someone who loves to share food as much as Bobby does!" —ROSANA RIVERA

1. Heat the annatto oil in a large sauté pan over high heat until shimmering. Add the ground chuck and cook until golden brown, about 5 minutes. Season with salt. Add the onion, garlic, potato, olives, capers, and adobo seasoning and cook for 2 minutes.

2. Add the wine and cook until reduced by half, about 3 minutes. Add the tomato sauce and bring to a boil. Reduce the heat to low and cook, stirring occasionally, until the flavors meld and the potato is tender, about 30 minutes. Season with salt. Transfer to a large plate and let cool before filling the empanadas, at least 30 minutes. The filling can be made 2 days in advance and stored, tightly covered, in the refrigerator.

3. Put about ⅓ cup of the filling into the center of each empanada round. Brush the edges with water and fold in half to close. Pinch the edges together and press to remove any air. Starting at a corner, fold and pinch the dough along the edge to create a rope design. Set aside and repeat with the remaining filling and rounds.

4. Pour 2 inches canola oil into a large deep sauté pan and heat over medium heat to 350°F on a deep-fry thermometer.

5. Line a sheet pan with paper towels. Working in batches of a few at a time, add the empanadas to the hot oil and cook until both sides are golden brown, about 5 minutes total. Remove with a large slotted spoon to the paper towels to drain. (Alternatively, you can

continued >

bake them in a 350°F oven: Arrange the empanadas in a single layer on a parchment-lined sheet pan. Brush the tops with egg wash—2 eggs beaten together with 2 tablespoons water—and bake until golden brown, 18 to 20 minutes.)

Annatto Oil

✖ **MAKES ½ CUP**

1 heaping tablespoon annatto seeds

½ cup extra-virgin olive oil

Place the annatto seeds and oil in a small saucepan and cook over medium-low heat until the oil turns orange and the seeds are black, 5 to 6 minutes. Strain the oil into a bowl. The oil can be stored, tightly covered, in the refrigerator for up to 1 month.

Adobo Seasoning

✖ **MAKES ABOUT 5 TABLESPOONS**

2 tablespoons kosher salt

2 teaspoons onion powder

2 teaspoons garlic powder

1 teaspoon dried oregano

1 teaspoon freshly ground black pepper

1 teaspoon ground cumin

1 teaspoon ground turmeric

Whisk together all the ingredients in a small bowl until combined. Store in an airtight container in a dark place for up to 6 months.

Empanada Rounds

✖ **MAKES TWELVE 6-INCH DOUGH ROUNDS**

3 cups all-purpose flour, plus more for dusting

1 teaspoon kosher salt

¼ cup very cold shortening

1 teaspoon distilled white vinegar

1 cup ice-cold water (chill with ice cubes or keep refrigerated)

1. Combine the flour and salt in a food processor and pulse a few times to combine. Add the shortening and pulse several times until it forms pea-size pieces.

2. Add the vinegar and, while pulsing, add about ¾ cup of the ice water through the feed tube, pulsing until a shaggy dough forms. If the dough seems very dry, add the remaining water, 1 tablespoon at a time, until moistened. Transfer the dough to a lightly floured surface and gently knead until a smooth dough forms. Shape the dough into a disc, wrap tightly with plastic wrap, and refrigerate until chilled, at least 1 hour and up to 3 days.

3. Divide the dough into 12 equal pieces and roll each into a ball. With a lightly floured rolling pin, roll each ball out into rough rounds that are ⅛ inch thick. Cut into uniform rounds using a 6-inch cookie cutter or by tracing the rim of a 6-inch bowl with a knife. Place on a parchment-lined sheet pan in a single layer and refrigerate until ready to use.

SPICE-CRUSTED LAMB GYROS

with Tangerine-Harissa Sauce & Pomegranate-Pickled Shallots

SERVES 6

LAMB

1½ pounds lamb loin, excess fat trimmed

Kosher salt and freshly ground black pepper

2 teaspoons ground coriander

2 teaspoons ground cumin

1 tablespoon sweet smoked Spanish paprika

Canola oil

TO FINISH

6 pitas

¼ cup canola oil

Tzatziki (recipe follows)

Tangerine-Harissa Sauce (recipe follows)

Pomegranate Pickled Shallots (recipe follows)

¼ cup fresh mint leaves, chopped

Pomegranate seeds, for garnish, optional

This was a fun one for me. Michael Ginor is a longtime friend, and he completely took me by surprise when he showed up in the *Beat* arena. He clearly brought his best, and I loved the idea of a lamb gyro because it allowed me to try and get creative with the garnishes and condiments to support the lamb. I pulled out all the flavor bombs for this one—pomegranate, harissa, and tangerine—and okay, so it's not classic Greek, but these are the flavors that get my juices flowing.

1. Cook the lamb: Preheat the oven to 425°F.

2. Season the lamb on both sides with salt and pepper. Combine the coriander, cumin, and smoked paprika in a small bowl and rub the entire loin with the mixture. Let sit at room temperature for 10 minutes.

3. Heat 2 tablespoons of oil in a large ovenproof sauté pan over high heat until shimmering. Add the lamb and cook until golden brown and a crust has formed on all sides, about 10 minutes. Transfer the pan to the oven and roast to medium-rare doneness or until an instant-read thermometer inserted into the center of the loin registers 135°F, about 8 minutes. Remove from the oven, transfer the lamb to a cutting board, and let rest for 5 minutes. Cut into ¼-inch-thick slices.

4. To finish: While the lamb is resting, heat a large sauté pan over high heat. Brush each side of a pita with 1 teaspoon oil. Toast in the pan until lightly golden on both sides and warmed through, about 1 minute total. Repeat with the remaining pitas.

5. Divide the pitas among the plates, put a dollop of the tzatziki in the center of each. Divide the lamb among the plates, drizzle with some of the tangerine sauce, and top with some of the pickled shallots. Garnish with the mint and pomegranate seeds, if using, and serve extra sauce and tzatziki on the side.

continued >

Tzatziki

✻ MAKES ABOUT 1½ CUPS

1 cup 2% Greek yogurt

½ cup grated cucumber, pressed in paper towels

3 garlic cloves, mashed to a paste with ¼ teaspoon kosher salt

Finely grated zest of 1 lemon

Juice of ½ lemon

Pinch of freshly ground black pepper

Stir together the yogurt, cucumber, garlic, lemon zest, lemon juice, and pepper in a medium bowl until combined. The tzatziki can be made up to 1 day in advance and stored, tightly covered, in the refrigerator.

Pomegranate-Pickled Shallots

✻ MAKES ABOUT 1 CUP

½ cup pomegranate juice

¼ cup red wine vinegar

2 tablespoons grenadine

2 tablespoons pure cane sugar

½ teaspoon kosher salt

4 large shallots, thinly sliced

Combine the pomegranate juice, vinegar, grenadine, sugar, and salt in a small saucepan. Bring to a boil and cook until the sugar has dissolved, 2 minutes. Put the shallots in a heatproof bowl and pour the liquid over top. Cover and refrigerate for at least 1 hour and up to 3 days before using.

Tangerine-Harissa Sauce

✻ MAKES 1¼ CUPS

2¼ cups tangerine juice

3 tablespoons clover honey

1 tablespoon red wine vinegar

2 tablespoons harissa

Kosher salt and freshly ground black pepper

¼ cup extra-virgin olive oil

Combine 2 cups of the tangerine juice and the honey in a deep medium sauté pan over high heat. Cook until thickened and reduced to about ½ cup, about 20 minutes. Transfer to a blender along with the remaining ¼ cup tangerine juice, the vinegar, harissa, salt, and pepper and blend until combined. With the machine running, add the oil and blend until emulsified. The sauce can be made up to 3 days in advance and stored, tightly covered, in the refrigerator.

EPISODE 1306:
"Familiar Names and Faces"
COMPETITOR: Stephen Kalt
DISH: Patty melts
WINNER: Stephen Kalt

STEPHEN KALT'S PATTY MELTS

SERVES 6

Extra-virgin olive oil

3 large Spanish onions, halved and thinly sliced

Maldon sea salt and freshly ground black pepper

4 small Italian eggplants (about 1½ pounds total), peeled and sliced crosswise into twelve ¼-inch-thick slices

2 pounds ground lamb shoulder

12 slices (¼ inch thick) from a bâtard or miche loaf, preferably made with rye flour

12 thin slices pecorino fresco cheese

12 thin slices Fontina cheese

¼ cup Dijon mustard, plus more (optional) for serving

1 stick (8 tablespoons) unsalted butter, at room temperature

"When I walked out into the middle of the studio, holding up a headshot of Bobby for all of the audience to see, then slowly tore the photo in half and tossed it to the ground, the gauntlet was thrown, and I knew it was the beginning of an incredibly fun day. Bobby is a good friend and one of the most talented and successful chefs in the food business—he has gone where most only dream. Though this was an old buddy and we wanted to make some good television, I knew we both wanted to win. I decided on a familiar dish, something simple that I could spin a bit and hopefully come out ahead: the patty melt, that old diner classic. I decided to use lamb in the patty and a combination of Fontina and pecorino fresco cheeses with a couple of slices of eggplant sautéed in olive oil added for texture and flavor—after all, my kitchen at Spartina is all Californian and Italian influences. As we battled, the clock ticking, Sunny Anderson distracted me with funny questions and a microphone in my face and the crowd above chanted, mostly for Bobby. In the end, the crunchy texture of the country bread griddled in butter won it for me." —STEPHEN KALT

1. Heat ¼ cup oil in a large sauté pan over medium heat until shimmering. Add the onions and cook, stirring occasionally, until very soft and light brown in color, about 30 minutes. Season with salt and pepper. Transfer to a bowl.

2. Meanwhile, in another large sauté pan, heat ¼ cup oil over high heat until shimmering. Working in batches, add the eggplant, season with salt and pepper, and cook until softened and golden brown on both sides, about 4 minutes per side. Remove to a sheet pan lined with paper towels. Add more oil to the pan if needed before cooking another batch of eggplant.

3. Divide the lamb into 6 equal portions (about 6 ounces each) and form into burgers. Generously season both sides with salt and pepper. Heat 2 tablespoons oil in a large sauté pan over high heat until shimmering. Cook the burgers (in batches if necessary; do not crowd the pan) until golden brown on both sides and cooked to rare doneness, about 2 minutes per side. Remove the patties with a metal spatula to a sheet pan lined with paper towels and let cool slightly, about 5 minutes.

4. Top 6 of the bread slices with 1 slice pecorino fresco and 1 slice Fontina. Top each with 2 slices eggplant, some caramelized onion, and a cooked lamb patty. Top each with a little more caramelized onion, 2 more slices eggplant, 1 more slice pecorino fresco, and 1 more slice Fontina. Spread a very thin layer of the Dijon onto the remaining 6 bread slices and place on top, mustard-side down, to form sandwiches.

5. Spread soft butter generously on the top of each sandwich. Heat a large nonstick or cast-iron skillet over medium heat for 1 minute. Place 2 or 3 of the patty melts in the pan, buttered-side down, and immediately spread the top slices of bread with butter. Cook until both sides are golden brown and the cheese has completely melted, about 8 minutes total. Remove to a sheet pan lined with paper towels. Transfer to a cutting board and slice on the diagonal. Serve with more Dijon on the side, if desired.

GEORGE RODRIGUES'S LAMB & CHORIZO CHILI
with Oaxaca Cheese

SERVES 6 TO 8

2 tablespoons extra-virgin olive oil

1 large Spanish onion, finely diced

5 garlic cloves, finely chopped

2 pounds ground lamb shoulder

1 pound Spanish chorizo, finely diced

1 (28-ounce) can tomato sauce

2 cups Light Chicken Stock (page 233) or store-bought low-sodium chicken stock or broth

1 heaping tablespoon tomato paste

1 (15.5-ounce) can black beans, rinsed and drained

2 tablespoons Dijon mustard

1 tablespoon clover honey

1 tablespoon finely chopped fresh thyme leaves

Kosher salt and freshly ground black pepper

8 ounces Oaxaca cheese, coarsely grated

Yellow corn tortilla chips

2 jalapeños, finely sliced

½ cup chopped fresh cilantro leaves

"Competing against one of the most famous chefs in America was a highlight of my career. Prior to this unforgettable experience, I had never been on TV, especially in a cooking competition, but I knew how hard it was to beat Bobby Flay, who is such a pillar in the American food world. After the first round, I felt slightly more confident, but still, the weight of his accolades and accomplishments as a chef made me worry about my chances of winning. Once the round started, I realized I was in my element—I regained my confidence to take him down and started cooking with all my heart. I chose chili as the surprise dish, fully knowing it was the type of food that Chef Flay had more experience with, because I wanted to not only compete but have him cooking at his best. Winning was a surreal and incredible experience, a feeling that I can still remember to this date. And gaining his respect and bragging rights was an awesome addition to my culinary skills." —**GEORGE RODRIGUES**

1. Heat the oil in a large Dutch oven over high heat until shimmering. Add the onion and cook until soft, about 4 minutes. Add the garlic and cook for 1 minute longer.

2. Crumble the lamb into the pan, add the chorizo, and cook, stirring often, until lightly golden brown, about 5 minutes. Add the tomato sauce, stock, and tomato paste and bring to a boil. Stir in the beans, mustard, honey, and thyme. Reduce the heat to medium and cook, stirring occasionally, until the liquid thickens and the lamb is tender, about 30 minutes. Season with salt and pepper.

3. Ladle into bowls and garnish with the cheese, a few chips, the jalapeño, and the cilantro.

SERVES 6 TO 8

LAMB SAUCE

4 tablespoons extra-virgin Greek olive oil

1 pound ground lamb

1 teaspoon ground cinnamon

¼ teaspoon ground allspice

¼ teaspoon ground ginger

⅛ teaspoon cayenne pepper

Kosher salt and freshly ground black pepper

1 large Spanish onion, halved and thinly sliced

1 red bell pepper, thinly sliced

5 garlic cloves, finely chopped

1 serrano chile, finely diced

2 tablespoons tomato paste

1 cup dry red wine

1 (28-ounce) can peeled whole tomatoes, puréed until smooth

2 tablespoons Calabrian chile paste

¼ cup dried currants, soaked in warm water for 30 minutes and drained

¼ cup chopped fresh flat-leaf parsley, plus more for garnish

2 tablespoons chopped fresh oregano

Clover honey (optional)

EGGPLANT

¾ cup extra-virgin Greek olive oil, plus more as needed

1½ pounds medium eggplants, peeled and cut crosswise into ¼-inch-thick slices

Kosher salt and freshly ground black pepper

MOUSSAKA

My friend and world-class chef Michael Symon, who has tons of Greek blood running through his veins, always laughs when I am tasked with making a classic Greek dish. I lucked out that this one—the actual national dish of Greece—was called on a day when Michael didn't have cohosting duties. I have to admit, this is a lot of work, especially in 45 minutes, but it's equally rewarding. Think of it as lamb-and-eggplant lasagna (hold the pasta) with tons of autumnal spices. It's warm and comforting, and as any Greek grandmother will tell you, moussaka will stick to your bones.

1. Make the lamb sauce: Heat 1 tablespoon of the oil in a large Dutch oven over high heat. Add the lamb, cinnamon, allspice, ginger, cayenne, and salt and black pepper to taste. Cook, stirring to break up the meat, until browned, about 5 minutes. Transfer the lamb to a large sieve set over a bowl and let drain.

2. Discard any liquid left in the pot, add the remaining 3 tablespoons oil, and heat over high heat until shimmering. Add the onion and bell pepper and cook until soft, about 5 minutes. Add the garlic and serrano and cook for 1 minute. Add the tomato paste and cook for 1 minute.

3. Return the lamb to the pot along with the wine and cook, stirring occasionally, until the wine is almost completely evaporated, about 5 minutes. Add the puréed tomatoes, chile paste, and currants and bring to a boil. Reduce the heat to medium-low and simmer, uncovered, stirring occasionally, until thickened, about 30 minutes. Stir in the parsley and oregano and season with salt and black pepper. Taste and add honey, if needed. Remove from the heat.

4. Prepare the eggplant: Heat the oil in a large skillet over medium-high heat until shimmering. Season the eggplant slices on both sides with salt and black pepper. Working in batches, add the eggplant slices to the skillet and fry until tender and lightly golden brown on both sides, about 5 minutes. Transfer the eggplant to a sheet pan lined with paper towels. Cook the remaining eggplant, adding more oil as needed.

5. Make the béchamel: Melt the butter in a medium saucepan over medium heat. Add the flour and cook, whisking constantly, until pale and smooth, about 2 minutes. While whisking, add the milk and bay leaf. Cook, whisking often, until thickened, about 7 minutes. Season with salt, and black pepper, the nutmeg, and the lemon zest. Let the sauce cool for 5 minutes (and discard the bay leaf).

BÉCHAMEL

6 tablespoons unsalted butter

½ cup all-purpose flour

2½ cups whole milk

1 bay leaf

Kosher salt and freshly ground black pepper

⅛ teaspoon freshly grated nutmeg

2 teaspoons grated lemon zest

3 large egg yolks

½ cup soft goat cheese

TO FINISH

1 cup grated Pecorino Romano cheese

Chopped fresh parsley, for garnish (optional)

6. Whisk together the egg yolks and goat cheese in a small bowl, then whisk the mixture into the béchamel sauce until smooth.

7. To finish: Preheat the oven to 400°F. Butter a 3-quart baking dish or casserole dish. Set the baking dish on a sheet pan.

8. Layer half of the eggplant slices on the bottom of the dish and cover with half of the lamb sauce. Top the sauce with the remaining eggplant slices and then the remaining lamb sauce. Pour the béchamel over the top and spread it evenly with a rubber spatula. Sprinkle the pecorino evenly over the top.

9. Bake until browned and bubbling, 55 to 65 minutes. Top with parsley, if desired. Let cool for at least 20 minutes before serving. Moussaka is best served at room temperature.

PORK

Chipotle Chilaquiles with Chorizo & Goat Cheese ✖ **135**

Spaghetti Carbonara ✖ **136**

Hoppin' John with Mustard Greens, Bacon & Eggs ✖ **139**

Hot & Sour Soup with Black Vinegar–Glazed Pork, Tofu & Eggs ✖ **140**

Scotch Eggs with Chorizo, Piquillo-Kalamata Relish & Saffron Mayonnaise ✖ **143**

Bubble & Squeak ✖ **146**

Classic Cuban Sandwich with Black Forest Ham, Swiss Cheese & Mustard ✖ **149**

Eggs Benedict with Smoked Paprika Olive Oil Toast, Serrano Ham, Chorizo & Toasted Fennel Hollandaise ✖ **150**

Pork Ragù with Homemade Pappardelle ✖ **153**

Adobo Grilled Pork Chops with Bourbon Pan Sauce & Green Apple–Green Chile Chutney ✖ **154**

Carrie Baird's Huevos Rancheros with Homemade Chorizo & Pico de Gallo Salsa Verde ✖ **157**

Jenny Dorsey's Pork & Shiitake Wonton Soup ✖ **160**

Ashley Gaboriault's Pork al Pastor Chili-Cheese Fries with Pineapple-Tomatillo Relish & Salsa Verde ✖ **163**

EPISODE 911: "Get in the Zone"
COMPETITOR: Kevin Templeton
DISH: Chilaquiles
WINNER: Bobby Flay

CHIPOTLE CHILAQUILES

with Chorizo & Goat Cheese

Think layers of corn tortillas, smoky chorizo, creamy goat cheese, and fiery chipotles—all laced with a green tomatillo sauce and topped with a fried egg or two. Oh, yeah. To me, it's the ultimate hangover brunch, and I like to make mine extra spicy with a good dose of hot sauce to kick-start the day. I'll leave that much at least up to you.

SERVES 4

3 tablespoons canola oil

8 ounces D'Artagnan chorizo, thinly sliced on the diagonal

1 (8-ounce) bag blue corn tortilla chips

4 ounces Monterey Jack cheese, coarsely grated

4 ounces sharp white cheddar cheese, coarsely grated

4 ounces goat cheese, crumbled

Kosher salt and freshly ground black pepper

4 large eggs

Tomatillo Sauce (recipe follows)

Store-bought chipotle hot sauce

Crème fraîche, for serving

¼ cup fresh cilantro leaves

1. Heat 1 tablespoon of the oil in a large nonstick skillet over high heat. Add the chorizo and cook until golden brown on both sides, 6 minutes. Remove to a plate lined with paper towels. Wipe out the pan.

2. Preheat the broiler. Spread the tortilla chips evenly on a sheet pan. Combine all three cheeses in a large bowl and season with salt and pepper. Scatter the cheese evenly over the tortilla chips. Broil until the cheese has melted and is lightly golden brown, 1 to 4 minutes.

3. Heat the remaining 2 tablespoons oil in the large nonstick skillet over high heat until shimmering. Crack the eggs into the pan, leaving room between them. Season with salt and pepper and cook until the edges of the whites are set, about 2 minutes. Cover and cook until the yolks are set but still runny, about 1 minute.

4. Divide the cheese-covered tortilla chips among four large shallow bowls and drizzle each with some of the tomatillo sauce. Top with an egg and drizzle with more tomatillo sauce. Arrange some of the chorizo slices around the egg, then drizzle with a few splashes of chipotle hot sauce and the crème fraîche. Garnish with the cilantro.

Tomatillo Sauce

✖ MAKES ABOUT 2 CUPS

1 large white onion, chopped

1½ pounds tomatillos, husked, rinsed, and halved

3 jalapeños, halved and seeded

7 garlic cloves, smashed

5 tablespoons canola oil

Kosher salt and freshly ground black pepper

½ cup fresh cilantro

Juice of 1 lime

Clover honey

1. Preheat the oven to 400°F.

2. Toss the onion, tomatillos, jalapeños, and garlic with 2 tablespoons of the oil and spread on a sheet pan. Roast until soft and slightly charred, stirring twice during roasting, 25 to 30 minutes.

3. Transfer to a food processor, and season with salt and pepper. Add the cilantro, lime juice, the 3 remaining tablespoons of the canola oil, and honey to taste and purée until smooth. Transfer to a bowl. The sauce can be made up to 3 days in advance and stored, tightly covered, in the refrigerator.

EPISODE 602: *"Settling the Score"*
COMPETITOR: *Bruce Kalman*
DISH: *Pasta carbonara*
WINNER: *Bruce Kalman*

SPAGHETTI CARBONARA

This classic dish is found in every great trattoria in Rome. In my house, I think it's fabulous as a midnight snack after a few Negronis. Think about it this way: It's like bacon and eggs, but on noodles—and with lots of cheese. I like to use grated Grana Padano for the sauce, since it melts better into the egg yolks and makes for a creamier texture, but I finish the dish with grated Parmigiano Reggiano. The tricky part is emulsifying the eggs and cheese, but the starchy pasta water is the big helper there, and the payoff is definitely worth the challenge.

This one is also known as the great "knife in the pasta roller" episode that Sunny Anderson has never let me live down.

SERVES 4

**4 ounces guanciale,
cut into ¼-inch dice**

**4 ounces slab bacon,
cut into ¼-inch dice**

½ cup canola oil

**¾ cup packed fresh parsley
leaves**

Kosher salt

6 large egg yolks

**2 ounces Grana Padano
cheese, finely grated
(about ¾ cup)**

**2 garlic cloves, mashed
to a paste with ¼ teaspoon
kosher salt**

**½ teaspoon freshly
ground black pepper**

**Black Pepper Pasta (page
235), cut into fettuccine,
or store-bought fresh or
dried fettuccine**

**2 ounces Parmigiano
Reggiano cheese, finely
grated (about ¾ cup)**

1. Combine the guanciale and bacon in a large sauté pan over medium heat. Slowly cook, stirring occasionally, until the fat has rendered and the meat is golden brown and crispy, about 12 minutes. Remove the pork to a plated lined with paper towels to drain. Pour the rendered fat into a small bowl and reserve.

2. Heat the oil in a small saucepan over medium heat until shimmering. Add ¼ cup of the parsley leaves and fry until just crispy, about 1 minute. Transfer with a slotted spoon to a plate lined with paper towels. Season with a pinch of salt, if desired. Coarsely chop the remaining ½ cup parsley leaves and set aside.

3. Bring a large pot of water to a boil and add 2 tablespoons salt.

4. While the water is coming to a boil, in a large heatproof bowl, whisk together the egg yolks, Grana Padano, garlic, pepper, and ½ teaspoon salt until very smooth. Stir in three-quarters of the pork and 2 tablespoons of the reserved rendered fat.

5. Add the pasta to the boiling water and cook until it rises to the top, then cook for about 1 minute longer, until just al dente. (If using store-bought dried fettucine, cook until al dente according to the package directions.)

6. Reserving a cup of the pasta cooking water, drain the pasta well. Immediately transfer the pasta to the egg mixture and, using tongs, mix quickly until the pasta is coated with the mixture. If the sauce seems too thick or dry, add a bit of the reserved pasta water a few tablespoons at a time. Stir in the chopped parsley.

7. Divide the pasta among four bowls. Garnish with the remaining pork, the Parmigiano, and the fried parsley. Serve immediately.

HOPPIN' JOHN
with Mustard Greens, Bacon & Eggs

SERVES 4 TO 6

3 tablespoons canola oil

8 thick-cut slices bacon, cut crosswise into ¼-inch-wide lardons

1 (15.5-ounce) can black-eyed peas, rinsed and drained

Kosher salt and freshly ground black pepper

1 poblano chile, finely diced

1 red bell pepper, finely diced

1 medium Spanish onion, finely diced

1 cup long-grain rice

2 cups Light Chicken Stock (page 233) or store-bought low-sodium chicken stock or broth

3 ounces mustard greens, stems removed, leaves coarsely chopped

Clover honey

4 large eggs

Homemade Hot Sauce (page 249) or store-bought hot sauce

2 scallions, green tops and pale-green parts only, thinly sliced, for garnish

Hoppin' John is a one-pot Southern staple of black-eyed peas and rice. I, of course, had to make an elaborate meal out of it—or at least I tried to. Chef Stephen Jones took me to hoppin' John school and beat me soundly! Mine may not have been the best hoppin' John of the day, but I do like it and think it stands on its own as a cool brunch dish. Think about it for New Year's Day, when the Southern tradition says eating hoppin' John will bring you a year of good luck.

1. Heat 1 tablespoon of the oil in a large sauté pan over medium heat. Add the bacon and cook, stirring occasionally, until it has rendered its fat and is golden brown and crispy, about 8 minutes. Remove with a slotted spoon to a plate lined with paper towels. Pour all but 2 tablespoons of the rendered fat into a small bowl and set aside for cooking the peppers.

2. Heat the rendered fat still in the pan over high heat until shimmering. Add the black-eyed peas and cook until warm, about 5 minutes. Season with salt and black pepper and transfer to a bowl.

3. Pour the reserved rendered bacon fat into a medium saucepan and heat over high heat. Add the poblano, bell pepper, and onion. Season with salt and black pepper and cook until soft, about 5 minutes. Stir in the rice and cook for 1 minute. Add the stock and season with salt and black pepper. Bring to a boil, then reduce the heat to medium and stir well. Cover and cook until the liquid is absorbed and the rice is tender, about 18 minutes.

4. While the rice is cooking, heat the remaining 2 tablespoons oil in a large deep sauté pan over high heat. Add the mustard greens, a splash of water, and salt and black pepper to taste and cook until wilted, about 10 minutes. Stir in a touch of honey to sweeten.

5. When the rice is done cooking, remove from the heat and let sit, covered, for 5 minutes. Uncover, fluff with a fork, and stir in the black-eyed peas and mustard greens. Transfer to a sheet pan in an even layer to stop further steaming and prevent the grains from clumping.

6. Preheat the oven to 425°F.

7. Spoon the rice into a 2-quart baking dish and make 4 indentations spaced a few inches apart. Crack an egg into each indentation and season the eggs with salt and black pepper. Bake until the whites are just set but the yolks are still runny, about 5 minutes. Remove, drizzle with a bit of hot sauce, and garnish with the bacon and scallions.

SERVES 4 TO 6

PORK BROTH

8 cups Light Chicken Stock
(page 233) or store-bought
low-sodium chicken stock
or broth

2 large chicken wings

8-ounce piece speck ham,
halved

3-inch piece fresh ginger,
peeled and coarsely chopped

8 garlic cloves, chopped

SOUP

3 tablespoons canola oil

1 pound shiitake mushrooms,
stems discarded, caps sliced
¼ inch thick

Kosher salt and freshly
ground black pepper

2 teaspoons cornstarch

2 large eggs

Vinegar-Glazed Pork
Tenderloin (recipe follows),
sliced or chopped

8 ounces firm tofu, cut into
½-inch dice

3 tablespoons Chinese black
vinegar or rice vinegar

3 tablespoons reduced-sodium
soy sauce

Minced fresh chives,
for garnish

Chili oil, for garnish

HOT & SOUR SOUP
with Black Vinegar–Glazed Pork, Tofu & Eggs

Even though I lost this one, I still liked the results. I had never attempted Chinese American hot-and-sour soup before this battle, but it made me a new fan of Chinese black vinegar. Made from fermented rice, Chinese black vinegar, also known as Chinkiang or Zhenjiang vinegar, has a mildly acidic, malty, slightly sweet complexity I now love. I used it in the broth and combined it with honey to glaze the pork in the soup. I didn't win, but I found a new ingredient to add to my home pantry— and that's a win in its own right.

1. Make the pork broth: Combine the stock, chicken wings, speck, ginger, and garlic in a pressure cooker and pressure-cook for 25 minutes. Quick-release the pressure. Strain the broth into a large Dutch oven.

2. Meanwhile, start the soup: Heat the canola oil in a large sauté pan over high heat until shimmering. Add the mushrooms and cook until golden brown and soft and their liquid has evaporated, about 12 minutes. Season with salt and black pepper.

3. Once the broth is in the Dutch oven, transfer the mushrooms to the broth and bring it to a boil over high heat. Whisk together the cornstarch and 1 tablespoon water in a small bowl until smooth. Add the slurry to the boiling broth and cook until it begins to thicken, about 5 minutes.

4. Whisk the eggs in a medium bowl until light and fluffy and uniform in color. While whisking constantly, add a few tablespoons of the hot broth, and whisk well. Repeat with a few more tablespoons of broth, then transfer the eggs to a spouted glass measuring cup. While you are whisking the soup with one hand, slowly drizzle the egg in a thin stream into the soup until it begins to make egg ribbons.

5. Stir in the pork, tofu, vinegar, and soy sauce. Ladle the soup into bowls, garnish with chives, and drizzle with a bit of chili oil.

continued >

½ cup Chinese black vinegar

3 tablespoons clover honey

1 tablespoon reduced-sodium soy sauce

1½ pounds pork tenderloin

Kosher salt and freshly ground white pepper

2 tablespoons canola oil

Vinegar-Glazed Pork

✖ MAKES 4 TO 6

1. Preheat the oven to 425°F.

2. Whisk together the vinegar, honey, and soy sauce in a small bowl.

3. Season the pork with salt and white pepper. Heat the oil in a large cast-iron skillet over high heat until shimmering. Add the pork to the pan and cook until golden brown on both sides, 8 minutes.

4. Brush the pork liberally with the glaze, transfer to the oven, and roast until the glaze is caramelized and the pork is cooked to 145°F on an instant-read thermometer, about 8 minutes.

5. Remove the pork to a cutting board and let rest for 5 minutes before slicing or chopping.

EPISODE 1409: *"Cracking a Win"*
COMPETITOR: *Blake Hartwick*
DISH: *Scotch eggs*
WINNER: *Bobby Flay*

SCOTCH EGGS
with Chorizo, Piquillo-Kalamata Relish & Saffron Mayonnaise

SERVES 4

SCOTCH EGGS

8 large eggs (make a few extra in case any break during the process)

½ cup all-purpose flour

Kosher salt and freshly ground black pepper

1¾ cups panko bread crumbs

½ cup Marcona almonds, toasted and thinly sliced (see Note)

7 ounces fresh Mexican chorizo

Canola oil, for frying

TO FINISH

6 thinly sliced pieces serrano ham

Saffron Mayonnaise (recipe follows)

Piquillo-Kalamata Relish (recipe follows)

✹ **NOTE:** Regular blanched whole almonds can be substituted for the Marcona almonds.

Scotch eggs—which call for wrapping boiled eggs first in sausage, then coating them with bread crumbs before baking or frying them—is a cool technique that I frankly never even thought about doing before this challenge. Eggs and chorizo is one of my favorite combinations, and it didn't let me down. If you don't want to make all the components, you should still bookmark the recipe for the perfect soft-cooked egg. It's a good one to have in your index.

1. Make the Scotch eggs: Fill a medium bowl with ice and water. Bring 8 cups of water to a boil in a medium saucepan. Slowly lower 6 of the eggs, one or two at a time, into the boiling water using a large slotted spoon and cook for exactly 6 minutes. Immediately remove with the slotted spoon and carefully put into the ice bath. Let sit until cool enough to peel, about 5 minutes. Carefully peel the eggs and place on a plate.

2. While the eggs are cooking, put the flour in a large shallow bowl and season with salt and pepper. Crack the remaining 2 eggs into a medium bowl and whisk with 2 tablespoons water until uniform in color and frothy. Combine the panko and almonds in a large shallow bowl and season with salt and pepper.

3. Divide the sausage into 4 equal portions. Pat 1 portion of sausage into a thin patty about the length of your palm. Lay 1 soft-boiled egg on top of the sausage and wrap the sausage around the egg, sealing the edges to completely enclose it. Repeat with remaining sausage and eggs.

4. Line a sheet pan with parchment paper. Dredge each sausage-wrapped egg in the flour and tap off the excess. Dip in the egg mixture and let the excess run off, then dredge in the panko mixture, completely coating the egg. Place on the parchment-lined sheet pan. At this point, the breaded eggs can be stored in the refrigerator on the sheet pan, uncovered, for up to 4 hours.

5. Fill a deep fryer or large Dutch oven halfway with oil and heat it over medium heat to 375°F on a deep-fry thermometer.

6. Fry the breaded eggs two at a time, turning them occasionally and maintaining an oil temperature of 375°F, until the sausage is cooked through and the breading is golden brown and crisp,

continued >

5 to 6 minutes. Use a slotted spoon to transfer the eggs to paper towels to drain. Season lightly with salt and repeat to fry the remaining eggs.

7. To finish: Fry the ham, a few slices at a time, in a large sauté pan with 2 tablespoons of oil, until it curls up slightly and becomes crispy, about 30 seconds. Drain on paper towels.

8. Slice each egg in half and put them yolk-side up on a plate. Top each half with saffron mayonnaise, relish, and the crispy ham.

Saffron Mayonnaise

✖ MAKES ABOUT 1¼ CUPS

3 tablespoons white wine vinegar

Pinch of saffron

1 cup mayonnaise

Juice of ½ lemon

Kosher salt and freshly ground black pepper

Combine the vinegar and saffron in a small bowl and let the saffron bloom for 2 minutes. Put the mayonnaise in a medium bowl, add the saffron mixture and lemon juice, and whisk until smooth. Season with salt and pepper. Cover and refrigerate for at least 30 minutes before serving. The mayonnaise can be made up to 3 days in advance and stored, tightly covered, in the refrigerator.

Piquillo-Kalamata Relish

✖ MAKES ABOUT 1½ CUPS

6 jarred or canned piquillo peppers, drained and coarsely chopped

1 cup kalamata olives, pitted and coarsely chopped

¼ cup white wine vinegar

1 tablespoon clover honey

¼ cup chopped fresh flat-leaf parsley

Kosher salt and freshly ground black pepper

Stir together the piquillos, olives, vinegar, and honey in a medium bowl until combined. Fold in the parsley and season with salt and pepper. The relish can be made up to 2 days in advance and stored, tightly covered, in the refrigerator.

EPISODE 1704: *"Flying Aubergines"*
COMPETITOR: Robert Aikens
DISH: Bubble and Squeak
WINNER: Robert Aikens

BUBBLE & SQUEAK

Bubble and squeak—an English dish that I clearly needed a little more practice at—includes some of my favorite ingredients: potatoes, onions, cabbage, sausage, bacon, and eggs. It's hearty and packed with flavor. Chef Aikens won this battle, and next time I'm starting with a pint or two of my favorite lager.

SERVES 4

1½ pounds russet potatoes, peeled and cut into 2-inch cubes

Kosher salt

Canola oil

1 tablespoon sweet Spanish paprika

Freshly ground black pepper

2 tablespoons unsalted butter

1 small Spanish onion, finely diced

½ head savoy cabbage, finely shredded

8 links best-quality breakfast sausage

8 ounces cremini mushrooms, stems discarded, caps quartered

1 small shallot, finely diced

4 plum tomatoes, halved crosswise

8 slices Oven-Roasted Crispy Bacon (page 246), cut into large pieces

4 Fried Eggs (page 242)

Homemade Hot Sauce (page 249) or store-bought hot sauce

✱ **IN IT TO WIN IT:** I chose savoy cabbage here instead of plain green cabbage because of its more vibrant color, the crinkly texture of the leaves, and the milder taste. You can sub regular green cabbage if you like. For the potatoes, it's best if you can boil and chill the potatoes 8 to 24 hours beforehand, as home fries work best with cold potatoes.

1. Put the potatoes in a large pot, add cold water to cover by 2 inches, and season with 2 tablespoons salt. Bring to a boil over high heat and cook until the potatoes are fork-tender, about 22 minutes. Drain well, spread on a sheet pan to cool slightly, and refrigerate until cold.

2. Heat ¼ cup oil in a 12-inch cast-iron or nonstick skillet over high heat until shimmering. Season the potatoes with salt and pepper and the paprika, then add them to the pan in a single layer. Using a heavy-duty metal spatula, smash them down into an even layer. Cook, undisturbed, until the bottom is golden brown and crusty, about 5 minutes. Turn the potatoes over, press down again with the spatula, and cook until the bottom is golden brown and crusty, about 5 minutes longer. Transfer the potatoes to a sheet pan in an even layer. Wipe out the skillet.

3. In the same pan heat the butter and 1 tablespoon oil over high heat. Add the onion, season with salt and pepper, and cook until just soft, about 4 minutes. Add the cabbage and ¼ cup water and cook, stirring occasionally, until it is wilted and lightly golden brown, about 20 minutes.

4. At the same time, in another large sauté pan, heat 2 tablespoons oil over high heat until shimmering. Add the sausage and cook until golden brown on all sides and just cooked through, about 4 minutes per side. Remove with a slotted spoon to a plate lined with paper towels, then cut each link crosswise into 4 pieces.

5. Return the sauté pan to high heat. Add the mushrooms and cook until they begin to release their liquid, about 8 minutes. Add the shallot, season with salt and pepper, and cook until golden brown, about 5 minutes.

6. Preheat the broiler. Brush the tomatoes with 1 tablespoon oil and season with salt and pepper. Put on a sheet pan and broil until lightly golden brown and soft, 2 to 5 minutes.

7. Stir the mushrooms and potatoes into the cabbage in the skillet. Using a heavy-duty metal spatula, press the mixture into a pancake shape and cook both sides until golden brown and crispy, about 5 minutes per side.

8. Divide the mixture among four plates and top each with a fried egg, 2 tomato halves, 2 slices bacon, the sausage, and hot sauce.

CLASSIC CUBAN SANDWICH

with Black Forest Ham, Swiss Cheese & Mustard

I am certainly a lover of sandwiches in general, but there are a few that I gravitate to more than others. It so happens that they're usually regional classics, like a Philly cheesesteak or a Juicy Lucy burger (page 106), for instance. And then there's this one, which will always remind me of late nights spent in Miami for the South Beach Wine and Food Festival. And I do love a Cuban sandwich. I really think the sweet edge of the Black Forest ham makes all the difference.

SERVES 6

3 pounds boneless pork shoulder, excess fat trimmed, cut into 2-inch chunks

1 large Spanish onion, chopped

5 garlic cloves, smashed

3 cups Light Chicken Stock (page 233) or store-bought low-sodium chicken stock or broth

Kosher salt and freshly ground black pepper

2 tablespoons Dijon mustard

2 tablespoons whole-grain mustard

2 tablespoons clover honey

6 soft Cuban hoagie rolls, halved lengthwise, insides scooped out, and lightly toasted

½ cup mayonnaise

24 thin slices Swiss cheese

12 thin slices Black Forest ham

Sliced dill pickles

6 tablespoons unsalted butter

6 tablespoons canola oil

1. Preheat the oven to 350°F.

2. Combine the pork, onion, garlic, and stock in a large Dutch oven and season with salt and pepper. Cover tightly, transfer to the oven, and cook until the meat is fork-tender, 2 to 2½ hours. Let rest for 10 minutes before pulling the pork into bite-size pieces.

3. In a small bowl, whisk together both mustards and the honey and season with salt and pepper. Spread the mixture on the tops of the rolls. Spread the bottoms of the rolls with the mayonnaise. Put 2 slices of the cheese on both the bottom and the top of each roll. Pile up some of the pork on the bottom and top with 2 slices of the ham and as many pickles as you like. Cover with the top of the rolls.

4. To cook, heat a large cast-iron skillet or grill pan over medium heat and add 2 tablespoons of the butter and 2 tablespoons of the oil. Place 2 of the sandwiches in the skillet, top-side down, and top with another heavy skillet and a couple of heavy weights (bricks or cans of tomatoes work well). Press down firmly and cook until the sandwich has compressed to about a third of its original thickness, the bread is super crispy, and the cheese has melted, 3 to 5 minutes. Flip the sandwiches, weight them again, and cook until the bottoms are crispy, about 3 minutes longer. Repeat with the remaining butter, oil, and sandwiches. Slice on the diagonal and serve immediately.

✖ **BEAT THE CLOCK:** Use a pressure cooker to save time: Instead of cooking the pork in the oven, combine the pork, stock, onion, and garlic in a pressure cooker and season with salt and pepper. Cook at high pressure for 35 minutes. Quick-release the pressure. Open the pressure cooker and let the pork rest for 10 minutes before pulling it apart. The sandwiches can be assembled ahead of time, wrapped in foil, and refrigerated. Press before serving.

EGGS BENEDICT
with Smoked Paprika Olive Oil Toast, Serrano Ham, Chorizo & Toasted Fennel Hollandaise

This is a Mediterranean version of the classic. In this case I substituted olive oil toast (spiced up with smoked paprika) for the English muffins, serrano ham for the Canadian bacon, and seasoned the hollandaise sauce with toasted fennel seeds. It might have been a *little* over the top for the judges, but I still think it would impress your family at brunch. Make sure you serve lots of brunch cocktails, and there's no doubt in my mind that they'll love it.

SERVES 4

HOLLANDAISE

1¼ sticks (10 tablespoons) unsalted butter, cut into pieces

4 large egg yolks

Juice of ½ large lemon

1 teaspoon fennel seeds, toasted (see Note) and finely ground

Kosher salt and freshly ground black pepper

EGGS BENEDICT

8 slices (1 inch thick) pain de mie

Kosher salt and freshly ground black pepper

1 teaspoon sweet smoked Spanish paprika

½ cup extra-virgin olive oil

¼ cup plus 2 tablespoons canola oil

4 thin slices serrano ham

8 large shrimp, peeled and deveined

½ pound D'Artagnan chorizo, diced

1 small poblano chile, roasted (see page 240) and thinly sliced

¼ cup chopped fresh flat-leaf parsley

8 Poached Eggs (page 241)

Finely chopped fresh chives, for garnish

Finely grated zest of 1 lemon, for garnish

✱ **NOTE:** Put fennel seeds in a small pan and toast over medium heat, stirring occasionally, until fragrant, about 4 minutes.

1. Make the hollandaise: Put the butter in a small saucepan and cook over high heat until melted and foamy, about 5 minutes. Remove from the heat; skim off and discard the white foam from the top. Keep warm.

2. Heat a few inches of water in a medium saucepan until barely simmering (or use a double boiler). Whisk the egg yolks in a medium stainless-steel bowl until the mixture is thickened and doubled in volume. Place the bowl over the saucepan (the water should not touch the bottom of the bowl) and continue to whisk rapidly; be careful not to let the eggs get too hot or they will scramble. Slowly drizzle in the melted butter and whisk until the sauce is thickened and doubled in volume. Remove from the heat and whisk in the lemon juice, fennel seeds, salt, and pepper. Cover and place in a warm spot until ready to use.

3. Prepare the eggs Benedict: Using a 3-inch round biscuit cutter, cut out the centers of the bread slices. Season the bread rounds on one side with salt, pepper, and the smoked paprika. Heat ¼ cup of the olive oil in a large nonstick sauté pan over high heat until shimmering. Add 4 rounds of bread, seasoned-side down, and cook until lightly golden brown, about 1½ minutes. Flip and cook until the bottoms are lightly golden brown, about 1 minute longer. Repeat with the remaining ¼ cup olive oil and bread. Transfer to a sheet pan and keep warm in a 200°F oven.

4. Heat ¼ cup of the canola oil in a large sauté pan over high heat until shimmering. Add the slices of serrano in an even layer and cook until crispy, turning once, about 1 minute per side. Remove to a plate lined with paper towels. Return the pan to the heat until the oil shimmers. Add the shrimp, season with salt and pepper, and cook for 1 minute on each side. Remove the shrimp to a plate.

5. Add the remaining 2 tablespoons canola oil to the pan over high heat until shimmering. Add the chorizo and cook until golden brown on both sides, about 4 minutes. Return the shrimp to the pan and cook until they are just cooked through, about 1 minute longer. Stir in the poblano and parsley.

6. Place 2 slices of the toast on each plate. Top each slice with some of the chorizo-shrimp mixture and a poached egg, then top the egg with a slice of the crispy serrano. Spoon some of the hollandaise sauce over top and garnish with chives and the lemon zest.

EPISODE 2401: *"Guess Who's Back"*
COMPETITOR: Ryan Lory
DISH: Pasta ragù
WINNER: Bobby Flay

SERVES 6

4 tablespoons canola oil

2½ pounds boneless pork shoulder, excess fat trimmed, cut into 1-inch chunks

Kosher salt and freshly ground black pepper

1 large Spanish onion, chopped

5 garlic cloves, chopped

¼ teaspoon Calabrian chile flakes

¼ cup tomato paste

1 cup dry red wine

3 cups Light Chicken Stock (page 233) or store-bought low-sodium chicken stock or broth

¼ cup veal demi-glace

¼ cup chopped fresh flat-leaf parsley, plus more for serving

Pasta Dough (page 235), cut into pappardelle, or 1 pound dried pappardelle

Grated Parmigiano Reggiano cheese

4 tablespoons unsalted butter, cut into pieces

2 teaspoons Calabrian chile paste

Extra-virgin olive oil, for drizzling

✖ **BEAT THE CLOCK:** As always, you can substitute dried pasta for homemade (it will take a few minutes longer to cook), or buy fresh pasta dough sheets and cut your own pappardelle by hand from those. You can use ground pork to make this sauce in a pinch. The end result will still be delicious, though not quite as rich and savory.

PORK RAGÙ
with Homemade Pappardelle

I know the title sounds like an old-school Sunday-night pasta dinner, but this might very well be one of my favorite dishes I've ever made in the arena. Something just clicked that day as the fresh homemade pasta folded itself around the savory pork ragù bathed in tomato, chiles, and red wine . . . yeah, I'm making this tonight. Even though ragù is often made with ground pork in Italy, I opt for rich pork shoulder cooked till it's fall-apart tender. On the show, since I'm pressed for time, I use a pressure cooker to get it done within 45 minutes. But here you'll be able to achieve the incredible slow-cooked effect for real.

1. Preheat the oven to 350°F.

2. Heat 2 tablespoons of the canola oil in a large Dutch oven over high heat until shimmering. Season the pork liberally in a large bowl with salt and pepper. Add half the pork to the pot and sear until golden brown on all sides, 5 minutes per side. Remove with a slotted spoon to another large bowl. Repeat with the remaining 2 tablespoons canola oil and pork.

3. Add the onion to the pan and cook until soft, about 4 minutes. Add the garlic and chile flakes and cook for 1 minute. Add the tomato paste and cook until deepened in color and fragrant, 2 minutes.

4. Add the wine and cook until reduced by half, about 5 minutes. Add the stock and demi-glace, bring to a boil, and return the meat to the pot. Cover, transfer to the oven, and cook until fork-tender, about 2 hours. Reserving the braising liquid, remove the pork with a slotted spoon to a large bowl and let rest for 10 minutes before mashing the meat with a potato masher into bite-size pieces.

5. Strain the braising liquid and return it to the pot (discard the solids). Cook over high heat until reduced by half, about 25 minutes. Add the pork to the liquid and cook to warm through and let the flavors absorb into the pork, 10 minutes. Season with salt and pepper and then stir in the parsley.

6. While the sauce is reducing, bring a large pot of water to a boil and season with 2 tablespoons salt. Add the pasta and cook until it rises to the top, count 10 seconds longer, and drain well. (If using dried pasta, cook to al dente according to the package directions.)

7. Add the pasta, ½ cup grated Parmigiano, the butter, and the chile paste to the sauce and toss well to combine. Serve in pasta bowls, topped with more cheese, parsley, and a drizzle of olive oil.

EPISODE 1211:
"Ghosts of Bobby's Past"
COMPETITOR: Leia Gaccione
DISH: Pork chops and applesauce
WINNER: Bobby Flay

ADOBO GRILLED PORK CHOPS

with Bourbon Pan Sauce & Green Apple–Green Chile Chutney

This is my Southwestern-style take on the classic combo of pork chops and applesauce, which my mother made often when I was growing up. Her chops were overcooked and her applesauce came from a jar—and if she was feeling extra fancy, she would add cinnamon to the sauce. Here I've updated the flavors with adobo, red chiles, and citrus and a bourbon sauce that ties it all together. I promise this dish is crazy satisfying. I have to give a special shout-out to my competitor on this one, too. Before opening her own successful restaurant, Central + Main in New Jersey, Leia Gaccione was my chef de cuisine at Bar Americain (among others) for years, and I watched her make a version of this dish nightly many times—I know she's got real chops! In fact, she's competed on *BBF* another time; check out her brunch burgers on page 111.

SERVES 4

PORK CHOPS

1 teaspoon finely grated tangerine zest or orange zest

½ teaspoon finely grated lime zest

1 cup tangerine juice

¼ cup fresh lime juice

¼ cup clover honey

1 or 2 chipotle chiles, to taste, finely chopped

1 teaspoon chile de árbol powder

Canola oil

Kosher salt and freshly ground black pepper

4 center-cut boneless pork chops (1½ to 2 inches thick)

BOURBON PAN SAUCE

2 tablespoons canola oil

1 medium Spanish onion, coarsely chopped

1 small head garlic, halved horizontally

1 cup bourbon

3 cups Light Chicken Stock (page 233) or store-bought low-sodium chicken stock or broth

12 black peppercorns

Kosher salt

2 heaping tablespoons crème fraîche

FOR SERVING

Green Apple–Green Chile Chutney (recipe follows)

Chopped fresh cilantro leaves

1. Marinate the pork chops: Combine both zests, both juices, the honey, chipotles, chile de árbol, and 2 tablespoons oil in a small bowl and season with salt and pepper. Season the pork chops on both sides with salt and pepper and brush the marinade over both sides of the pork chops. Let sit at room temperature for 30 minutes.

2. Meanwhile, make the bourbon pan sauce: Heat the oil in a large deep sauté pan over high heat until shimmering. Add the onion and garlic, cut-sides down, and cook until the onion is soft and the cut side of the garlic begins to turn a light golden brown, about 4 minutes. Remove the pan from the heat, slowly add the bourbon, and stand back, as it could ignite quickly. Return the pan to the stove and cook until completely reduced, about 4 minutes.

3. Add the stock and peppercorns, bring to a boil, reduce the heat to medium, and cook, stirring occasionally, until reduced by half, about 15 minutes. Strain the sauce into a bowl (discard the solids). Wipe out the pan and return the sauce to the pan. Season with salt and whisk in the crème fraîche. Keep warm.

continued >

4. Cook the pork chops: Heat a few tablespoons oil in a cast-iron skillet or grill pan over high heat until shimmering. (Alternatively, heat a grill to high heat.) Reserving the marinade, add the chops to the pan (or grill) and cook, brushing with the marinade once more before finishing, until golden brown on both sides and cooked to medium doneness, about 5 minutes per side. Remove and let rest for 5 minutes before slicing.

5. To serve: Put a chop in the center of each plate. Ladle the sauce lightly over the top and around the plate. Put a large dollop of the chutney on the side of the chop and garnish with cilantro.

Green Apple–Green Chile Chutney

✻ **MAKES ABOUT 2 CUPS**

Finely grated zest of 1 tangerine or ½ orange

1 cup tangerine juice

2-inch piece fresh ginger, finely grated

3 large Granny Smith apples, peeled, halved, and diced

1 large poblano chile, roasted (see page 240) and diced

Clover honey

¼ cup chopped fresh cilantro leaves

1. Combine the tangerine zest, tangerine juice, and ginger in a medium saucepan and bring to a boil over high heat. Add the apples and cook until softened, about 10 minutes.

2. Stir in the poblano and season with honey to taste. Remove from the heat and fold in the cilantro. Serve at room temperature. The chutney can be made up to 1 day in advance and stored, tightly covered, in the refrigerator. Bring to room temperature before serving.

CARRIE BAIRD'S HUEVOS RANCHEROS

with Homemade Chorizo & Pico de Gallo Salsa Verde

SERVES 6

HOMEMADE CHORIZO

1 pound pork shoulder, cut into 1-inch cubes

½ pound pork fatback, cut into 1-inch cubes

1 red onion, cut into 1-inch chunks

2 tablespoons fresh oregano, chopped

1 tablespoon ground cumin

1 tablespoon sweet smoked Spanish paprika

1 tablespoon cayenne pepper

2 tablespoons chile de árbol powder

1 whole clove, crushed

1 cinnamon stick, broken into pieces

6 garlic cloves, chopped

Sea salt

½ cup cider vinegar

Freshly ground black pepper

ROASTED SALSA VERDE

1 pound tomatillos, husked and rinsed, large ones halved

1 large poblano chile, coarsely chopped

2 Anaheim chiles, coarsely chopped

2 jalapeños

2 serrano chiles

2 tablespoons canola oil

Kosher salt and freshly ground black pepper

ingredients continued >

"It was so exciting (and intimidating) to be on *BBF*, as Bobby very rarely gets beat. I've always thought my pork green chili was the best, so challenging him on huevos rancheros was an easy choice. It's a hard dish to make pretty, and challenging Bobby to a Southwestern dish was a bold move. I didn't get a chance to try his version, but I made my chorizo fresh, which is always best!" —CARRIE BAIRD

1. Make the chorizo: Combine the pork, fatback, onion, oregano, cumin, smoked paprika, cayenne, chile de árbol, clove, cinnamon stick, garlic, and 2 teaspoons salt in a large bowl and mix well to combine. Cover and refrigerate for at least 1 hour or put in the freezer for 20 minutes.

2. Using the medium die of a meat grinder attachment for a stand mixer and working in batches, grind the mixture into the bowl.

3. Remove the grinder attachment and attach a chilled paddle attachment to the mixer. Add the vinegar to the ground meat and beat until combined. Season with salt and black pepper. Use immediately or cover and refrigerate the chorizo for up to 48 hours.

4. Make the roasted salsa verde: Preheat the oven to 425°F.

5. Combine the tomatillos, poblano, Anaheims, jalapeños, and serranos in a large bowl. Add the oil, season with salt and black pepper, and toss well to coat.

6. Spread the mixture onto a sheet pan in an even layer (set the bowl aside) and roast until the tomatillos and chiles are slightly charred and soft, stirring once, about 25 minutes. Remove from the oven (reduce the oven temperature to 200°F) and when cool enough to handle, coarsely chop and return them to the bowl.

✘ **NOTE:** If you don't want to make your own chorizo, you can buy 1 pound fresh Mexican chorizo, loose or in links.

continued >

HUEVOS

6 (6-inch) flour tortillas

Canola oil

6 (6-inch) yellow or white corn tortillas

Sea salt

Black Beans (recipe follows)

Pico de Gallo Salsa Verde (recipe follows)

6 Fried Eggs (page 242)

Chopped fresh cilantro leaves, for garnish

7. Prepare the huevos: Wrap the flour tortillas tightly with foil and keep warm in the oven until ready to assemble the dish.

8. Heat 2 tablespoons oil in a large deep skillet over high heat until shimmering. Put the chorizo in the pan and cook, stirring, until golden brown, about 7 minutes. Add the roasted salsa verde and bring to a boil. Reduce the heat to medium and simmer until the chorizo is cooked through, 25 minutes.

9. Line a sheet pan with paper towels. Pour 2 inches of oil into a deep sauté pan and heat over medium heat to 350°F on a deep-fry thermometer. Fry the corn tortillas, one at a time, until lightly golden brown, 30 seconds. Remove to the sheet pan and season with salt.

10. To serve, put a flour tortilla on each plate and top with some of the black beans. Put a fried tortilla on top and spoon some of the chorizo mixture over it. Put a fried egg on top of the chorizo, top with the pico de gallo salsa verde, and garnish with cilantro.

Black Beans

✖ MAKES 1 QUART

1 pound dried black beans, picked over and soaked overnight in cold water

1 quart pork stock, Light Chicken Stock (page 233), or water

1 medium Spanish onion, coarsely chopped

6 garlic cloves, smashed and peeled

1 teaspoon ground coriander

1 teaspoon ground cumin

Kosher salt and freshly ground black pepper

Drain the beans and add to a large pot. Add stock to cover by 2 inches. Add the onion, garlic, coriander, and cumin and bring to a boil. Reduce the heat to medium and simmer, stirring occasionally, until tender, about 1 hour. Season with salt and black pepper.

> ✖ **BEAT THE CLOCK:** On the show, I cooked the beans in a pressure cooker due to time constraints. You can use your pressure cooker (it takes about 20 minutes) or stovetop (above). You can also use two 15-ounce cans of canned black beans, drained, rinsed, and cooked with the stock and aromatics until heated through.

Pico de Gallo Salsa Verde

✖ MAKES ABOUT 3 CUPS

½ pound tomatillos, husked, rinsed, and finely diced

½ pound green tomatoes, finely diced (see Note)

1 medium onion, finely diced

1 jalapeño, finely diced

1 serrano chile, finely diced

½ cup chopped fresh cilantro leaves

Juice of 2 limes

Few dashes of green habanero sauce, such as El Yucateco

Kosher salt

Combine the tomatillos, tomatoes, onion, jalapeño, serrano, cilantro, lime juice, and habanero sauce in a large bowl and season with salt to taste. Let sit at room temperature for at least 15 minutes before serving to allow the flavors to meld or cover and refrigerate for up to 4 hours.

> ✖ **NOTE:** If you can't find green tomatoes, you can just use all tomatillos. If you can't find tomatillos, you can use all green tomatoes.

EPISODE 910: *"Age Is Just a Number"*
COMPETITOR: Jenny Dorsey
DISH: Wonton soup
WINNER: Jenny Dorsey

JENNY DORSEY'S PORK & SHIITAKE WONTON SOUP

SERVES 8

FILLING

1 cup chopped pencil asparagus (about 8 stalks)

1 tablespoon canola oil

1 teaspoon kosher salt

8 ounces ground pork

½ teaspoon fish sauce

½ teaspoon pure maple syrup

½ teaspoon Maggi seasoning

¼ teaspoon pure cane sugar

Freshly ground white pepper

3 teaspoons soy sauce

3 teaspoons mirin

3 tablespoons peanut oil

2 medium scallions, green tops and pale-green parts only, thinly sliced

3 garlic cloves, thinly sliced

1-inch piece fresh ginger, peeled and finely chopped

3 shiitake mushrooms, stems discarded, caps coarsely chopped

2 links Chinese sausage, chopped

1 teaspoon Shaoxing cooking wine

1 teaspoon Chinese black vinegar

1 teaspoon toasted sesame oil

¼ cup finely chopped fresh cilantro leaves

WONTON SOUP

40 wonton wrappers

Pork Neck Broth (recipe follows)

3 scallions, thinly sliced

"It was nerve-wracking and exciting to compete against Bobby in front of a live audience. Having grown up watching him cook on *Iron Chef America*, the experience felt incredibly surreal. When the producers told me to stare directly at Bobby for a few minutes (the 'face off' shot), I remember pinching myself, thinking 'That's Bobby Flay!' Bobby was a lot of fun to cook alongside—he was a generous competitor, giving me 'home turf' tips as he worked (like where the paper towels were) and he was utterly gracious when I beat him. It was so rewarding to hear his encouraging words, telling me to go on and pursue my culinary career with the confidence of my win. (Hearing Bobby tell me he was impressed with how I moved in the kitchen? Truly wild.) Being on *Beat Bobby Flay* was such a memorable experience, and it's an episode I hold near and dear to my heart." —JENNY DORSEY

1. Make the filling: Preheat the oven to 375°F.

2. Toss the asparagus with the canola oil and salt and spread on a sheet pan. Roast until tender, stirring once, about 10 minutes. Set aside.

3. Combine the pork, fish sauce, maple syrup, Maggi seasoning, sugar, ⅛ teaspoon white pepper, and 1½ teaspoons each of the soy sauce and mirin in a large bowl. Set aside.

4. Heat the peanut oil in a large skillet over medium heat until shimmering. Add the scallions, garlic, ginger, shiitakes, and sausage and cook until the vegetables begin to soften, about 5 minutes. Reduce the heat to medium-low. Add the Shaoxing wine, black vinegar, ¼ teaspoon white pepper, and the remaining 1½ teaspoons each soy sauce and mirin. Cook until the mushrooms have released their moisture and are beginning to caramelize, 10 minutes.

5. Transfer this mixture to a food processor and add the sesame oil and roasted asparagus. Pulse until the consistency matches that of the ground pork mixture. Transfer to a bowl and let cool completely. Add to the ground pork mixture and mix until well combined. Mix in the cilantro.

continued >

✖ NOTE: If you have extra filling, you can vacuum-seal and freeze it for up to 1 month, or you can sauté it in a pan with a few teaspoons of oil until golden brown and cooked through and use it as a filling for an omelet. To freeze the filled wontons, place them on a parchment-lined plate and cover loosely with plastic wrap. Place in the freezer until completely frozen, about 1 hour, then transfer them to a zip-top freezer bag. They can be cooked directly from frozen; just add 1 to 2 minutes to the cooking time.

✖ IN IT TO WIN IT: It's a good idea to keep your wonton wrappers and wontons covered with a lightly damp towel as you make them so they don't dry out. Maggi and maple syrup add complexity of flavor beyond salty/sweet that gives this filling a lot of umami.

4 pounds pork necks

¼ cup chopped, peeled fresh ginger

Kosher salt

Pure cane sugar

Freshly ground white pepper

6. Test the seasoning of the filling by scooping 1 teaspoon onto a small plate and microwaving it for 20 to 30 seconds or searing it in a touch of oil in a pan until golden brown and cooked through. Taste and season the raw mixture with additional soy sauce, Maggi, fish sauce, and maple syrup as needed.

7. Make the wonton soup: Using your finger, wet the edges of a wonton wrapper with water. Place ½ tablespoon of the pork filling in the center of the wonton wrapper. Fold the wonton in half diagonally to create a triangle and seal the edges. Fold the two identical corners in on each other and press again to seal. Repeat until all the wonton wrappers are filled.

8. Bring a large pot of water to a boil over high heat. Working in batches, add the wontons and cook until the filling is cooked through, about 8 minutes. Remove with a slotted spoon to a sheet pan in a single layer.

9. While the wontons are cooking, bring the pork neck broth to a boil over high heat.

10. To serve, put 5 to 7 wontons in a large bowl and ladle the broth over them. Garnish with the scallions and serve.

Pork Neck Broth

✖ MAKES ABOUT 16 CUPS

1. Put the pork necks in a large stockpot, add cold water to cover by 2 inches, bring to a boil, and cook for 5 minutes. Drain.

2. Return the necks to the pot, add 8 quarts (32 cups) cold water, the ginger, and 2 tablespoons salt, and bring to a boil over high heat. Reduce the heat to medium-low and simmer, skimming away any of the scum that rises to the surface from time to time, and cook until reduced by half and flavorful, about 6 hours.

3. Strain the stock into a large bowl and taste for seasoning, adding sugar, white pepper, and more salt, if needed. Use immediately or let cool to room temperature and store in airtight containers in the refrigerator for up to 3 days or in the freezer for up to 3 months.

ASHLEY GABORIAULT'S PORK AL PASTOR CHILI-CHEESE FRIES

with Pineapple-Tomatillo Relish & Salsa Verde

SERVES 6

POTATOES

10 to 12 russet potatoes, peeled or unpeeled, whichever you prefer

GRILLED PINEAPPLE AND TOMATILLOS

½ fresh pineapple, peeled, quartered lengthwise, and cored

10 tomatillos, husked and rinsed

Canola oil

PORK AL PASTOR

12 guajillo chiles, seeded

6 mulato chiles, seeded

Boiling water

10 garlic cloves, peeled

½ cup fresh lime juice

¼ cup achiote paste

2 tablespoons dried Mexican oregano

1 tablespoon ground cumin

½ fresh pineapple, peeled, quartered lengthwise, cored, and chopped

Kosher salt

3 pounds boneless pork shoulder, excess fat removed, cut into 1-inch chunks

ingredients continued >

"It was an honor to be selected to compete on *BBF*. Shout-out to the whole crew who made it possible! Seeing all the work that goes on behind the scenes was such a cool experience, and everyone was so excited and helpful. It was super stressful, and I was full of anxiety to be running around cooking, talking, and filming, but it was so rewarding and fun at the same time! I had a blast and would do it again in a heartbeat, but then again, I've already beat him—so really, who's next?! So much fun and such a great experience!"

—ASHLEY GABORIAULT

1. Prepare the potatoes: Trim the sides of the potatoes to create rectangles. Cut them lengthwise into 4 planks each and then cut the planks into ¾-inch-wide fries. Put the potatoes in a large bowl and cover with cold water. Drain, then cover with cold water again and refrigerate for at least 2 hours and up to 24 hours (changing the water about every 4 hours).

2. Grill the pineapple and tomatillos: Heat a grill to high or a grill pan over high heat. Brush the pineapple and tomatillos with oil and grill until both are slightly charred on all sides and the tomatillos are soft, about 8 minutes. Remove the pineapple to a cutting board, let cool slightly, then cut into bite-size pieces. Put the tomatillos in a large bowl and reserve them for the relish and salsa verde.

3. Make the pork al pastor: Preheat the oven to 400°F.

4. Combine the chiles in a large heatproof bowl and cover with boiling water. Let sit at room temperature until softened, about 30 minutes.

5. Put the chiles in a blender, reserving the soaking liquid in case you need to thin the sauce. Add the garlic, lime juice, achiote paste, oregano, cumin, and pineapple. Blend until smooth. The sauce should be the thickness of marinara sauce. If it is too thick, add some chile soaking liquid a few tablespoons at a time until you reach the desired consistency. Season with salt to taste.

continued >

SALSA VERDE

2 garlic cloves, peeled

2 serrano chiles, seeded

½ cup chopped fresh cilantro leaves

¼ cup fresh lime juice

Kosher salt

PINEAPPLE-TOMATILLO RELISH

2 serrano chiles, finely diced

¼ red onion, finely diced

¼ cup chopped fresh cilantro leaves

Juice of 2 limes

Kosher salt

TO FINISH

Canola oil, for frying

Kosher salt

1 pound Oaxaca cheese, grated

1 pound Cotija cheese, grated

Chopped fresh cilantro leaves, for garnish (optional)

6. Combine the pork and the sauce in a large Dutch oven, making sure that the pork is covered with the sauce and adding some of the chile soaking liquid or water if needed. Cover the pot tightly, transfer to the oven, and cook for 1 hour. Reduce the oven temperature to 300°F and cook until the pork is fork-tender, 1½ to 2 hours longer.

7. Remove the pork with a slotted spoon to a large bowl and, using two forks, shred it into bite-size pieces. Return the pork to the sauce and keep warm.

8. Make the salsa verde: Combine 5 of the grilled tomatillos, the garlic, serranos, cilantro, lime juice, and salt to taste in a blender and blend until smooth.

9. Make the pineapple-tomatillo relish: Combine the remaining 5 grilled tomatillos and the grilled pineapple in a bowl. Add the serranos, onion, cilantro, and lime juice and season with salt. Let sit at room temperature for at least 30 minutes before serving. The relish can be made up to 8 hours in advance.

10. To finish: Drain the potatoes and pat them dry with paper towels. (It is important that the potatoes be very dry before you add them to the hot oil.) Line two large sheet pans with several layers of paper towels.

11. Fill the Dutch oven halfway with oil and heat over medium heat to 300°F on a deep-fry thermometer.

12. Working in batches, blanch the fries in the hot oil until slightly softened and a pale blonde color, about 4 minutes. Remove with a slotted spoon to one of the sheet pans lined with paper towels.

13. Increase the heat of the oil to 375°F. Fry the blanched fries again until golden brown and crispy, about 2 minutes. Remove to the remaining sheet pan and season immediately with salt. Keep warm.

14. Preheat the broiler.

15. Combine the two cheeses in a large bowl. Divide the fries among six large shallow broilerproof bowls. Top with several spoonfuls of the pork and as much of the cheese as you like. Place the bowls until the broiler and broil until the cheese is melted and bubbling, 2 to 5 minutes.

16. Serve topped with the relish and salsa verde and more cilantro, if desired.

POULTRY

SERVES 4 TO 6

BROTH

2 tablespoons schmaltz (chicken fat) or canola oil

3 pounds chicken wings

3 pounds duck legs

3 pounds chicken feet

5 medium Spanish onions, unpeeled, chopped

3 carrots, chopped

2 large parsnips, chopped

1 large leek, white and pale-green parts only, cleaned and coarsely chopped

1 head garlic, halved horizontally

1 bay leaf

15 sprigs flat-leaf parsley

15 sprigs dill

3 quarts Light Chicken Stock (page 233), store-bought low-sodium chicken stock or broth, or water

Kosher salt and freshly ground black pepper

MATZOH BALLS

1 cup matzoh meal

2 teaspoons baking powder

1 teaspoon baking soda

1 tablespoon kosher salt

1 teaspoon freshly ground black pepper

2 large eggs

½ cup schmaltz (chicken fat), melted and cooled

½ cup seltzer water

2 tablespoons finely chopped fresh flat-leaf parsley

4 large egg whites

ALEX REZNIK'S MATZOH BALL SOUP

"Who would want to watch us cook matzoh ball soup, I thought, old Jewish men sitting around Canter's Deli kibitzing? I grew up watching my Babushka cooking in her tiny four-by-six-foot kitchen in Brooklyn every day, all day, but matzoh ball soup was reserved only for Passover or if any of her grandchildren got sick. Laughingly, I said to my wife, 'Oy vey, what have I done? How can I possibly cook it in forty-five minutes? It took Baba all day, slowly simmering the soup, gently shaping the matzoh balls, letting them rest. . . .' The day of shooting was one big blur. Not only was I cooking against an Iron Chef, but I had my mom and dad in the audience rooting for me, judging from above. As soon as I saw Bobby bring out the pasta machine, I knew I'd had it! With nervous energy, I channeled the souls of generations of little Jewish grandmothers and made one amazing soup. Even before they announced it, I could tell by Bobby's face he knew it was all over. Rematch?" —**ALEX REZNIK**

1. Make the broth: Heat the schmaltz in a large stockpot or Dutch oven over high heat. Working in batches, brown the chicken wings, duck legs, and chicken feet until golden brown. Remove with tongs to a large bowl. Discard the rendered fat once cool.

2. Return the chicken wings and feet and the duck to the pot, along with the onions, carrots, parsnips, leek, garlic, bay leaf, parsley, dill, and stock. Bring to a boil over high heat, then reduce the heat to medium and simmer, skimming the scum that rises to the top, until the broth is reduced by a third, about 4 hours. Strain the broth and let cool, then remove the fat from the top. Transfer to a large Dutch oven and season with salt and pepper to taste.

3. Make the matzoh balls: Stir together the matzoh meal, baking powder, baking soda, salt, and pepper in a medium bowl. Whisk together the eggs, melted schmaltz, seltzer, and parsley in a large bowl until smooth. Add the dry ingredients and mix until just combined. Beat the egg whites until they hold soft peaks. Fold in the egg whites until there are no visible streaks and use immediately. The matzoh mixture can be made up to 1 day in advance, tightly covered, and refrigerated. If doing this, do not fold in the egg whites until just before using.

TO FINISH

2 pieces duck leg confit

¼ cup finely chopped fresh flat-leaf parsley

¼ cup finely chopped fresh dill fronds

✖ **BEAT THE CLOCK:** On the show, I had to use a pressure cooker to achieve my full-flavored stock. If you want to save time, too, it will take about 25 minutes.

4. Using damp hands, roll the matzoh mixture into 1-inch balls. Bring the broth to a simmer. Add the matzoh balls and cook until light and fluffy and cooked through in the center, 30 to 40 minutes.

5. To finish: Put the confited duck legs in a nonstick skillet, turn the heat to medium-high, and cook until the fat renders and the skin becomes very crispy, about 15 minutes. Turn the legs over and cook until golden brown, crispy, and just cooked through, about 10 minutes longer. Let cool slightly, then remove the meat from the bones and shred it into bite-size pieces.

6. To serve, ladle the broth and matzoh balls into bowls. Garnish with the shredded duck, parsley, and dill.

CHICKEN SHAWARMA
with Red Pepper Tahini, Mint Yogurt Sauce & Pickled Shallots

SERVES 4 TO 6

3-inch piece fresh ginger, peeled and chopped

6 garlic cloves, peeled

½ cup canola oil

1 pound boneless, skinless chicken thighs

2 tablespoons light brown sugar

1 tablespoon ground coriander

1 tablespoon ground cumin

1 teaspoon ground cinnamon

1 teaspoon ground turmeric

½ teaspoon ground allspice

Kosher salt and freshly ground black pepper

4 to 6 pitas

Red Pepper Tahini (recipe follows)

Mint Yogurt Sauce (recipe follows)

½ cup Pickled Shallots (page 248)

2 tablespoons finely chopped fresh mint leaves, for garnish

Chef Gail Arnold gave me one of my most important jobs early on in my cooking career. She hired me as a line cook at a restaurant called Bud's, which was Jonathan Waxman's California-style restaurant with a Southwestern touch. It was in Gail's kitchen where I first learned about the world of fresh and dried chiles, blue corn, and so many of the elements that make up the palate of the American Southwest. Those flavors inspired me to continue my education in that genre and led to the opening of Mesa Grill. Now, why Gail challenged me to chicken shawarma, I'll never know. The flavors are big and bold, and I'm always here for that, wherever the idea came from.

1. Combine the ginger, garlic, and oil in a food processor and process until almost smooth. Put the chicken in a large bowl, add the marinade, and toss well to coat. Cover and refrigerate for at least 30 minutes and up to 24 hours.

2. Combine the brown sugar, coriander, cumin, cinnamon, turmeric, and allspice in a small bowl. Remove the chicken from the marinade and pat dry. Season on both sides with salt and pepper and the spice rub.

3. Heat a grill to high or a grill pan over high heat. Grill the chicken until golden brown and slightly charred on both sides and just cooked through, about 5 minutes per side. Remove and let rest for 5 minutes before slicing crosswise into ¼-inch-thick slices. Grill the pita on both sides until lightly marked and soft, about 30 seconds per side.

4. Place the pitas on plates. Slather some of the red pepper tahini on top of each pita, top with some of the chicken, then drizzle some of the yogurt sauce on top of the chicken. Garnish with the pickled shallots and mint.

continued >

Red Pepper Tahini

✳ **MAKES 1½ CUPS**

1 cup tahini

4 jarred piquillo peppers, drained and patted dry

1 tablespoon harissa

1 teaspoon fresh lemon juice

Kosher salt and freshly ground black pepper

Combine the tahini, piquillos, harissa, and lemon juice in a food processor and process until smooth. Season with salt and pepper to taste. Cover and let sit for at least 30 minutes to allow the flavors to meld. The sauce can be made up to 24 hours in advance and stored, tightly covered, in the refrigerator. Bring to room temperature before using.

Mint Yogurt Sauce

✳ **MAKES 1½ CUPS**

¼ cup fresh mint leaves

¼ cup fresh cilantro leaves

1 cup 2% Greek yogurt

2 teaspoons Champagne vinegar or white wine vinegar

Kosher salt and freshly ground black pepper

Combine the mint, cilantro, yogurt, and vinegar in a food processor and process until smooth. Season with salt and pepper. The sauce can be made up to 12 hours in advance and stored, tightly covered, in the refrigerator.

SERVES 4

CHICKEN

3-inch piece fresh ginger, peeled and chopped

1 medium Spanish onion, chopped

12 garlic cloves, chopped

1 cup packed fresh cilantro leaves

½ cup canola oil

2 (4-pound) whole chickens, excess fat trimmed, butterflied (see How to Butterfly a Chicken, page 174) and halved

GREEN SAUCE

1 cup packed fresh cilantro

2 large scallions, green top and pale-green parts only, thinly sliced

2 tablespoons red wine vinegar

¼ cup canola oil

Kosher salt and freshly ground black pepper

SMOKED PAPRIKA POTATOES

2 pounds small yellow new potatoes

Kosher salt

3 tablespoons unsalted butter

3 tablespoons canola oil

1 tablespoon sweet smoked Spanish paprika

Freshly ground black pepper

4 ounces ricotta salata cheese, crumbled

¼ cup chopped fresh flat-leaf parsley

ingredients continued >

PIRI PIRI CHICKEN
with Apricot-Chile Hot Sauce & Smoked Paprika Potatoes

I absolutely love this dish. Spicy chile-laced chicken with crispy skin is welcome at my table anytime. This hot sauce features a great combination of Fresno chiles for fruity heat plus tart vinegar and dried apricots for a lovely balance. Actually, as I write this, I'm thinking about making it—I'll be back in a little while.

On the show, I juice the ingredients for the chicken marinade—ginger, onion, cilantro, garlic, oregano—so that I can really get those flavors into my chicken in the short time that I have, and if you have a juicer at home, you should try doing that, too. But if not, then just combine all the ingredients in a food processor with oil, as described in the recipe, and let it marinate for a minimum of four hours and preferably overnight.

1. Marinate the chicken: Combine the ginger, onion, garlic, cilantro, and oil in a food processor and process until smooth. Put the chickens in a large baking dish or two large zip-top bags. Add the marinade and make sure both chickens are entirely coated. Refrigerate for at least 4 hours and up to 24 hours.

2. Make the green sauce: Combine the cilantro, scallions, vinegar, oil, and a splash of water in a blender and blend until smooth. Season with salt and pepper. Transfer to a bowl and set aside.

3. Make the smoked paprika potatoes: Put the potatoes in a large saucepan, add cold water to cover by 2 inches, and season with 2 tablespoons salt. Bring to a boil over high heat and cook until fork-tender, about 25 minutes. Drain well and transfer to a sheet pan to cool for a few minutes. Slice crosswise into ½-inch-thick slices.

4. Heat the butter and oil in a large cast-iron skillet over high heat until shimmering. Stir in the smoked paprika and cook for 10 seconds. Season the potatoes with salt and pepper, then add to the pan and toss in the oil. Press the potatoes down with a metal spatula into an even layer and cook until the bottoms are golden brown and crusty, about 5 minutes. Flip the potatoes over, press down on them again with the spatula, and cook until the bottoms are golden brown and crusty, about 5 minutes longer. Stir in the ricotta salata and parsley and cook for 1 minute longer. Transfer to a platter or large shallow bowl and keep warm.

continued >

TO FINISH

Canola oil

Apricot–Chile Hot Sauce
(recipe follows)

5. To finish: Remove the chicken from the refrigerator 30 minutes before grilling. Preheat the oven to 400°F.

6. Heat a grill pan or large cast-iron skillet over medium heat. Drizzle some of the oil over two of the chicken halves and grill, skin-side down, until the fat has rendered and the skin is golden brown and crispy, about 10 minutes. Turn the chicken halves over and cook until the bottoms are golden brown, about 5 minutes. Transfer to a sheet pan. Repeat with the other chicken halves and more oil.

7. Brush the chicken liberally with some of the apricot-chile hot sauce, transfer to the oven, and roast until just cooked through, about 12 minutes longer. Remove from the oven and brush with more of the hot sauce. Let rest for 10 minutes.

8. To serve, put half a chicken on each plate, spoon some of the green sauce over the top, and place the potatoes on the side.

Apricot–Chile Hot Sauce

✖ **MAKES ABOUT 1½ CUPS**

5 dried apricots, soaked in boiling water for 15 minutes

8 large Fresno chiles, roasted (see page 240)

2 tablespoons Dijon mustard

½ cup red wine vinegar

Kosher salt and freshly ground black pepper

Reserving the soaking liquid, drain the apricots and transfer to a blender. Add the chiles, mustard, vinegar, and a splash of the apricot soaking water and blend until smooth. Season with salt and pepper. Let sit for at least 30 minutes before using to allow the flavors to meld. The sauce will keep, tightly covered, in the refrigerator for up to 2 weeks.

HOW TO BUTTERFLY A CHICKEN

I butterfly (spatchcock) my chickens so I can grill them more quickly and get more surface area for a crispy skin.

Put your whole chicken on a cutting board breast-side down with the legs facing you. Using kitchen shears or a sharp chef's knife, start at the tail end and cut up either side of the backbone, and fully removing the backbone so the chicken starts to lie flat. (Save the backbone for making stock.)

Once you've taken out the backbone, open the chicken up and flip it breast-side up, flattening it as much as possible. Then, using your palms, press down firmly at the top between the breasts—you will hear a crack—to flatten it even more.

TORTILLA SOUP
with Avocado Relish

It seems like every culture has its version of a comforting and healing chicken soup. This one is inspired by the flavors of Mexico and the American Southwest, and I've been making a version of this dish at Mesa Grill for thirty years! Think rich chicken broth enhanced with red chiles that both flavor and thicken the soup. I like to use spice-rubbed chicken thighs instead of the usual poached chicken—the thighs add more flavor and richness to the soup and are harder to overcook. The flavor-charged base becomes a vehicle for all of the fun garnishes like cheese, chiles, avocado, and tortilla chips.

SERVES 4

1 ancho chile, seeded

Boiling water

1 or 2 canned chipotle peppers in adobo sauce, to taste

4 tablespoons canola oil

1 medium Spanish onion, chopped

3 garlic cloves, chopped

2 tablespoons tomato paste

1 quart Rich Chicken Stock (page 233) or store-bought low-sodium chicken stock or broth

1 pound boneless, skinless chicken thighs

3 tablespoons Bobby's Spice Rub (page 243)

Kosher salt and freshly ground black pepper

Avocado Relish (page 240)

½ cup grated Monterey Jack cheese

¼ cup grated Cotija cheese

4 ounces store-bought blue and yellow tortilla chips, coarsely chopped

Cilantro leaves, for garnish

1. Put the ancho chile in a heatproof bowl, cover with boiling water, and let sit for 15 minutes. Reserving the soaking liquid, drain the chile and transfer to a food processor. Add ¼ cup of the soaking liquid and the chipotle peppers. Purée until smooth, scraping the sides and bottom of the processor and processing again, if needed.

2. Heat 2 tablespoons of the oil in a medium Dutch oven over high heat until shimmering. Add the onion and cook until soft, about 4 minutes. Add the garlic and cook for 1 minute longer. Add the tomato paste and cook, stirring constantly, until fragrant and deepened in color, about 2 minutes.

3. Add the stock and ancho paste and bring to a boil. Reduce the heat to medium and cook until slightly reduced and the flavors have melded, about 30 minutes. Strain the soup into a large bowl (discard the solids). Rinse out the Dutch oven, return the soup to the pot, and cook over high heat until warmed through and slightly reduced, about 10 minutes.

4. While the soup is cooking, preheat the oven to 400°F.

5. Put the chicken thighs in a bowl and add remaining 2 tablespoons oil, the spice rub, and salt and black pepper. Toss well to coat the chicken evenly. Heat a grill pan or cast-iron skillet over high heat. Add the chicken and cook until golden brown and charred on both sides, about 4 minutes per side. Transfer the pan to the oven and roast until cooked through, 10 minutes. Remove to a cutting board and let rest for 5 minutes before cutting into ¼-inch-thick slices.

6. Divide the chicken among four bowls. Ladle the soup over the chicken, top with a dollop of the relish, sprinkle with both cheeses, and top with a handful of tortilla chips. Garnish with cilantro leaves.

SERVES 4

2 tablespoons canola oil

2 carrots, coarsely chopped

1 medium red onion, coarsely chopped

5 garlic cloves, coarsely chopped

1 cup Cognac

1 (750 ml) bottle red wine (Burgundy or Pinot Noir)

6 ounces slab bacon, cut into ½-inch dice

2 tablespoons fennel seeds

2 tablespoons coriander seeds

8 bone-in, skin-on chicken thighs, skin removed and reserved

Kosher salt and freshly ground black pepper

1 pound cremini mushrooms, stems discarded, caps coarsely chopped

4 tablespoons unsalted butter

Homemade Butter & Parsley Noodles (recipe follows)

Crispy Chicken Skin (page 245), made using reserved skin from above

COQ AU VIN
with Homemade Butter & Parsley Noodles & Crispy Chicken Skin

Let's call coq au vin what it is: chicken and wine sauce but with a French accent. One of my favorite touches is to crisp up the chicken skin for the contrasting crunchy texture. I use chicken thighs rather than a whole bird, because thighs cook faster and stay moist. Sometimes egg noodles simply tossed with butter and parsley are better than a fancy pasta with tons of ingredients. In the battle, I had to make fresh noodles so my cohosts wouldn't shame me, but I don't think anyone will think less of you for using dried, store-bought noodles— everyone will be too busy licking their plates clean.

1. Heat the oil in a large Dutch oven over high heat until shimmering. Add the carrots and onion and cook until soft, 5 minutes. Add the garlic and cook for 1 minute longer. Remove the pan from the heat, slowly add the Cognac, and stand back as it could ignite quickly. Cook until reduced by half, 5 minutes. Add the wine and cook over high heat until reduced by half, about 20 minutes.

2. Put the bacon in a large cast-iron skillet and turn the heat to medium. Cook until the fat has rendered and the bacon is crisp, about 8 minutes. Remove the bacon with a slotted spoon to a plate lined with paper towels. Reserve the skillet with the bacon fat.

3. Combine the fennel seeds and coriander seeds in a coffee or spice grinder and grind to a fine powder. Season the chicken on both sides with salt and pepper and the ground spices.

4. Heat the skillet with the bacon fat over high heat until the fat begins to shimmer. Add the chicken and cook until golden brown on both sides, about 4 minutes per side. Remove the chicken to a bowl.

5. Add the mushrooms and 2 tablespoons of the butter to the pan and cook until golden brown and their liquid has evaporated, about 8 minutes. Transfer the mushrooms to the bowl with the chicken.

6. Add the chicken, mushrooms, and half of the bacon to the wine sauce in the Dutch oven. Bring to a boil, then reduce the heat to medium-low, cover, and simmer until the chicken is tender, about 20 minutes. Remove the chicken with a slotted spoon to a bowl.

7. Bring the sauce to a boil over high heat and cook until reduced to a sauce consistency, about 10 minutes. Stir in the remaining 2 tablespoons butter and season with salt and pepper.

8. Serve the chicken thighs on top of the noodles, garnished with more sauce, crispy chicken skin, and the remaining bacon.

Homemade Butter & Parsley Noodles

✖ **SERVES 4**

Kosher salt

1 stick (8 tablespoons) unsalted butter

¼ cup finely chopped fresh flat-leaf parsley

Freshly ground black pepper

Pasta Dough (page 235), cut into 1-inch-wide noodles

1. Bring a large pot of water to a boil and add 2 tablespoons salt.

2. While the water is coming to a boil, melt the butter in a large sauté pan over low heat. Add the parsley and season with salt and pepper.

3. Add the noodles to the boiling water and cook until they rise to the top, about 1 minute. Drain the noodles well in a colander and immediately transfer to the melted butter. Toss to coat.

EPISODE 1709: *"Skating By"*
COMPETITOR: Adam Greenberg
DISH: Chicken scarpariello
WINNER: Adam Greenberg

CHICKEN SCARPARIELLO
with Fried New Potatoes

A Sunday-night special. Perfectly cooked chicken, nestled in a fragrant sauce along with sausage and peppers, and served with crispy potatoes. It's an Italian American classic that my friend Jimmy V. refers to as "Chicken Scarp." This is the kind of dish that screams for a great bottle of wine—and then a nap!

SERVES 4

4 boneless, skin-on chicken breasts

4 boneless, skin-on chicken thighs

1 tablespoon sweet smoked Spanish paprika

Kosher salt and freshly ground black pepper

¼ cup canola oil

4 links sweet or hot Italian sausage (or a combination)

1 small Spanish onion, coarsely chopped

5 garlic cloves, coarsely chopped

1 cup dry white wine

3 cups Light Chicken Stock (page 233) or store-bought low-sodium chicken stock or broth

3 tablespoons unsalted butter, cold

Finely grated zest and juice of 1 lemon

6 Peppadew peppers, drained and coarsely chopped

¼ cup chopped fresh flat-leaf parsley, plus more for garnish

Fried New Potatoes (recipe follows)

Lemon wedges, for squeezing

✖ **IN IT TO WIN IT:** To get your chicken skin extra crispy, use a cast-iron skillet and weight the chicken down with another heavy pan (or even a brick wrapped in foil).

1. Preheat the oven to 425°F. Set a wire rack over a sheet pan.

2. Season the chicken all over with the smoked paprika and salt and pepper. Heat the oil in a cast-iron skillet over medium-high heat until shimmering. Put the chicken breasts in the pan, skin-side down, and immediately top with another cast-iron skillet or other heavy pot and cook until the skin is evenly golden brown and crispy, about 6 minutes. Turn the breasts over and cook on the other side until lightly golden brown, about 4 minutes longer. Transfer to the rack in the sheet pan. Repeat with the chicken thighs.

3. Transfer the chicken to the oven and roast until just cooked through, about 7 minutes. Remove the chicken from the skillet and let rest before serving.

4. Pour off and discard all but 2 tablespoons of the oil from the skillet that you cooked the chicken in. Add the sausage and cook over high heat, turning to ensure even browning, until golden brown, about 5 minutes. Transfer to a cutting board and let cool slightly, about 5 minutes. Slice the sausages into 1-inch rounds. Return the sausage to the skillet and cook over high heat until crispy, about 3 minutes more. Transfer the sausage to a plate, reserving the fat in the skillet.

5. Add the onion to the skillet and cook until soft, about 4 minutes. Add the garlic and cook for 1 minute longer. Stir in the wine, scraping the bottom of the pan with a wooden spoon, and cook until the wine is reduced by half, 5 minutes. Add the stock and cook until reduced by half, about 15 minutes. Stir in the butter, lemon zest, lemon juice, Peppadews, and parsley, return the sausage to the pan, and season with salt and pepper.

6. To serve, put a breast and a thigh on each plate, spoon the sauce over half of the meat, and scatter the potatoes around the plate. Garnish with parsley and a squeeze of lemon juice.

continued >

2 pounds yellow new potatoes

Kosher salt

½ cup canola oil

Freshly ground black pepper

✻ **BEAT THE CLOCK:** The potatoes can
be boiled up to 2 days in advance and
stored whole, tightly covered, in the
refrigerator.

Fried New Potatoes

✻ SERVES 4

1. Put the potatoes in a large saucepan, add cold water to cover by 2 inches, and season with 2 tablespoons salt. Bring to a boil and cook until fork-tender, about 12 minutes. Drain well and let sit until just cool enough to handle.

2. Slice the potatoes crosswise into ½-inch-thick slices. Heat the oil in a large nonstick or cast-iron skillet over high heat until shimmering. Working in batches, if necessary, arrange the potatoes in a single layer in the oil and cook until golden brown on the bottom, about 4 minutes. Flip and cook until golden brown on the second side, about 4 minutes more. Season with salt and pepper and keep warm until serving.

MARCUS SAMUELSSON'S DORO WAT

SERVES 4

2 medium red onions, diced

Kosher salt

4 tablespoons Spiced Butter (recipe follows) or unsalted butter

¼ teaspoon ground cardamom, preferably freshly ground

¼ teaspoon freshly ground black pepper

3 whole cloves

2 garlic cloves, finely chopped

1½-inch piece fresh ginger, peeled and chopped

1 tablespoon berbere or chili powder

2½ cups Light Chicken Stock (page 233) or store-bought low-sodium chicken stock or broth

¼ cup dry red wine

1 (4- to 5-pound) whole chicken, cut into 8 pieces, wings reserved for another use

Juice of 1 lime, plus wedges for garnish

4 hard-cooked eggs, peeled and halved

"It was so much fun cooking on *Beat Bobby Flay*, and I can't wait to come back again. Bobby is a food icon and such an incredible competitor. Only a chef like Bobby can go up against so many different chefs constantly and transition between cuisines like Chinese, Ethiopian, and Italian. Do you know how hard that is? It's really difficult. In many ways, Bobby and I are similar in our love for food and sports, and our competitiveness.

"I remember we both gave it our all for that round, and his version of doro wat was so tasty. I remember how confident I felt until I walked over to taste his berbere coconut rice and thought, 'Jeez, that's so good.' His passion for food is obvious and he demonstrates that in his dishes. Bobby is a natural at bringing flavors together and translating his skills to different cuisines. As a chef you want to go up against the best, and that's what Bobby's doing all the time." —MARCUS SAMUELSSON

1. Combine the onions, a pinch of salt, and 2 tablespoons of the spiced butter in a Dutch oven or other large deep pot over low heat. Cook, stirring occasionally, until the onions are golden, about 15 minutes. Add the remaining 2 tablespoons butter, the cardamom, pepper, cloves, garlic, ginger, and berbere and cook until the onions soften and take on the color of the spices, about 10 minutes.

2. Add the stock and wine and bring to a simmer. Add the chicken drumsticks and thighs. Bring back to a simmer and cook for 15 minutes. Add the chicken breasts and simmer until just cooked through, 15 minutes longer. Gently stir in the lime juice and eggs and simmer for 5 minutes longer. The sauce will be loose and soupy. Season with salt to taste and serve, with lime wedges alongside for squeezing.

continued >

Spiced Butter

✖ MAKES ABOUT ¾ CUP

1 stick (8 tablespoons) unsalted butter, cut into pieces

⅛ medium red onion, coarsely chopped

½ garlic clove, minced

1-inch piece fresh ginger, peeled and finely chopped

¼ teaspoon cardamom seeds

¼ teaspoon ground cumin

¼ teaspoon fenugreek seeds

¼ teaspoon dried oregano

⅛ teaspoon ground turmeric

2 fresh basil leaves

1. Melt the butter in a medium saucepan over low heat, stirring frequently. As the foam rises to the top, skim and discard it. Continue cooking, without letting the butter brown, until no more foam appears, about 2 minutes.

2. Add the onion, garlic, ginger, cardamom, cumin, fenugreek, oregano, turmeric, and basil and cook, stirring occasionally, for 15 minutes.

3. Remove from the heat and let stand until the spices settle. Strain through a fine-mesh sieve before using. The butter will keep in the refrigerator for up to 3 days or in the freezer for up to 3 months.

SERVES 4

CHICKEN

2 (4-pound) whole chickens, excess fat removed, butterflied (see How to Butterfly a Chicken, page 174), backbones reserved for the Pan Gravy (recipe follows)

Kosher salt and freshly ground black pepper

Canola oil

SPANISH TORTILLA DRESSING

4 tablespoons canola oil

2 large shiitake mushrooms, stems discarded, caps coarsely chopped

Kosher salt and freshly ground black pepper

1 medium Spanish onion, finely diced

1 large carrot, finely diced

1 medium celery stalk, finely diced

2 garlic cloves, mashed to a paste with ¼ teaspoon kosher salt

½ cup Light Chicken Stock (page 233) or store-bought low-sodium chicken stock or broth

2 teaspoons finely chopped fresh thyme

¼ cup chopped fresh flat-leaf parsley

4 slices (½ inch thick) day-old sourdough bread, crusts removed, cut into 1-inch squares

8 large eggs, beaten until light and fluffy

2 tablespoons unsalted butter

ingredients continued >

ROAST WHOLE CHICKEN
with Pan Gravy, Spanish Tortilla Dressing & Cranberry-Tangerine Relish

Perhaps the elements of this dish seem like an odd combination, but hey, that's what happens sometimes when you're under the gun trying to pull off a Thanksgiving-esque meal during a 45-minute competition. That said, it works! Not only that, but any one of these components would work really well on its own, too. Here's a recommendation: Roast the chicken and serve it with the cranberry relish. The next day, serve the Spanish tortilla dressing for brunch. Two meals in one!

1. Roast the chicken: Liberally season the chickens on all sides with salt and pepper. Let sit at room temperature for 20 minutes.

2. Preheat the oven to 425°F.

3. Heat 2 tablespoons of the oil in a 14-inch cast-iron skillet over medium heat until shimmering. Put one chicken in the pan, skin-side down, and cook, undisturbed, until the skin turns golden brown and crispy and releases easily from the pan, about 8 minutes. Turn the chicken over and cook on the other side until golden brown, about 5 minutes longer. Repeat with the other chicken.

4. Transfer the chickens to a sheet pan and roast until golden brown and an instant-read thermometer inserted into the thigh registers 160°F, about 25 minutes.

5. Meanwhile, make the Spanish tortilla dressing: Preheat the broiler. Heat 2 tablespoons of the oil in a large nonstick or cast-iron skillet over high heat until shimmering. Add the mushrooms and cook until golden brown and tender and their liquid has evaporated, about 8 minutes. Season with salt and pepper and transfer to a large bowl.

6. Add the remaining 2 tablespoons oil to the skillet and heat over high heat until shimmering. Add the onion, carrot, and celery and cook until soft, about 5 minutes. Add the garlic and cook for 1 minute longer. Return the mushrooms to the pan and add the stock, thyme, and parsley. Stir well and season with salt and pepper. Transfer to the bowl with the mushrooms, fold in the bread, and let cool slightly.

continued >

FOR SERVING

Cranberry-Tangerine Relish (recipe follows)

Pan Gravy (recipe follows)

✖ **BEAT THE CLOCK:** Properly roasting a whole chicken in 45 minutes is impossible unless you butterfly (spatchcock) the bird, which allows it cook more quickly and evenly. It is actually my favorite way to prepare a chicken.

½ **cup tangerine juice**

⅓ **cup clover honey, or ½ cup pure cane sugar**

Pinch of kosher salt

1 (12-ounce) bag cranberries, fresh or thawed frozen

2 **tablespoons canola oil**

2 **tablespoons unsalted butter**

Chicken backbones (reserved from butterflying the chickens)

Kosher salt and freshly ground black pepper

1 medium Spanish onion, coarsely chopped

1 small carrot, chopped

1 small celery stalk, chopped

¼ **cup all-purpose flour**

½ **cup dry white wine**

½ **cup dry red wine**

3 cups Light Chicken Stock (page 233) or store-bought low-sodium chicken stock

3 sprigs thyme

5 sprigs flat-leaf parsley

7. Stir the eggs into the mixture until well combined. Let sit for 10 minutes to allow the bread to absorb the eggs.

8. Return the skillet to high heat, add the butter, and cook until melted and shimmering. Add the bread mixture and cook, stirring once to distribute the solids, until the bottom of the tortilla is set and lightly golden brown, about 7 minutes. Transfer the pan to the broiler and broil until puffed and the top is lightly golden brown, 2 to 5 minutes, depending on your broiler. Run a knife around the edges. Let cool for 5 minutes and cut into wedges.

9. To serve: Transfer the chicken to a cutting board and let rest for 10 minutes before carving it. Serve with the tortilla dressing, cranberry sauce, and gravy.

Cranberry-Tangerine Relish

✖ **MAKES ABOUT 2 CUPS**

Bring the tangerine juice to a boil in a medium saucepan over high heat. Add the honey, salt, and cranberries and cook until the cranberries soften and pop and the mixture thickens, about 10 minutes. Transfer to a bowl and serve at room temperature or chilled. The cranberry sauce can be made 2 days in advance and stored, tightly covered, in the refrigerator.

Pan Gravy

✖ **MAKES ABOUT 2¼ CUPS**

1. Heat the oil and butter in a large deep sauté pan over high heat until shimmering. Add the chicken backbones, season with salt and pepper, and cook until golden brown on both sides, about 8 minutes. Remove to a plate.

2. Add the onion, carrot, and celery to the pan and cook until soft and lightly golden brown, about 6 minutes. Sprinkle in the flour and cook, stirring constantly with a wooden spoon, until lightly golden brown, about 2 minutes. Stir in the both wines and cook until reduced by half, about 5 minutes.

3. Return the backbones to the pan and add the stock, thyme, and parsley. Bring to a boil, then reduce the heat to medium and cook, stirring occasionally, until the gravy is thickened and the flour taste has been cooked out, about 12 minutes. Strain the gravy into a bowl. Wipe out the saucepan, return the gravy to the pan, and season with salt and pepper to taste. Keep warm until serving. The gravy can be made up to 1 day in advance and stored, tightly covered, in the refrigerator. Warm over low heat before serving.

JOEY WARD'S VIETNAMESE-STYLE CHICKEN & WAFFLES

SERVES 6

NUOC CHAM MAPLE SYRUP

2 shallots, finely diced

2-inch piece fresh ginger, peeled and finely diced

6 garlic cloves, mashed to a paste with ¼ teaspoon kosher salt

4 Thai bird's eye chiles, finely diced

1 cup packed light brown sugar

1 teaspoon kosher salt

1 cup fish sauce, preferably Red Boat or Squid

Juice of 3 large limes

2 cups pure maple syrup

FRIED CHICKEN

8 boneless, skinless chicken thighs, cut into 1½-inch chunks

1 cup well-shaken buttermilk

Kosher salt

1 cup all-purpose flour

⅓ cup cornstarch

⅓ cup rice flour

1 tablespoon garlic powder

1 tablespoon onion powder

1 teaspoon sweet Spanish paprika

1 teaspoon freshly ground black pepper

Canola or peanut oil

LIME BUTTER

4 tablespoons unsalted butter, at room temperature

Finely grated zest of 2 limes

ingredients continued >

"This dish is particularly special to me as it is responsible for me meeting my wife! When I was the chef of Gunshow, I had put the dish on my menu for the first time the very night that my wife, Emily, had decided to try out the restaurant, on a date with another gentleman. She wrote a Yelp review a few days later about her visit, raving about the chicken and waffles, which feature some of my favorite Vietnamese flavors. When I read it, I reached out to her, and the rest is history. Beating Bobby was an amazing experience, as I got to share with the world the dish that got me on the road to love, and I got to compete against (and defeat!) a great champion." —**JOEY WARD**

1. Make the nuoc cham maple syrup: Combine the shallots, ginger, garlic, chiles, brown sugar, and salt in a mortar and pound into a paste with the pestle. (Alternatively, you can combine the ingredients in a food processor and pulse a few times until finely chopped to a paste.) Transfer the mixture to a large bowl and stir in the fish sauce, lime juice, and maple syrup.

2. Fry the chicken: Combine the chicken, buttermilk, and 1 tablespoon salt in a large bowl. Cover and marinate for 20 minutes in the refrigerator.

3. Meanwhile, in a medium bowl, combine the all-purpose flour, cornstarch, rice flour, 1 tablespoon salt, the garlic powder, onion powder, paprika, and pepper and mix well.

4. Fill a deep fryer or large Dutch oven halfway with oil and heat over medium heat to 325°F on a deep-dry thermometer.

5. Remove the chicken from the marinade and dredge in the flour mixture. Working in batches, carefully add the chicken to the hot oil and fry until golden and cooked through, about 6 minutes. Drain on paper towels and season lightly with salt.

6. Make the lime butter: Stir together the lime zest and butter in a small bowl until smooth. The butter can be made 3 days in advance and stored, tightly covered, in the refrigerator. Bring to room temperature before using.

continued >

FOR SERVING

6 Peanut Waffles (recipe follows)

½ cup roasted peanuts, finely chopped

1 ounce micro cilantro or 1 cup cilantro leaves

Finely grated zest of 3 limes, for garnish (optional)

1½ cups all-purpose flour

⅓ cup pure cane sugar

½ teaspoon kosher salt

1 teaspoon baking powder

½ teaspoon baking soda

¾ cup roasted peanuts, coarsely chopped

1 large egg

1 cup whole milk

½ cup well-shaken buttermilk

1 tablespoon extra-chunky peanut butter

¼ cup roasted peanut oil (see Note) or peanut oil

Cooking spray

7. To serve: Serve one waffle per plate, topped with some of the fried chicken. Drizzle with the nuoc cham maple syrup and top with the peanuts, cilantro, and lime butter. Garnish with lime zest, if desired.

Peanut Waffles

✖ MAKES 6 WAFFLES

1. Whisk together the flour, sugar, salt, baking powder, baking soda, and peanuts in a large bowl until combined. Whisk together the egg, milk, buttermilk, peanut butter, and oil in a medium bowl until smooth. Add the wet ingredients to the dry ingredients and whisk until the mixture just comes together. Let rest for 10 minutes.

2. Set a wire rack over a sheet pan. Heat your waffle maker to medium-high heat according to the manufacturer's directions. Mist the plates with cooking spray. Pour a heaping ¼ cup of batter onto each plate of the waffle iron and cook until golden brown and crispy, about 4 minutes. Remove to the wire rack on the sheet pan. Keep the waffles warm in a 200°F oven until ready to serve.

> ✖ NOTE: Peanuts can be roasted prior to their oil being extracted. The roasting provides a deep nutty flavor and dark golden brown color, and the oil is generally used for flavoring, rather than cooking.

EPISODE 1710: *"Fit to Flay"*
COMPETITOR: Nate Appleman
DISH: Chicken adobo
WINNER: Bobby Flay

SERVES 4

CHICKEN

½ cup canola oil

4 bone-in, skin-on chicken thighs, skin removed and reserved

4 skin-on chicken drumsticks

5 shallots, halved and thinly sliced

2-inch piece fresh ginger, peeled and chopped

8 garlic cloves, smashed

5 dried Thai chiles

2 cups Light Chicken Stock (page 233) or store-bought low-sodium chicken stock or broth

1 cup reduced-sodium soy sauce

½ cup coconut vinegar or cider vinegar

3 tablespoons pure cane sugar

1 teaspoon freshly ground black pepper

2 bay leaves

CRISPY COCONUT CHICKEN LIVER RICE

5 chicken livers, patted dry

Kosher salt and freshly ground black pepper

3 large eggs

Crispy Rice (page 243)

TO FINISH

Crispy Chicken Skin (page 245), made using reserved skin from above

2 scallions, green tops and pale-green parts only, thinly sliced

CHICKEN ADOBO
with Crispy Coconut Chicken Liver Rice & Crispy Chicken Skins

I lucked out on this challenge, which features a classic Filipino chicken dish. I work with some amazing Filipino people who have taught me the characteristic balance of vinegar, garlic, soy, and sweetness that creates an amazing umami sensation, one that works beautifully on chicken but also roasted pork or beef.

1. Make the chicken: Heat 2 tablespoons of the oil in a large Dutch oven over medium heat until shimmering. Add the chicken thighs and cook until the fat renders, the skin is crispy, and both sides are golden brown, about 5 minutes per side. Remove to a large plate.

2. Add 2 tablespoons of the oil to the pan and heat until shimmering. Add the drumsticks and cook until golden brown on both sides, about 3 minutes per side. Remove to a plate.

3. Leaving 2 tablespoons of the fat in the pan, pour off the rest of the fat and reserve 3 tablespoons of it to cook the chicken livers. Add the shallots and ginger to the pan and cook over high heat, stirring occasionally, until soft, about 5 minutes. Add the garlic and dried chiles and cook for 1 minute. Add 1 cup water, the stock, soy sauce, vinegar, sugar, pepper, and bay leaves and stir until combined.

4. Return the chicken to the pot and bring to a boil. Reduce the heat to low, cover, and cook until the chicken is tender, about 1 hour. If the liquid reduces too quickly or becomes too salty, add a bit of water. Remove the chicken from the pot to a sheet pan in an even layer.

5. Heat the remaining ¼ cup oil in a large nonstick pan over medium heat until shimmering. Cook the chicken, in batches if necessary, until crispy on both sides, about 2 minutes per side.

6. Make the rice: Heat the reserved 3 tablespoons chicken fat in a large nonstick sauté pan over high heat until shimmering. Add the chicken livers, season with salt and pepper, and cook until golden brown on both sides and pink in the center, about 2 minutes per side. Remove and let cool for 5 minutes before coarsely chopping.

7. Return the pan to high heat until the fat shimmers. Crack the eggs into the pan, season the tops with salt and pepper, and cook until the whites are firm and set and the yolks are almost set, about 2 minutes. Break the eggs into large pieces.

8. To finish: Place the crispy rice in a large bowl. Add the eggs and chopped chicken livers and gently mix to combine. Put the rice in bowls, top with a leg and a thigh, spoon sauce over the top, and garnish with crispy chicken skin and the scallions.

EPISODE 2403:
"The Queen Returns"
COMPETITOR: Sarah Wade
DISH: Fried chicken sandwich
WINNER: Bobby Flay

FRIED CHICKEN SANDWICHES
with Yuzu-Scallion Slaw & Ají Amarillo Aioli

There are few things that hit the spot better than a crispy-coated, juicy piece of fried chicken—and when it's served up in a sandwich, you get more room to layer in fun and flavorful condiments and toppings. I brought the crunch with a citrusy slaw and for a flavorful, luscious spread, I utilized some yellow chile paste from Peru, folding it into mayonnaise for an aioli with extra fruity, spicy flavor. This might show up on my menu at Bobby's Burgers. Stay tuned!

SERVES 4

MARINATED CHICKEN

2 cups buttermilk

Juice of 2 limes

2 teaspoons onion powder

2 teaspoons garlic powder

2 teaspoons sweet Spanish paprika

2 teaspoons New Mexico chile powder

Kosher salt and freshly ground black pepper

1½ pounds boneless, skinless chicken thighs (6 ounces each)

YUZU-SCALLION SLAW

¼ cup yuzu juice

2 tablespoons rice vinegar

Juice of ½ lemon

2 teaspoons reduced-sodium soy sauce

1 teaspoon pure cane sugar

1 teaspoon toasted sesame oil

¼ cup canola oil

½ small head napa cabbage, finely shredded

2 large scallions, thinly sliced

AJÍ AMARILLO MAYONNAISE

1 cup mayonnaise

2 tablespoons aji amarillo paste

Kosher salt and freshly ground black pepper

FRIED CHICKEN

Canola oil, for frying

1 cup buttermilk

Kosher salt and freshly ground black pepper

1. Marinate the chicken: Whisk together the buttermilk, lime juice, onion powder, garlic powder, paprika, chile powder, and salt and pepper in a large baking dish or bowl. Add the chicken thighs and turn to coat them in the mixture. Cover and marinate in the refrigerator for at least 1 hour and up to 4 hours.

2. Make the yuzu-scallion slaw: Whisk together the yuzu juice, vinegar, lemon juice, soy sauce, sugar, sesame oil, and canola oil in a large bowl until combined. Stir in the cabbage and scallions, cover, and refrigerate for at least 30 minutes and up to 8 hours.

3. Make the ají amarillo mayonnaise: Whisk together the mayonnaise and ají amarillo paste. Season with salt and pepper. Cover and refrigerate for at least 30 minutes and up to 3 days.

4. Preheat the oven to 350°F. Put a wire rack over a sheet pan.

5. Remove the chicken from the marinade, letting any excess run off. Transfer to the rack and season on both sides with salt and pepper. Bake until three-quarters of the way cooked through, about 12 minutes. Remove from the oven and let sit at room temperature for 15 minutes. Transfer to a large plate and refrigerate until just chilled, about 30 minutes.

6. Fry the chicken: Pour 2 inches of canola oil into a large cast-iron skillet and heat over medium heat to 375°F on a deep-fry thermometer.

7. Set a wire rack over a sheet pan. Put the buttermilk in a small baking dish and season with salt and pepper. Combine the flour and cornstarch in a large baking dish and season with the onion powder, garlic powder, and salt and pepper. Dip a thigh in the buttermilk, let the excess drain off, then dredge in the flour mixture, making sure the entire thigh is coated evenly. Tap off the excess and transfer to the rack. Let sit for 5 minutes to allow the flour to be absorbed. Repeat with the remaining thighs.

2 cups all-purpose flour

1 cup cornstarch

2 teaspoons onion powder

2 teaspoons garlic powder

SANDWICHES

4 soft sesame-seed hamburger buns, insides scooped out, lightly toasted

Pickled Red Onions (page 248, optional)

8. Working in batches, fry the chicken until golden brown, about 2 minutes per side. Remove and let drain on the rack. Immediately season with a bit of salt.

9. Make the sandwiches: Spread some of the ají amarillo mayonnaise on the top and bottom of each bun. Put a thigh on the bottom bun, then top with a large dollop of slaw, a few pickled onions (if using), and the top bun. Serve with extra slaw on the side.

EPISODE 1806: *"Drop the Mic"*
COMPETITOR: Ryan Hackney
DISH: *Gai yang (Thai-style grilled chicken)*
WINNER: Bobby Flay

THAI-STYLE GRILLED CHICKEN

I love Southeast Asian food, and although I'm admittedly not very well-versed in it, I love learning more about it. Though it originated in Laos (where it's called *pin gai*), this marinated grilled chicken dish is now popular all over Thailand, where it's often served up hot off the grill in open-air markets. Garlic, ginger, chiles, lemongrass: all so fragrant and so flavorful. I'm sure my version is not anywhere near authentic, but it tastes pretty good. This would be a great dish for an outdoor cocktail party.

SERVES 4

SPECIAL EQUIPMENT

Twelve 12-inch skewers (optional)

8 garlic cloves, chopped

3-inch piece fresh ginger, peeled and chopped

2 lemongrass stalks, trimmed and pounded with the back of the knife

12 sprigs cilantro

¼ cup fish sauce

¼ cup reduced-sodium soy sauce

¼ cup canned unsweetened full-fat coconut milk

1 Fresno chile, chopped

2 red Thai bird's eye chiles, chopped

¼ cup canola oil

6 boneless, skin-on chicken thighs (about 2½ pounds total)

Crispy Rice (page 24)

3 limes, quartered

Sweet Chili Dipping Sauce (recipe follows)

1. Combine the garlic, ginger, lemongrass, cilantro, fish sauce, soy sauce, coconut milk, both chiles, and oil in a food processor and process until smooth. Put the chicken in a large bowl, pour the marinade over, and toss well to make sure all the thighs are coated in the marinade. Cover and refrigerate for at least 4 hours and up to 24 hours.

2. Preheat the oven to 450°F. Set a wire rack over a sheet pan.

3. Heat a grill pan or cast-iron skillet over medium heat until smoking. Remove the chicken from the marinade and place in the pan, skin-side down. Cook until the fat renders and the skin becomes crispy, about 5 minutes. Turn over and cook on the other side until golden brown, about 4 minutes longer. Transfer to the wire rack and roast in the oven until just cooked through, about 5 minutes. Remove to a cutting board and let rest for 5 minutes.

4. To serve, slice the thighs lengthwise in half and skewer each half, if desired. Put the rice in bowls, top with the skewered chicken, and squeeze lime juice over. Serve the dipping sauce on the side.

Sweet Chili Dipping Sauce

✖ **MAKES ABOUT 1¼ CUPS**

1 cup Thai sweet chili sauce

2 tablespoons cider vinegar

Finely grated zest and juice of 2 limes

1 fresh Thai chile, finely diced

1 tablespoon finely chopped fresh chives

Whisk together the sweet chili sauce, vinegar, lime zest, lime juice, chile, and chives until combined. Let sit for at least 15 minutes and up to 3 days, covered, in the refrigerator to allow the flavors to meld.

SERVES 4 TO 6

PIMENTO CHEESE DUMPLINGS

Kosher salt

3 cups whole-milk ricotta cheese

2 large eggs

¼ cup extra-virgin olive oil

2 tablespoons your favorite Cajun spice blend

1 cup coarsely grated sharp white or yellow cheddar cheese

5 cups all-purpose flour

4 teaspoons baking powder

CHICKEN AND SAUCE

2 teaspoons mustard powder

2 teaspoons ground coriander

2 teaspoons ground cumin

Kosher salt and freshly ground black pepper

4 bone-in, skin-on chicken leg quarters

4 tablespoons extra-virgin olive oil

1 cup medium-diced Spanish onion

1 cup medium-diced carrots

1 cup medium-diced celery

10 garlic cloves, chopped

8 cups Light Chicken Stock (page 233) or store-bought low-sodium chicken stock or broth

2 cups heavy cream

¼ teaspoon xanthan gum (see Note), such as Bob's Red Mill

1 tablespoon finely chopped fresh flat-leaf parsley

KENNY GILBERT'S CHICKEN & DUMPLINGS

"Being able to stand in the same kitchen and cook against Bobby was a huge honor. I used to watch Bobby on *Grillin' & Chillin'* many moons ago. To see his growth and accomplishments based on flavorful delicious food has been so impressive, and beating him was an amazing achievement. Not many have beat him, so to do this was a big feather in my cap. For a rematch, I want to see him in Kitchen Stadium, Iron Chef–style!"

—KENNY GILBERT

1. **Make the pimento cheese dumplings:** Bring a large pot of water to a boil, and add 2 tablespoons salt. Line a sheet pan with parchment paper.

2. Whisk together the ricotta, eggs, oil, 2 tablespoons salt, and the Cajun spice blend in a large bowl until smooth. Stir in the cheddar. Add the flour and baking powder, and mix until the mixture just comes together and forms a dough. Using a 2-ounce ice cream scoop, scoop the dough onto the prepared sheet pan. Roll each scoop into a ball.

3. Fill a large bowl with ice and water. Lower the dumplings into the boiling water and cook until they float to the top, then cook for 2 minutes longer. Remove the dumplings carefully with a slotted spoon and transfer to the ice bath to cool, about 2 minutes. Once cool, remove with a slotted spoon and place on a sheet pan until ready to use. The dumplings can be stored, tightly covered, in the refrigerator for up to 1 day.

4. **Make the chicken and sauce:** Mix together the mustard powder, coriander, cumin, 1 teaspoon salt, and 2 teaspoons pepper in a small bowl. Season the chicken on all sides with the spice mixture.

5. Heat 3 tablespoons of the oil in a large Dutch oven or large deep skillet over high heat until shimmering. Cook the chicken until golden brown on both sides, about 3 minutes per side. Remove the chicken (it will not be cooked through) to a large plate.

6. Add the remaining 1 tablespoon oil to the pan and heat until shimmering. Add the onion, carrots, and celery and cook until lightly golden brown, about 5 minutes. Stir in the garlic and cook for 1 minute longer. Add the stock and bring to a boil, scraping up any brown bits on the bottom of the pan. Add the cream and 1 teaspoon salt and bring to a simmer. Return the chicken to the pan. Cover and

1 tablespoon finely chopped fresh sage

1 tablespoon finely chopped fresh rosemary

¼ cup picked fresh celery leaves, for garnish

✱ **NOTE:** Xanthan gum is ideal in this recipe as a thickener. It makes the sauce lighter than a roux, and you don't have to use a lot. Plus, the base is gluten-free.

reduce the heat to medium. Cook until the chicken is tender and cooked through, about 12 minutes.

7. Remove the chicken to a plate and let rest until cool enough to handle. Discard the bones and skin and cut the meat into 1-inch cubes.

8. While the chicken is cooling, carefully transfer the cooking liquid, in batches if needed, to a blender. Add the xanthan gum and blend until smooth. Strain into a bowl and then return to the pan. Bring to a simmer over medium heat, then add the chicken, dumplings, parsley, sage, and rosemary and cook until heated through, about 5 minutes.

9. Spoon the stew into bowls and garnish with the celery leaves.

✖ **IN IT TO WIN IT:** Serve the meatloaf alongside whipped or mashed sweet potatoes and/or sautéed green beans for a winning combination.

✖ **NOTE:** For the competition, I was required to make my own no-salt seasoning mix. For ease, I recommend you use a store-bought variety, such as Mrs. Dash. —T. L.

EPISODE 2212:
"Gobble Till You Wobble"
COMPETITOR: Tirzah Love
DISH: Turkey meatloaf
WINNER: Bobby Flay

TIRZAH LOVE'S TURKEY MEATLOAF
with Cranberry Relish

"My experience on *Beat Bobby Flay* was magical. Coming out in a turkey costume to celebrate Thanksgiving had to be one of silliest, yet most liberating things I've ever done! Guest judges Alex Guarnaschelli and Jay Pharoah kept me giggling the whole time with their banter, and Jay comparing me to Beyoncé had to be one of the best compliments I ever received. Bobby was so gracious, and we both worked really hard on our dishes, even though he used pork in his turkey meatloaf (cheater!). I feel like we had a fair fight, but I am ready for my rematch. My turkey meatloaf recipe is so special to me, as it represents everything I love to eat on Thanksgiving Day, all in one. Even though I didn't beat Bobby, it's still a winning dish." —**TIRZAH LOVE**

SERVES 6 TO 8

MEATLOAF

Cooking spray

2 cups crumbled day-old cornbread, homemade (page 237) or store-bought

⅓ cup heavy cream, plus more as needed

2 large eggs

2 tablespoons unsalted butter, cut into pieces

1 small Spanish onion, grated

1 small celery stalk, finely chopped

2 small carrots, grated

¼ cup dried cranberries

½ teaspoon Himalayan pink salt

¼ teaspoon freshly ground black pepper

2 tablespoons no-salt seasoning (see Note)

1 tablespoon minced fresh sage

1 teaspoon minced fresh rosemary

2 pounds ground turkey (80/20)

CRANBERRY RELISH

1 (10-ounce) bag frozen cranberries

1 cup pure cane sugar

2 teaspoons Sriracha

Finely grated zest of 1 lemon

3 tablespoons fresh lemon juice

1. Make the meatloaf: Preheat the oven to 375°F. Line a sheet pan with foil or parchment paper and mist with cooking spray.

2. Combine the cornbread and cream in a large bowl. Let stand for 10 minutes until the bread absorbs the cream. If the bread seems dry, add more cream. Whisk the eggs in a small bowl until light and fluffy.

3. Melt the butter in a large sauté pan over medium-high heat until shimmering. Add the onion, celery, carrots, and dried cranberries and cook until the vegetables are soft and the cranberries are plump, about 5 minutes. Season with the salt, pepper, and no-salt seasoning. Transfer the vegetables to a large bowl and let cool slightly.

4. Add the soaked cornbread, eggs, sage, and rosemary to the sautéed vegetables and mix well to combine. Crumble the turkey over the mixture and gently mix to combine.

5. Transfer the meat mixture to the prepared sheet pan and shape into a 9 × 5-inch loaf. Smooth the top and bake until an instant-read thermometer inserted into the center registers 160°F, about 45 minutes. Loosely tent with foil and let rest for 20 minutes before slicing.

6. Make the cranberry relish: Combine the cranberries, sugar, Sriracha, lemon zest, lemon juice, and ½ cup cold water in a medium saucepan. Bring to a boil over high heat, reduce the heat to low, and simmer until thickened and the berries have popped, about 15 minutes. Transfer to a bowl and let cool to room temperature.

7. Cut the meatloaf into slices and serve with the cranberry relish.

DESSERTS

Vanilla Cream Puffs with Blackberry-Bourbon Caramel Sauce & Toasted Pecans ✳ **205**

Vanilla Bean Cheesecake with Apple-Blackberry Compote & Spiced Crumble Topping ✳ **207**

Red Hot Cinnamon Apple Dumplings with Caramel Sauce & Spiced Crème Fraîche ✳ **211**

Bittersweet Chocolate Soufflé with Blackberry Whipped Cream ✳ **213**

Bananas Foster Cream Pie with Praline Pecans ✳ **216**

Key Lime Pie with Toasted Coconut Whipped Cream ✳ **219**

Upside-Down Carrot Cake with a Rum-Caramel Pineapple & Cream Cheese Drizzle ✳ **220**

Spiced Chocolate Cream Pies with Chocolate-Hazelnut Crust & Bourbon Whipped Cream ✳ **223**

Roy Breiman's Dutch Baby Pancake with Sautéed Apples & Fromage Blanc ✳ **224**

Clarice Lam's S'mores ✳ **226**

Shelby Sieg's Lemon Thyme Olive Oil Cake with Fig Caramel, Candied Hazelnuts & Lemon Whipped Cream ✳ **228**

MAKES 16 CREAM PUFFS

VANILLA BEAN PASTRY CREAM

2 cups whole milk

1 vanilla bean, split lengthwise, or 2 teaspoons pure vanilla extract

4 large egg yolks

⅓ cup pure cane sugar

¼ cup cornstarch

¼ teaspoon kosher salt

CREAM PUFFS

1 stick (8 tablespoons) unsalted butter, cut into pieces

½ cup whole milk

2 teaspoons pure cane sugar

½ teaspoon kosher salt

1 cup all-purpose flour

4 large eggs

Egg wash: 1 egg beaten with 1 teaspoon water

TO FINISH

Blackberry–Bourbon Caramel Sauce (recipe follows)

Powdered sugar

✳ **BEAT THE CLOCK:** The unfilled baked choux shells freeze perfectly. Just thaw them in a hot oven on a sheet pan for a few minutes before using them. The pastry cream and caramel can be made up to 2 days in advance and stored, tightly covered, in the refrigerator.

VANILLA CREAM PUFFS
with Blackberry-Bourbon Caramel Sauce & Toasted Pecans

I have known Caprial Pence for a very long time, and her accomplishments are vast, so the fact that I won this battle—with a dessert!—was a big surprise to me. When pushed into the dessert realm and feeling overwhelmed, I usually reach for some of my "crutch" ingredients that I know will serve me well. So when this battle brought me to the uncharted waters of pâte à choux, I went straight for one of my favorite combinations: blackberries, caramel, and toasted nuts. I know these three ingredients always work well in unison—even enough to distract from my less-than-stellar cream puff execution!

1. Make the vanilla bean pastry cream: Place the milk in a medium saucepan. Scrape in the vanilla seeds and add the pod (if using extract, do not add it yet). Bring to a simmer over medium heat. Remove the saucepan from the heat and discard the vanilla pod.

2. Whisk together the yolks and cane sugar in a large bowl until pale and thick, 2 minutes. Add the cornstarch and salt and whisk until combined. Slowly whisk in the hot milk mixture little by little to temper the eggs, being careful not to scramble the eggs and whisking constantly until combined.

3. Return the mixture to the saucepan and return to high heat. Cook, whisking constantly, until it just begins to thicken, about 2 minutes. Once thickened, allow it to bubble for 60 seconds, whisking a few times. Remove from the heat (if using vanilla extract, stir it in now). Scrape the mixture into a medium bowl. Press a piece of plastic wrap on the surface of the custard and refrigerate until cold, at least 4 hours and up to 2 days.

4. Make the cream puffs: Preheat the oven to 425°F. Line two sheet pans with parchment paper. Lightly brush the parchment with water, which creates a humid environment for the pastry shells, allowing them to puff up without drying out or burning.

5. Combine ½ cup water with the butter, milk, cane sugar, and salt in a medium saucepan. Bring to a boil over medium-high heat and quickly stir in the flour with a wooden spoon. Continue to cook, stirring until a film forms on the bottom of the pan, about 2 minutes. Remove from the heat and transfer the contents to the bowl of a stand mixer fitted with the paddle. Beat the mixture on high speed

continued >

for 45 seconds to allow some of the steam to escape and to cool it. Add the eggs, one at a time, making sure each egg is entirely incorporated before adding the next.

6. Transfer the choux pastry dough to a piping bag fitted with a plain Wilton 1A tip. (You can also use a zip-top plastic bag and cut off the corner for easy piping.) Pipe 2-inch mounds about 3 inches apart on the prepared sheet pans. Using a water-moistened finger, smooth down the peaks and lightly brush each with egg wash.

7. Bake for 20 minutes. Reduce the oven temperature to 350°F. Continue to bake until golden brown, 10 to 15 minutes longer. Do not open the oven while the pastries cook, as cool air will prevent them from properly puffing up. Remove from the oven and transfer to a wire rack. Let cool completely before filling.

8. To finish: When ready to fill the cream puffs, whisk the pastry cream to loosen and make it creamy. Scrape into a pastry bag or plastic zip-top bag (or you can just spoon the custard onto the choux bottoms). Slice the puffs horizontally in half and fill the bottoms with the pastry cream. Put the tops on.

9. Ladle some of the sauce onto a plate and top with 3 of the puffs. Dust with powdered sugar and garnish with some of the remaining ¼ cup chopped pecans (from making the caramel sauce). Serve with the remaining blackberry-bourbon caramel sauce on the side.

Blackberry-Bourbon Caramel Sauce

✖ **MAKES ABOUT 2 CUPS**

¾ cup whole pecans

1 pint fresh blackberries

1 cup plus 2 tablespoons pure cane sugar

1 tablespoon corn syrup

½ cup heavy cream

¼ cup bourbon

1 teaspoon pure vanilla extract

Pinch of kosher salt

1. Put the pecans in a small sauté pan and cook over medium heat, shaking the pan occasionally, until fragrant, about 5 minutes. Remove to a cutting board, let cool, and coarsely chop.

2. Combine the blackberries and 2 tablespoons of the sugar in a small saucepan and let macerate for 10 minutes. Cook over high heat until the berries just begin to break down and the sugar has completely dissolved, about 5 minutes.

3. Combine the remaining 1 cup sugar, the corn syrup, and ¼ cup water in a medium saucepan and bring to a boil over high heat. Cook until it turns a deep amber color, about 8 minutes.

4. Slowly whisk in the cream and cook, whisking constantly, until smooth. Remove the pan from the heat, slowly add the bourbon, and stand back, as it could ignite quickly. Cook about 1 minute more. Remove from the heat and stir in the vanilla, salt, blackberry mixture, and ½ cup of the pecans. The caramel can be made 7 days in advance and stored, tightly covered, in the refrigerator. Reheat over low heat.

VANILLA BEAN CHEESECAKE

with Apple-Blackberry Compote & Spiced Crumble Topping

MAKES ONE 9-INCH CHEESECAKE

GRAHAM CRACKER CRUST

Cooking spray

10 graham crackers, broken into pieces

½ cup walnuts, lightly toasted (see page 247), and chopped

3 tablespoons pure cane sugar

6 tablespoons unsalted butter, melted

½ teaspoon kosher salt

CHEESECAKE

3 (8-ounce) packages Philadelphia cream cheese, at room temperature

½ cup pure cane sugar

½ cup packed light brown sugar

3 large eggs

1 cup heavy cream

½ teaspoon kosher salt

1 vanilla bean, split lengthwise, or 1 tablespoon pure vanilla extract

FOR SERVING

Apple-Blackberry Compote (recipe follows)

Blackberry-Bourbon Caramel Sauce (page 206)

Spiced Crumble Topping (recipe follows)

Okay, so I lost this battle to chef and good friend Anne Burrell, but I wanted to include this recipe because the dessert's components worked well at the time—and still do. The cheesecake itself is dense but silky, and the blackberry-bourbon caramel sauce will work on almost any vanilla-based dessert (including a scoop of ice cream). The allspice-and-fennel-laced compote proved to be a little much for the judges, including the legendary pastry chef Jacques Torres. I was bummed to lose, but Anne deserved the win for sure!

1. Make the graham cracker crust: Preheat the oven to 350°F. Mist a 9-inch springform pan with cooking spray and place it on a sheet pan.

2. Combine the graham crackers, walnuts, and cane sugar in a food processor and process until finely chopped. Add the melted butter and salt and process until the butter is incorporated. Scrape the bottom and sides of the processor with a rubber spatula and process for 10 seconds longer. Press the mixture firmly over the bottom and slightly up the sides of the prepared pan.

3. Bake until fragrant and golden brown, 8 minutes. Set the pan on a wire rack and let cool while you make the filling. (Leave the oven on.)

4. Make the cheesecake: In the bowl of a stand mixer fitted with the paddle, combine the cream cheese, cane sugar, and brown sugar and beat until light and fluffy, stopping to scrape the bottom and sides of the bowl with a rubber spatula as needed, about 5 minutes. Add the eggs, one at a time, allowing each to be incorporated before adding the next one. Add the cream and salt. Scrape in the vanilla seeds (or add the extract) and mix until just combined. Scrape the bottom and sides of the bowl again and beat for 10 seconds more.

5. Pour the batter into the crust. Transfer to the oven and bake until the edges are lightly golden brown and puffed but the center still jiggles slightly, about 1 hour.

6. Remove the cheesecake from the oven and let cool to room temperature, about 1 hour. Once the cheesecake has cooled, cover and refrigerate for at least 4 hours and up to 24 hours.

continued >

7. To serve: Slice into wedges, top with some of the apple-blackberry compote, drizzle with the blackberry-bourbon caramel sauce, and sprinkle with the crumb topping.

Apple-Blackberry Compote

✖ **MAKES ABOUT 1 QUART**

4 tablespoons unsalted butter

¼ teaspoon ground fennel

¼ teaspoon ground allspice

2 Granny Smith apples, peeled and thinly sliced

2 tablespoons pure cane sugar

Pinch of kosher salt

Squeeze of lemon juice

1 pint fresh blackberries

Melt the butter in a large sauté pan over high heat until shimmering. Add the fennel and allspice and cook for 20 seconds. Add the apples, sugar, and ¼ cup water and cook until the apples are soft and lightly caramelized, about 10 minutes. Stir in the salt and lemon juice and mix to combine. Remove from the heat and fold in the blackberries. Compote can be refrigerated, tightly covered, for up to 3 days. Warm in a saucepan over low heat before serving or serve at room temperature.

Spiced Crumble Topping

✖ **MAKES 1½ CUPS**

1 cup all-purpose flour

⅓ cup packed light brown sugar

½ teaspoon ground cinnamon

¼ teaspoon kosher salt

6 tablespoons unsalted butter, cut into pieces

½ teaspoon ground fennel

¼ teaspoon ground allspice

1. Preheat the oven to 350°F.

2. Whisk together the flour, brown sugar, cinnamon, and salt in a small bowl.

3. Melt the butter in a small saucepan over high heat. Stir in the fennel and allspice and cook for 20 seconds. Pour the butter over the flour mixture and stir until the mixture creates coarse crumbs. Spread onto a sheet pan and bake until lightly golden brown, about 12 minutes. Remove from the oven and let cool on the pan. Use immediately or store, tightly covered, at room temperature for 1 day.

RED HOT CINNAMON APPLE DUMPLINGS

with Caramel Sauce & Spiced Crème Fraîche

SERVES 6

POACHED APPLES

6 large Gala apples

4 cups apple cider

½ cup pure cane sugar

3 cinnamon sticks

8 whole cloves

5 whole star anise

Juice of ½ lemon

Pinch of kosher salt

FILLING

2 tablespoons unsalted butter

1 Granny Smith apple, peeled and finely diced

1 Gala apple, peeled and finely diced

2 tablespoons pure cane sugar

1 teaspoon ground cinnamon

Pinch of kosher salt

½ cup dried cranberries or dried cherries

½ cup walnuts or pecans, toasted (see page 247), and coarsely chopped

DUMPLINGS

3 tablespoons pure cane sugar

1 teaspoon ground cinnamon

Dough from ½ recipe Biscuits (page 236), chilled

All-purpose flour, for dusting

2 tablespoons unsalted butter, cut into 6 pieces

An apple dumpling is one of those dishes I would probably never have made unless challenged, but I'm so happy because it was delicious. If you watch the show at all, you know I don't love to make desserts, but I think Chef DeLost wanted to give me a chance, because she took it easy on me with this delicious choice. My guess is, that's not happening next time! I pulled out a favorite biscuit dough recipe to come to my rescue, and it was clutch. The apples, cinnamon, and caramel filled the arena with the most intoxicating aromas—just imagine what they'll do to your kitchen!

1. Poach the apples: Peel the apples. Starting at the stem end, core the apple, but stop short of cutting all the way through so that you create a well for holding the filling.

2. Combine the apple cider, sugar, cinnamon sticks, cloves, star anise, lemon juice, and salt in a large Dutch oven and bring to a boil over high heat. Reduce the heat to medium, add the apples, and cook until the apples are fork-tender, 9 to 12 minutes. Reserving the poaching liquid, use a large slotted spoon to transfer the apples to a sheet pan and refrigerate the apples until chilled. The apples can be poached up to 8 hours in advance and stored, tightly covered, in the refrigerator.

3. Make the filling: Measure out ½ cup of the reserved poaching liquid. Melt the butter in a large sauté pan over high heat until shimmering. Add the diced apples, sugar, cinnamon, salt, and a splash of the poaching liquid and cook until the apples are beginning to release their juices and have begun to soften and caramelize, about 5 minutes. Add the cranberries and the remaining poaching liquid and cook until the liquid is absorbed, about 5 minutes. Fold in the nuts and transfer the mixture to a medium bowl to cool slightly.

4. Use a spoon to lightly pack the filling into the poached apples. (Use any leftover filling to spoon over oatmeal or yogurt for breakfast.)

ingredients continued >

continued >

CARAMEL SAUCE

1 cup pure cane sugar

¼ cup heavy cream

2 tablespoons unsalted butter

Pinch of kosher salt

SPICED CRÈME FRAÎCHE

1 cup crème fraîche

1 tablespoon pure cane sugar

½ teaspoon ground cinnamon

Pinch of cayenne pepper

TO FINISH

Canola oil, for deep-frying

✖ **BEAT THE CLOCK:** The caramel sauce can be made a few days in advance and gently reheated over low heat. The biscuit dough can be made a day in advance, tightly wrapped in plastic, and stored in the refrigerator.

5. Wrap the dumplings: Mix the sugar and cinnamon together in a small bowl. Divide the biscuit dough into 6 portions. Roll each on a lightly floured surface into a 7-inch square about ⅛ inch thick. Place an apple on each square. Place 1 piece of butter and a heaping teaspoon of the cinnamon-sugar mixture in the center of each apple. Gently bring the corners of the pastry square up to the center, trimming any excess, and pinch the edges to seal. Transfer the wrapped apples to a parchment-lined sheet pan and refrigerate for at least 30 minutes to chill the dough (or freeze for 15 minutes).

6. Make the caramel sauce: Measure out ½ cup of the reserved poaching liquid. Combine the sugar and ¼ cup of the poaching liquid in a medium saucepan and bring to a boil over high heat. Cook, without stirring, until the mixture becomes a deep amber color, about 12 minutes. Slowly whisk in the remaining ¼ cup poaching liquid, the cream, butter, and salt and whisk until smooth. Keep warm. The caramel sauce will keep, tightly covered, in the refrigerator for up to 7 days. Reheat over low heat before using.

7. Make the spiced crème fraîche: Whisk together the crème fraîche, sugar, cinnamon, and cayenne in a small bowl until combined. Set aside.

8. To finish: Preheat the oven to 350°F. Fill a deep fryer or a large Dutch oven halfway with oil and heat over medium heat to 360°F on a deep-fry thermometer.

9. Working with two at a time, fry the dumplings until golden brown and the dough is cooked through, about 5 minutes. Drain on paper towels and transfer to a sheet pan. Keep warm in the oven while you cook the remaining apples.

10. To serve, spoon some of the caramel sauce into large shallow bowls and top with a dumpling. Drizzle a bit more of the sauce over the top, along with some of the spiced crème fraîche.

EPISODE 1701: *"Waltz Up a Win"*
COMPETITOR: Olivier Palazzo
DISH: Chocolate soufflé
WINNER: Olivier Palazzo

BITTERSWEET CHOCOLATE SOUFFLÉ
with Blackberry Whipped Cream

Blackberries and chocolate are one of my favorite sweet combos. Melting chocolate and pouring it over some gorgeous sweet and tart berries would be fine with me. In this case, I got challenged to a soufflé. Not exactly easy to pull off under pressure, even if the flavor pairing is spot on! Sure enough, Chef Palazzo got the win, and I got to eat blackberries and chocolate, so we both won—kind of.

SERVES 6

1 stick (8 tablespoons) plus 3 tablespoons unsalted butter, at room temperature

½ cup plus 4 tablespoons pure cane sugar

8 ounces bittersweet chocolate (I prefer Valrhona Guanaja 70% cacao), either pastilles or block chocolate, finely chopped

1 teaspoon instant espresso powder

¼ teaspoon kosher salt

6 large eggs, separated, at room temperature

½ teaspoon cream of tartar

¼ teaspoon pure vanilla extract

Blackberry Whipped Cream (recipe follows)

✖ **BEAT THE CLOCK:** Make sure that your ramekins are buttered and sugared perfectly and ready to go on a sheet pan before you begin to make the soufflé batter.

1. Preheat the oven to 400°F. Butter six 8-ounce ramekins with 3 tablespoons of the butter and coat the bottom and sides with ½ cup of the sugar, tapping out any excess. Put the ramekins on a sheet pan, leaving a few inches of space between them.

2. Combine the chocolate, the remaining 1 stick butter, the espresso powder, and salt in a large heatproof bowl. Set the bowl over a pot of simmering water and whisk constantly until the butter and chocolate are melted, a few minutes. Remove from the heat and let cool slightly; the mixture should still be warm (but not hot) when the egg yolks are mixed in.

3. In the bowl of a stand mixer fitted with the whisk, beat the egg whites and cream of tartar until soft peaks form. Begin adding the remaining 4 tablespoons sugar, 1 tablespoon at a time, and continue beating until stiff peaks form.

4. Add the egg yolks to the warm chocolate mixture and whisk until smooth. Whisk in the vanilla. Gently fold a few dollops of the beaten whites into the chocolate mixture to lighten it. Fold in the remaining whites in two additions until completely combined and no white streaks are showing. Divide the batter among the ramekins. Rub your thumb around the inside edge of each ramekin to create a ¼-inch gap between the side of the ramekin and the soufflé mixture.

5. Transfer the soufflés to the oven and immediately reduce the oven temperature to 375°F. Bake until puffed and the center moves slightly when the ramekin is shaken, about 18 minutes. Remove from the oven and, using silicone-tipped tongs, transfer the ramekins to dessert plates. Serve the soufflés topped with some of the glazed blackberries and with the blackberry whipped cream on the side.

continued >

2 pints blackberries

¼ cup plus 2 tablespoons pure cane sugar

2 teaspoons fresh lemon juice

1 cup cold heavy cream

2 tablespoons crème fraîche

Blackberry Whipped Cream

✖ MAKES 3 CUPS

1. Combine 1 pint of the blackberries, ¼ cup of the sugar, and the lemon juice in a medium bowl and let macerate at room temperature for 15 minutes, stirring a few times. Transfer to a blender and blend until smooth. Strain the purée through a fine-mesh sieve into a bowl (discard the solids).

2. Combine the remaining pint of blackberries and remaining 2 tablespoons sugar in a large sauté pan and cook over high heat until the berries are just soft and lightly glazed in the sugar, about about 3 minutes. Transfer to a plate.

3. In the bowl of a stand mixer fitted with the whisk, whip the cream and crème fraîche until soft peaks form. Carefully fold in the blackberry purée and serve immediately with the soufflés and glazed berries.

EPISODE 1212: *"Salty and Sweet"*
COMPETITOR: *Michelle Gayer*
DISH: *Banana cream pie*
WINNER: *Bobby Flay*

BANANAS FOSTER CREAM PIE
with Praline Pecans

My first job in a kitchen was at a place called Joe Allen restaurant in New York City's theater district. The head baker there was a talented gentleman named Mr. Mack—I can *still* taste his banana cream pie. Mr. Mack made his classic banana cream pie with vanilla wafers. This one gets a little indulgent, injecting New Orleans flavor via a custard inspired by bananas Foster and transforming pecans into praline deliciousness.

MAKES ONE 9-INCH PIE

CRUST

Cooking spray

6 tablespoons unsalted butter, melted

10 graham crackers, broken into pieces

¼ cup pure cane sugar

¼ teaspoon kosher salt

CARAMELIZED BANANAS

3 tablespoons unsalted butter, cut into pieces

½ cup packed light brown sugar

2 large ripe bananas, cut into 1-inch cubes

½ teaspoon ground cinnamon

FILLING

5 large egg yolks

¼ cup pure cane sugar

8 ounces mascarpone cheese, at room temperature

1 teaspoon pure vanilla extract

3 large ripe bananas, cut into ½-inch-thick slices

TO FINISH

1 cup cold heavy cream

3 tablespoons powdered sugar

Candied Nuts (page 247), made with pecans

Rum Caramel Sauce (recipe follows, optional)

1. Make the crust: Preheat the oven to 350°F. Place a 9-inch tart pan with a removable bottom on a sheet pan and liberally mist with cooking spray.

2. Combine the melted butter, graham crackers, cane sugar, and salt in a food processor and process until coarsely chopped. Scrape down bottom and sides and process again until finely ground. Press the mixture over the bottom and up the sides of the prepared tart pan. Bake until lightly browned and just set, about 8 minutes. Remove and let cool.

3. Meanwhile, make the caramelized bananas: Combine the butter and brown sugar in a large sauté pan and cook over high heat until the brown sugar melts and the mixture thickens slightly, about 4 minutes. Add the bananas and cinnamon and cook until the bananas soften and caramelize, about 5 minutes. Transfer to a sheet pan and let cool.

4. Make the filling: In the bowl of a stand mixer fitted with the whisk, combine the egg yolks and cane sugar and beat until pale and thick and tripled in volume, about 5 minutes. Add the mascarpone and vanilla and mix until just incorporated, about 10 seconds. Fold in the caramelized bananas and spread half of the mixture into the prepared crust. Arrange the banana slices over the filling, then spread the remaining filling over the bananas. Press a piece of plastic wrap directly on the surface of the custard and refrigerate until just set, at least 30 minutes and up to 8 hours.

5. To finish: In the bowl of a stand mixer fitted with the whisk, combine the cream and powdered sugar and beat to soft peaks. Spread the whipped cream over the custard and sprinkle the candied nuts over the top. Cut into slices. If desired, drizzle with rum caramel sauce.

Rum Caramel Sauce

✖ **MAKES 1¼ CUPS**

1 cup pure cane sugar

¼ cup heavy cream

2 tablespoons unsalted butter

2 tablespoons dark rum

Pinch of kosher salt

Combine the sugar and ¼ cup water in a medium saucepan and bring to a boil over high heat. Cook, without stirring, until the mixture becomes a deep amber color, about 12 minutes. Slowly whisk in the cream, butter, rum, and salt and whisk until smooth. Keep warm. The caramel sauce will keep, tightly covered, in the refrigerator for up to 7 days. Reheat over low heat before using.

EPISODE 1810:
"Sweet, Sweet Revenge"
COMPETITOR: Caroline Schiff
DISH: Key lime pie
WINNER: Bobby Flay

MAKES ONE 9-INCH PIE

Cooking spray

7 tablespoons unsalted butter, cut into pieces

10 graham crackers, broken into pieces

⅓ cup pure cane sugar

1 teaspoon kosher salt

6 large egg yolks

2 (14-ounce) cans sweetened condensed milk

1 teaspoon finely grated lime zest

1 cup Key lime juice, store-bought or freshly squeezed

½ teaspoon pure vanilla extract

TOASTED COCONUT WHIPPED CREAM

1 cup cold heavy cream

¼ cup sweetened cream of coconut, such as Coco López

½ teaspoon pure vanilla extract

½ cup Toasted Coconut (page 247), made with sweetened, flaked coconut

✖ **BEAT THE CLOCK:** I use Nellie & Joe's Key lime juice for this recipe, which is delicious and beats having to juice a bunch of small Key limes.

KEY LIME PIE
with Toasted Coconut Whipped Cream

You may have noticed how often I use some form of coconut whenever I'm challenged to make a dessert. My feeling is, if I'm going to lose—which I do a lot in the sweet department—at least I can get a few tastes of something I like! And coconut is one of my favorites. My first taste of Key lime pie was definitely not in the Florida Keys (it was in NYC), but regardless of where it happened, I've been a fan ever since.

1. Preheat the oven to 350°F. Mist a 9-inch tart pan with a removable bottom liberally with cooking spray and set it on a sheet pan.

2. Place the butter in a light-colored saucepan over medium heat. (The light color of the pan means you can monitor the color change in the butter, an important factor in this process.) Stir the butter the entire time to keep it moving. Once melted, the butter will begin to foam and sizzle around the edges; keep stirring. In 5 to 8 minutes from when you started, the butter will turn golden brown. Some foam will subside, the milk solids at the bottom of the pan will be toasty brown, and it will smell intensely buttery and nutty. Immediately remove the pan from the heat and pour the brown butter into a heatproof bowl to stop the cooking process (if left in the hot pan, the butter will burn).

3. Combine the graham crackers, sugar, and salt in a food processor and process until the mixture is coarsely ground. With the motor running, slowly add the brown butter through the feed tube and process until combined. Scrape down the bottom and sides and pulse a few more times to make sure it is totally combined.

4. Use the flat bottom of a measuring cup to press the mixture over the bottom and up the sides of the prepared tart pan. Make sure it is tight and compact. Bake the crust until set, 8 minutes. Remove and let cool for a few minutes. (Leave the oven on.)

5. Meanwhile, whisk the egg yolks in a large bowl until pale and thickened, about 5 minutes. Add the condensed milk, lime zest, lime juice, and vanilla and whisk until smooth. Pour the custard into the crust.

6. Bake until the top is set, about 11 minutes. Remove, let cool to room temperature, and refrigerate until chilled completely, at least 4 hours.

7. Make the toasted coconut whipped cream: In the bowl of a stand mixer fitted with the whisk, combine the heavy cream, cream of coconut, and vanilla and beat until soft peaks form. Fold in half of the toasted coconut just before serving. Serve the pie with a dollop of the coconut whipped cream and garnish with the remaining toasted coconut.

EPISODE 2006: *"Grapes of Wrath"*
COMPETITOR: *Zac Young*
DISH: *Carrot cake*
WINNER: *Zac Young*

UPSIDE-DOWN CARROT CAKE
with a Rum-Caramel Pineapple & Cream Cheese Drizzle

I love Zac Young. He's so knowledgeable and talented, and he has a competitive spirit I like. All that said, I really wanted to beat him for bragging rights since he's a Food Network regular and part of our family. In the end, it didn't go the way I hoped, but I know he was nervous for at least thirty seconds! My thoughts on the carrot cake flavors: Where there is pineapple, there must be rum.

MAKES ONE 9-INCH CAKE

CARAMELIZED PINEAPPLE

Cooking spray

4 tablespoons unsalted butter

1 cup light brown sugar

1 cup crushed fresh pineapple

¼ cup dark rum

½ teaspoon kosher salt

CARROT CAKE

1 cup all-purpose flour

1 teaspoon baking soda

1 teaspoon ground cinnamon

½ teaspoon ground ginger

⅛ teaspoon grated nutmeg

½ teaspoon kosher salt

2 large eggs

¾ cup pure cane sugar

¼ cup light brown sugar

4 tablespoons unsalted butter, melted and cooled

¼ cup canola oil

1 teaspoon pure vanilla extract

1½ cups grated carrots, pressed dry with paper towels

2 teaspoons grated fresh ginger

¼ cup diced crystallized ginger

½ cup chopped pecans, toasted (see page 247)

CREAM CHEESE DRIZZLE

4 ounces Philadelphia cream cheese, at room temperature

¼ cup powdered sugar

1 teaspoon pure vanilla extract

¼ cup whole milk

1. Preheat the oven to 350°F.

2. Caramelize the pineapple: Mist the sides of a 9-inch cast-iron skillet thoroughly with cooking spray. Melt the butter in the pan over high heat. Add the brown sugar and cook until melted and slightly thickened, about 5 minutes. Add the pineapple and cook for 2 minutes longer. Add the rum and cook, stirring constantly, until reduced by half, about 2 minutes. Remove the pan from the heat and set aside while you make the cake batter.

3. Make the carrot cake: Whisk together the flour, baking soda, cinnamon, ground ginger, nutmeg, and salt in a medium bowl until combined.

4. In the bowl of a stand mixer fitted with the paddle, combine the eggs and both sugars and mix until smooth. Add the melted butter, oil, and vanilla and mix until combined. Add the carrots, fresh ginger, and crystallized ginger and mix for 10 seconds. Add the flour mixture and mix until the batter just comes together.

5. Scrape the batter over the pineapple in the skillet and smooth the top. Transfer to the oven and bake until a toothpick inserted into the center comes out dry, about 25 minutes. Transfer the skillet to a wire rack and let rest for 10 minutes. Carefully run a butter knife around the outside of the skillet and, using oven mitts, unmold the cake onto a large platter. Let cool for at least 15 minutes.

6. Meanwhile, prepare the cream cheese drizzle: Whisk together the cream cheese, powdered sugar, vanilla, and milk in a medium bowl until smooth with a spreadable frosting consistency, adding more milk if too thick or more powdered sugar if too thin.

7. To serve: Drizzle some of the cream cheese icing on plates, top with a wedge of the cake, and drizzle more of the cream cheese icing over the top. Garnish with the toasted pecans.

EPISODE 2308:
"Chocolate Covered Clash"
COMPETITOR: DaVee Harned
DISH: Chocolate cream pie
WINNER: Bobby Flay

SPICED CHOCOLATE CREAM PIES
with Chocolate-Hazelnut Crust & Bourbon Whipped Cream

Chocolate cream pie was always a favorite of mine when I was kid—so much so, in fact, that I asked my pastry chef Josephine Pacquing to devise an upside-down version for my restaurant Bar Americain. I poured my love of Mexican chocolate into this particular version, flavoring the rich chocolate cream with red chile, cinnamon, and sugar.

SERVES 8

CHOCOLATE-HAZELNUT CRUST

20 chocolate sandwich cookies, such as Oreos

¾ cup skinless hazelnuts, lightly toasted (see page 247)

1 teaspoon ground pure chile powder, such as ancho

½ teaspoon ground cinnamon

Pinch of kosher salt

6 tablespoons unsalted butter, melted and slightly cooled

FILLING

⅓ cup pure cane sugar

¼ cup cornstarch

2 tablespoons Dutch-process cocoa powder, such as Valrhona

½ teaspoon kosher salt

3 cups whole milk

2 cinnamon sticks

2 cascabel chiles or 1 teaspoon ancho chile powder

6 ounces bittersweet chocolate (such as Valrhona Manjari, 64% cacao), coarsely chopped

2 tablespoons unsalted butter, cut into pieces

2 teaspoons pure vanilla extract

BOURBON WHIPPED CREAM

1½ cups cold heavy cream

3 tablespoons powdered sugar

2 tablespoons bourbon

FOR ASSEMBLY

Toasted hazelnuts (see page 247), chopped

1. Make the chocolate-hazelnut crust: Preheat the oven to 350°F. Line a sheet pan with a silicone baking mat or parchment paper.

2. Combine the cookies, hazelnuts, chile powder, cinnamon, and salt in a food processor and process until coarsely chopped. With the motor running, slowly add the melted butter through the feed tube and process until finely chopped and the mixture comes together.

3. Transfer the mixture to the prepared sheet pan and press into an even layer about ¼ inch thick. Bake until fragrant and just set, about 8 minutes. Remove and let cool to room temperature on a wire rack. Refrigerate until firm, 30 minutes. Using a 3½-inch round cookie cutter or a very sharp knife, carefully cut out 8 discs.

4. Make the filling: Whisk together the cane sugar, cornstarch, cocoa powder, and ¼ teaspoon of the salt in a medium saucepan. Slowly whisk in the milk until smooth. Add the cinnamon sticks and chiles. Bring to a boil over high heat and cook, whisking constantly, until the mixture begins to thicken, about 5 minutes. Let boil for exactly 1 minute. Remove the pan from the heat (discard the cinnamon stick and chiles).

5. Whisk in the chocolate and butter until melted and smooth. Stir in the remaining ¼ teaspoon salt and the vanilla and transfer the pudding to a bowl. Press a piece of plastic wrap directly against the surface of the pudding and cool to room temperature, about 30 minutes. Refrigerate until chilled through, about 4 hours.

6. Make the bourbon whipped cream: Just before assembling the pies, in the bowl of a stand mixer fitted with the whisk, combine the cream, powdered sugar, and bourbon and beat to soft peaks.

7. Assemble the pies: Spoon ½ cup of the pudding into each of 8 shallow bowls. Sprinkle some of the hazelnuts over the pudding and spoon a large dollop of the whipped cream over the nuts. Smooth into a slightly even layer and top with a cookie crust.

ROY BREIMAN'S DUTCH BABY PANCAKE
with Sautéed Apples & Fromage Blanc

"I came out guns blazing with my version of a Dutch baby pancake, a family recipe that has been proven through the generations to be a winner. Bobby would need his A-game to beat me, and I knew I had it in the bag when he let his batter sit before cooking—a cardinal sin in the Dutch baby world because the batter deflates. A high-speed blender is my secret to a light, airy, soufflé-like texture straight out of the oven. The judges loved my version, while they said Bobby's did not 'rise' to the occasion. It was an exciting day, and I felt the support and encouragement from everyone on the set—a first-class team!" —ROY BREIMAN

SERVES 4 TO 6

SAUTÉED APPLES

6 tablespoons unsalted butter, cut into pieces

¼ cup packed light brown sugar

½ teaspoon pumpkin pie spice

1 vanilla bean, split lengthwise

3 large Fuji apples, peeled and thinly sliced

APPLE-VANILLA SYRUP

4 cups filtered apple juice

2 vanilla beans, split lengthwise

FROMAGE BLANC

2 ounces cream cheese, at room temperature

1½ ounces creamy goat cheese, at room temperature

2 teaspoons finely grated lemon zest

¾ cup very cold heavy cream

2 tablespoons pure cane sugar

DUTCH BABY PANCAKE

1 cup whole milk

⅔ cup all-purpose flour

2 tablespoons pure cane sugar

½ teaspoon fine sea salt

4 tablespoons unsalted butter, cut into tablespoons

FOR SERVING

Powdered sugar, for dusting

1. Make the sautéed apples: Melt the butter in a large sauté pan over high heat. Add the brown sugar and pumpkin pie spice and cook until the sugar has melted, about 5 minutes. Scrape in the vanilla seeds and add the pod. Add the apples and cook, stirring occasionally, until the apples are softened and caramelized, about 7 minutes. Discard the vanilla pod. Keep warm.

2. Make the apple-vanilla syrup: Place the apple juice in a medium saucepan. Scrape in the vanilla seeds and add the pods. Bring to a boil over high heat and cook until thickened and reduced to about 1 cup, about 20 minutes. Discard the vanilla pods. Cover and keep warm.

3. Prepare the fromage blanc: In the bowl of a stand mixer fitted with the paddle, combine the cream cheese, goat cheese, and lemon zest and beat until light and creamy, about 2 minutes. Add the heavy cream and cane sugar and beat until light and fluffy, about 2 minutes longer. Scrape into a bowl and keep cold until ready to serve, up to 2 hours.

4. Make the Dutch baby pancake: Preheat the oven to 400°F. Combine the milk, flour, cane sugar, and salt in a blender and blend until smooth, about 30 seconds.

5. Put the butter in a 9-inch pie plate and put the pie plate in the oven. When the butter has melted, pour the batter into the pie plate and top with some of the sautéed apples. Bake until puffy and golden brown, 25 to 30 minutes.

6. Slice into wedges and top each with the remaining sautéed apples, the apple-vanilla syrup, a dollop of the fromage blanc, and powdered sugar.

EPISODE 1603: *"Sticky Situation"*
COMPETITOR: *Clarice Lam*
DISH: *S'mores*
WINNER: *Bobby Flay*

SERVES 6

MARSHMALLOW

¾ cup pure cane sugar

½ cup light corn syrup

¼ teaspoon kosher salt

23 grams unflavored powdered gelatin (scant 5 teaspoons)

2 to 3 large egg whites

1 tablespoon pure vanilla extract

S'MORES

12 Graham Crackers (recipe follows) or 12 store-bought honey graham cracker sheets

6 ounces Cacao Barry 58% cacao bar chocolate, broken into 1-ounce squares, or any high-quality bittersweet chocolate bar up to 60% cacao

CLARICE LAM'S S'MORES

"Appearing on *Beat Bobby Flay* was one of the best and funniest things I have ever done in my career. Bobby has a certain reputation for being arrogant, so I was shocked when he was *so* nice and cool! I had so much fun ripping on him and dishing it out to the judges, and I think they found it entertaining as well. It honestly felt like a group of friends just hanging out, baking, and having a good time. I did not beat Bobby because I forgot the baking soda in my graham crackers, which meant they did not have the nice crunchy bite that you would expect from a s'more. However, I loved competing on the show so much—it was truly a blast and has helped me and my business so much. Every time something good happens from it (more orders and recognition), my sous chef, Lauren, and I look at each other and say, 'God bless Bobby Flay!'" —CLARICE LAM

1. Make the marshmallow: Combine the sugar, corn syrup, salt, and ½ cup water in a medium saucepan and bring to a boil over high heat. Cook, without stirring, until it reaches 248°F on a candy thermometer.

2. While the sugar mixture is coming to a boil, pour ½ cup cold water into the bowl of a stand mixer, sprinkle the gelatin over it, and let soften, about 5 minutes.

3. When the sugar syrup reaches 220°F, add the egg whites to the mixer bowl and beat on high speed until soft peaks form.

4. When the sugar syrup reaches 248°F, reduce the speed of the mixer to medium-low and slowly and carefully begin to add the hot syrup to the whites in a thin, steady stream. Once the syrup has been added, increase the speed to high again and beat until stiff, glossy peaks form and the mixture has cooled, about 6 minutes. Add the vanilla and mix for 30 seconds longer.

5. Assemble the s'mores: Preheat the broiler. Put 6 graham crackers on a sheet pan and top with squares of chocolate to fill the entire surface. Place dollops of the marshmallow on top. Broil until the marshmallow is golden brown, 45 seconds to 2 minutes. (Alternatively, use a kitchen blowtorch.) Top each with another cracker and push down slightly. Serve immediately.

Graham Crackers

✖ MAKES 12

3 cups whole wheat flour, plus more for dusting

⅔ cup dark brown sugar

1 teaspoon baking soda

1 teaspoon kosher salt

½ teaspoon ground cinnamon

7 tablespoons cold unsalted Plugrá butter, cut into small pieces

¼ cup clover honey

¼ cup plus 1 tablespoon whole milk

1 tablespoon pure vanilla extract

1. Preheat the oven to 350°F. Line two sheet pans with parchment paper.

2. Combine the flour, brown sugar, baking soda, salt, and cinnamon in a food processor and pulse a few times to combine. Scatter the butter over the top of the flour and pulse until the mixture looks like coarse bread crumbs.

3. Whisk together the honey, milk, and vanilla in a measuring cup. With the food processor running, add the milk mixture to the flour mixture through the feed tube and process until the dough just comes together. Wrap the dough in plastic and refrigerate until chilled, at least 1 hour and up to 3 days.

4. On a well-floured surface, roll out the dough to a little more than ¼ inch thick. Using a pizza cutter, cut the dough into 2 × 5-inch rectangles. Using a knife, score the cookies down the center lengthwise, then crosswise in half. Using a fork, prick the crackers on either side of the scored lines. This will create the classic graham cracker pattern. Gently transfer the crackers to the prepared sheet pans.

5. Bake the crackers, one pan at a time, for 10 to 12 minutes— 10 minutes will yield a slightly softer texture and 12 minutes a crunchier texture. Let cool completely on a wire rack, about 20 minutes. The crackers will keep, tightly covered, at room temperature for up to 5 days.

SHELBY SIEG'S LEMON THYME OLIVE OIL CAKE with Fig Caramel, Candied Hazelnuts & Lemon Whipped Cream

MAKES ONE 9-INCH CAKE

CAKE

Cooking spray

2 cups all-purpose flour

1 teaspoon baking powder

1½ teaspoons kosher salt

Grated zest of 1 lemon

5 or 6 sprigs thyme, leaves picked and chopped

⅓ cup unsalted butter, at room temperature

1⅓ cups pure cane sugar

2 medium eggs

⅓ cup high-quality extra-virgin olive oil

⅔ cup whole milk

FIG CARAMEL

1¼ cups pure cane sugar

5 ounces dried figs

LEMON WHIPPED CREAM

1 cup cold heavy cream

4 teaspoons pure cane sugar

Finely grated zest of 1 lemon

FOR SERVING

High-quality extra-virgin olive oil, for drizzling

1 cup Candied Nuts (page 247), made with hazelnuts, chopped

"When I was first approached about competing on *Beat Bobby Flay*, I was terrified! But I chose this cake because I was extremely confident in it. I competed on another Food Network competition show the year before; I made it to the final round but didn't win. This time, I was determined to come out on top. Having to come face-to-face (and I mean *directly* face-to-face!) with the Iron Chef himself was very intimidating, and cooking in that environment—the audience talking to you and sometimes heckling, trying to stay on track and handle your nerves, watching the clock—was nothing I had ever experienced. When they announced I was the winner, it took quite a while to set in, and it didn't feel entirely real until the episode aired. Ultimately, it gave me a chance for redemption, and I am so thankful to the Bobby Flay team for the opportunity!" —SHELBY SIEG

1. Make the cake: Preheat the oven to 325°F. Mist a 9-inch cake pan with cooking spray and line it with a round of parchment paper.

2. Combine the flour, baking powder, salt, lemon zest, and thyme in a bowl and set aside.

3. In the bowl of a stand mixer fitted with the paddle, beat the butter and sugar on medium-high speed until very light in color, about 5 minutes, scraping the bowl a few times. Reduce the speed to medium, and add the eggs, one at a time, blending well after each addition. Reduce the speed to medium-low, and slowly pour in the oil. Alternate adding the milk and the flour mixture until the batter is blended, 2 to 3 minutes. Pour the batter into the prepared pan.

4. Bake until golden brown and the cake begins pulling away from the sides of the pan, about 35 minutes. Let cool in the pan for 20 minutes. Remove from the pan and let cool completely.

5. Meanwhile, make the fig caramel: Combine the sugar and ¼ cup water in a medium saucepan, bring to a boil over high heat, and cook, without stirring, until it becomes a deep amber color, about 8 minutes. Slowly add 1 cup water (be careful, it will bubble up) and cook until smooth. Add the figs and cook until very soft, about 15 minutes. Remove from the heat and let cool for 10 minutes.

6. Carefully transfer the mixture to a blender and blend until smooth. Return to the pan and cook over low heat until heated through. Use immediately or let cool to room temperature and store, tightly covered, in the refrigerator for up to 3 days. Reheat in a saucepan over low heat before serving.

7. Meanwhile, make the lemon whipped cream: Combine the cream, sugar, and lemon zest in a large bowl and beat to soft peaks, 3 to 5 minutes.

8. To serve: Cut the cake into wedges. Pour some of the fig caramel onto a plate and place a piece of cake on top. Add a dollop of the lemon whipped cream, sprinkle the candied hazelnuts, and drizzle olive oil on top. Arrange additional candied hazelnuts on the plate around the cake and serve.

MY BASIC RECIPE ARSENAL

Every chef has an arsenal of recipes that he or she can pull out whenever needed. You will see these recipes appear often (some really often: Crispy Rice and Anchovy Bread Crumbs) in my battles and in this book. Whether they are the backbone of a dish (i.e., the crust for pizza) or the garnish that finishes it, the following recipes make up my basics—and they're anything but basic.

TAKE STOCK

Everyone needs a good homemade meat stock and seafood stock recipe. Homemade stocks are not only the foundation of soups but are imperative for battle-winning sauces. The gelatin from the meat bones helps give sauces natural body without the need to add starchy thickeners such as flour or cornstarch.

There are some good-quality ones prepared in supermarkets and at your butcher these days, and while you can swap those in, nothing beats homemade. You get to be in control of the flavor profile and salt content, and homemade stock will always be fresher—even when pulled from the freezer. Fun battle fact: I am only permitted to use previously prepared homemade stocks as the base of a sauce, a poaching or braising liquid, or to cook rice or grains. I am *not* permitted to use it as the sole base of a soup (like the Hot & Sour Soup with Black Vinegar–Glazed Pork, Tofu & Eggs on page 140).

Beef Stock

I don't use beef stock as often as I use chicken stock for a few reasons: I don't make that many sauces or soups that require a deep beefy base, it's time-consuming to make, and I really do think that chicken stock can substitute for beef stock very nicely the majority of the time. That said, it is always good to have a solid recipe for one in your arsenal, and this is a winner. Like all stocks, it freezes well for months.

MAKES 4 QUARTS

✖ **IN IT TO WIN IT:** Freeze stock in ice cube trays.

4 pounds bone-in beef shank, crosscut

1 large Spanish onion, quartered

2 celery stalks, cut into 2-inch pieces

1 large carrot, cut into 2-inch pieces

2 tablespoons canola oil

Kosher salt and freshly ground black pepper

1 small bunch parsley stems (reserve the leaves for something else)

8 sprigs thyme

4 bay leaves

1 tablespoon black peppercorns

1. Preheat the oven to 400°F.

2. Combine the beef, onion, celery, and carrot in a large roasting pan. Add the oil and season with salt and pepper. Roast until the meat and vegetables are deep golden brown, stirring a few times, about 40 minutes.

3. Transfer the meat and vegetables to a large stockpot. Pour the fat in the roasting pan into a bowl and discard. Add 1 cup cold water to the roasting pan, scrape the bottom to remove the brown bits, and add to the stockpot with the meat and vegetables. Add 6 quarts cold water, the parsley stems, thyme, bay leaves, and peppercorns. Bring to a boil over high heat, then reduce the heat to medium-low. Cook, skimming the top periodically, for 6 hours.

4. Strain the stock into a large bowl or another large pot and let cool to room temperature. Divide into quart containers and refrigerate for up to 3 days or freeze for up to 6 months.

Light Chicken Stock

The king of all stocks, in my opinion, good chicken stock really can do everything. I always have two variations in my freezer at home: Light Chicken Stock, which I use to cook rice or polenta and when I want just a mild chicken flavor in my dish, and Rich Chicken Stock (see below) for when the sauce, gravy, or soup calls for a deeper color and deeper flavor.

MAKES 4 QUARTS

3 pounds chicken backs, cleaned and rinsed, kidneys removed

3 pounds chicken wings

3 pounds chicken feet, cleaned and rinsed

2 large Spanish onions, quartered

6 celery stalks, chopped

2 large carrots, chopped

1 small bunch thyme

12 black peppercorns

1 head garlic, halved horizontally

1. Combine the backs, wings, feet, onions, celery, carrots, thyme, peppercorns, and garlic in a large stockpot and add 6 quarts water. Bring to a boil over high heat, then reduce the heat to medium-low. Season with salt and simmer, skimming periodically, for 3 hours.

2. Strain the stock into another clean large pot or bowl and let cool to room temperature. Divide into quart containers and refrigerate for up to 3 days or freeze for up to 6 months.

Rich Chicken Stock

Browning the bones and vegetables and reducing the stock to intensify the flavor is what you need to do to create an enriched chicken stock. The ingredient amounts are the same as for light chicken Stock (see above), with a few additions. You just need to add two extra steps: browning and reducing the stock to cook out some of the water.

MAKES 3 QUARTS

1. Preheat the oven to 400°F.

2. Combine the backs, wings, feet, onions, celery, and carrots in a large roasting pan. Drizzle with 3 tablespoons oil and season with salt and pepper. Roast in the oven until the chicken parts and vegetables are a deep golden brown, stirring a few times, about 40 minutes.

3. Transfer the contents of the roasting pan to a large stockpot. Add 2 cups water to the roasting pan and stir to scrape up the brown bits in the pan. Add the liquid to the stockpot and add 6 quarts of cold water. Bring to a boil over high heat, reduce the heat to low, and simmer, skimming periodically, for 3 hours.

4. Strain the stock into another clean large pot or bowl, then return it to the pot it cooked in. Cook over high heat until reduced to 12 cups, about 30 minutes.

Lobster Stock & Shrimp Stock

I love using lobster stock for bisque, chowders, and risotto (and shrimp stock for shrimp and grits, pastas, scampi, etc.). There's really no better way to amp up your shellfish flavor. If you eat a lot of lobster and shrimp in your house, this is a good way to use up those shells (keep them in the freezer till it's stock time), and you really can use one or the other interchangeably. Like all stocks, these freeze beautifully, too.

Lobster Stock

MAKES 3 QUARTS

¼ **cup canola oil**

5 **lobster bodies, halved, cleaned, gills and tomalley removed, excrement washed out**

¼ **cup tomato paste**

½ **cup French brandy**

3 **leeks, white parts only, chopped**

1 **medium fennel bulb, sliced**

4 **celery stalks, cut into 2-inch lengths**

2 **carrots, cut into large dice**

5 **garlic cloves, smashed**

12 **parsley stems**

2 **sprigs thyme**

1 **large bay leaf**

1 **teaspoon black peppercorns**

1. Heat the oil in a large Dutch oven or stockpot over high heat until shimmering. Add the lobster bodies and cook until golden brown, 7 minutes. Add the tomato paste and cook, stirring constantly, until it deepens in color, 3 minutes.

2. Crush the lobster bodies with a potato masher or wooden mallet and cook until dry and caramelized, 5 minutes. Add the brandy and cook, scraping the bottom of the pan with a wooden spoon, until completely reduced, 4 minutes. Stir in the leeks, fennel, celery, carrots, and garlic and cook, stirring, for 2 minutes.

3. Add 4 quarts water, the parsley, thyme, bay leaf, and peppercorns. Bring to a boil, then reduce the heat to low. Simmer, skimming periodically, for 3 hours.

4. Strain the stock into a large bowl and let cool to room temperature. Divide into quart containers and refrigerate for up to 2 days or freeze for up to 6 months.

Shrimp Stock

MAKES ABOUT 4 QUARTS

3 **tablespoons canola oil**

½ **pound head-on, shell-on medium shrimp**

1 **pound shrimp shells**

2 **tablespoons tomato paste**

¼ **cup dry vermouth or dry white wine**

3 **leeks, white parts only, chopped**

4 **celery stalks, cut into 2-inch lengths**

2 **carrots, cut into large dice**

5 **garlic cloves, smashed**

12 **parsley stems**

2 **sprigs thyme**

1 **large bay leaf**

1 **teaspoon black peppercorns**

1. Heat the oil in a large stockpot over high heat until shimmering. Add the whole shrimp and cook until lightly golden brown, about 4 minutes. Stir in the shrimp shells and cook for 2 minutes longer.

2. Stir in the tomato paste and cook until it deepens in color, about 2 minutes. Crush the shrimp and shells with a potato masher and cook, stirring occasionally, until dry and caramelized, about 5 minutes.

3. Add the vermouth and cook, scraping the bottom of the pot with a wooden spoon, until completely reduced, 4 minutes. Add 4 quarts cold water, the leeks, celery, carrots, garlic, parsley, thyme, bay leaf, and peppercorns. Bring to a boil, reduce the heat to low, and simmer, skimming periodically, for 1 hour.

4. Strain the stock into a large bowl. Let cool to room temperature. Divide into quart containers and refrigerate for up to 2 days or freeze for up to 6 months.

KNOCKOUT DOUGHS

These doughs and baked goods—from pasta to pizza—are my go-tos on set, and the best part is you can make many of them ahead of time and have them on hand whenever you need.

Pasta Dough

I'm called upon to make homemade pasta often on *Beat Bobby Flay,* and that's okay by me because pasta is one of my favorite things to make *and* to eat. I use this winning recipe to make everything from ravioli to tortelloni, fettuccine to egg noodles. The good thing about pasta dough is that you can make it a day or two in advance and keep it tightly wrapped in the refrigerator.

✱ **NOTE:** To refrigerate or freeze pasta dough after step 1, form it into a ball, dust it with a bit of flour, wrap it well in plastic wrap, and then put it into a zip-top freezer bag.

MAKES ABOUT 1½ POUNDS

2 cups all-purpose flour, plus more for rolling

3 large eggs

1 large egg yolk

1. Combine the flour, whole eggs, and egg yolk in a food processor and pulse until a dough comes together. Transfer to a counter dusted lightly with flour and knead gently until the dough is smooth, about 1 minute. Wrap in plastic wrap and refrigerate for at least 30 minutes and up to 24 hours.

2. Divide the dough into 4 pieces. With your hands, flatten and shape one piece of dough into a rectangle ½ inch thick. Dust it lightly with flour and pass it through a pasta machine on the thickest setting. If the dough comes out oddly shaped, reshape into a rectangle. Fold it in thirds, like a letter, and, if necessary, flatten it to a ½-inch thickness. Pass it through the pasta machine on the thickest setting again, with the seam of the letter perpendicular to the rollers. Repeat this folding-and-rolling step 10 to 12 times, dusting the dough with flour if it becomes sticky.

3. Without folding the dough, pass it through the pasta machine on the next thinnest setting. Keep reducing the space between the rollers after each pass, lightly dusting the pasta with flour on both sides each time, until the pasta sheet is about $\frac{1}{16}$ inch thick.

4. Lay the sheet of rolled-out dough on a counter and cover it with a kitchen towel. Roll out the remaining dough. Cut each sheet crosswise into 11-inch lengths. Use a sharp knife to cut the dough into your desired noodle shape: fettuccine, pappardelle, etc. (Alternatively, if you have a cutting attachment on your pasta machine, use that.)

5. If you're not cooking the pasta right away, let it dry on a sheet pan for 1 to 2 minutes. Dust well with flour so the strands do not stick together and loosely fold or form them into small nests. Let dry for about 30 minutes more, then wrap in plastic wrap and store in the refrigerator for up to 2 days or freeze for up to 30 days.

VARIATIONS

Black Squid Ink Pasta

Add 1 tablespoon squid ink to the eggs and whisk until combined.

Black Pepper Pasta

Add 2 tablespoons coarsely ground black pepper to the flour.

Smoked Paprika Pasta

Add 2 teaspoons sweet smoked Spanish paprika to the flour.

Saffron Pasta

Add 1 large pinch or about a tablespoon of saffron threads to the whisked eggs and let it bloom for a minute before adding to the flour.

Pizza Dough

There are a few things you just can't cram into 45 minutes, and this pizza dough is one of them. Pizza dough has to be made at least 24 hours and up to 2 days in advance of cooking. Now I have no idea if it will be a pizza battle till it's revealed on screen, but since pizza dough can't be made and baked in the allotted time, the kitchen will have made it for me in advance so it's ready to go when the competition starts. (My assistant supplies the Food Network kitchen staff with many of my recipes in advance, should they be needed for a battle.) This is my all-time favorite pizza dough, based on chef Chris Bianco's recipe. I have been making it for years at home and in my restaurants.

MAKES 4 PIZZAS

2¼ cups warm water

0.6 ounce fresh yeast or 1 (7 g) envelope active dry yeast

1 tablespoon kosher salt

2 tablespoons extra-virgin olive oil, plus more for the bowl

5 cups all-purpose flour, plus more for rolling

1. Place ¼ cup of the warm water in the bowl of a stand mixer fitted with the dough hook. Add the fresh yeast and mix until dissolved (if using dry yeast, stir and let it stand for a few minutes to rehydrate). Add 1½ cups of the warm water, the salt, and oil and mix a few seconds. Add the flour, 1 cup at a time, until the dough comes together; if it appears too dry, add a little more of the remaining water. Turn the dough out of the bowl and knead on a floured surface until smooth. Shape into a ball.

2. Place the dough in a lightly oiled bowl, cover, and let stand at room temperature until double in size, about 45 minutes.

3. Divide the dough into 4 balls, place them on a sheet pan, cover, and let rise in the refrigerator for at least 8 hours and up to 2 days. The dough will rise slightly in the refrigerator. Remove from the refrigerator and let sit for 30 minutes before using.

Biscuits

I serve biscuits alongside many savory dishes, and sweet ones, too—I wrap apples in this very dough for my show-winning apple dumplings (page 211). The key to competition-winning biscuits is to keep the butter very cold and to make sure you don't overwork the dough.

MAKES 8 BISCUITS

4 cups all-purpose flour, plus more for rolling

4 teaspoons baking powder

1 teaspoon baking soda

1 teaspoon salt

1½ sticks (12 tablespoons) cold unsalted butter, cut into small pieces

1½ cups very cold well-shaken buttermilk

½ cup heavy cream

2 teaspoons freshly ground black pepper, not superfine or coarse—somewhere in between (optional)

1. Preheat the oven to 450°F. Line a sheet pan with parchment paper.

2. Combine the flour, baking powder, baking soda, and salt in a large bowl. Cut in the butter using your fingers or a pastry cutter until the mixture resembles coarse meal. Add the buttermilk and gently mix until the dough just begins to come together.

3. Scrape the dough onto a lightly floured counter. Pat the dough into a 10 × 12-inch rectangle about ¾ inch thick. Use a 3-inch round cutter to cut out biscuits. Press the scraps of dough together and repeat the process to make a total of 8 biscuits.

4. Put the biscuits on the prepared sheet pan. Brush the tops with cream and sprinkle with the pepper (if using). Bake the biscuits until lightly golden brown, 12 to 15 minutes. Cool on a wire rack.

✖ **NOTE:** You can also cut the biscuits into squares so that you don't need special equipment and there are no scraps to rework or waste.

Cast-Iron Skillet Cornbread

This is another of my favorite recipes to make at home and on *Beat Bobby Flay*. There are two must-haves: buttermilk—which adds a great tang, ensures a tender crumb, and keeps the bread moist—and a cast-iron skillet. Preheating the skillet in the oven before baking guarantees a beautiful crust every time.

MAKES ONE 9-INCH ROUND CORNBREAD

1¼ **cups coarsely ground yellow cornmeal**

¾ **cup all-purpose flour**

¼ **cup pure cane sugar**

1 **teaspoon kosher salt**

2 **teaspoons baking powder**

½ **teaspoon baking soda**

1⅓ **cups well-shaken buttermilk**

2 **large eggs, lightly beaten**

1 **stick (8 tablespoons) unsalted butter, melted**

Cooking spray

FOR SERVING (OPTIONAL)

Unsalted butter, at room temperature

Hot sauce

1. Preheat the oven to 400°F. Put a 9-inch cast-iron skillet in the oven to heat while you make the batter.

2. Whisk the cornmeal, flour, sugar, salt, baking powder, and baking soda in a large bowl. Whisk the buttermilk and eggs together in a measuring cup. Add to the dry ingredients and whisk until almost combined. Add the melted butter and whisk until just smooth.

3. Remove the skillet from the oven using oven mitts and mist liberally with cooking spray. Scrape the batter into the pan and smooth the top. Bake until a toothpick inserted into the center comes out with a few moist crumbs attached (remember that the cornbread will continue to bake in the hot pan as it cools), 18 to 22 minutes.

4. Serve warm with butter and hot sauce, if desired.

ANYTHING-BUT-BASIC BASICS

These are essentials that I've had in my repertoire for years—sure, you can get some of these items store-bought, but nothing beats homemade. Plus, many of these recipes are easy to double or triple—the future you will thank you.

Bobby's Barbecue Sauce

This is my go-to barbecue sauce and it has been for years. I slather it on chicken, ribs, and steak and even use it as a base for other sauces. I bring it to the table often in my battles (e.g., Carolina Veggie Burger with Smoked Gouda & Dijon-Scallion Slaw, page 27), and its perfect balance of sweet and spicy is responsible for many wins.

MAKES ABOUT 3 CUPS

3 tablespoons canola oil

1 large Spanish onion, coarsely chopped

5 garlic cloves, coarsely chopped

3 tablespoons ancho chile powder

1½ tablespoons sweet Spanish paprika

1 teaspoon chile de árbol powder or cayenne pepper

2 cups ketchup

2 heaping tablespoons Dijon mustard

2 tablespoons red wine vinegar

2 tablespoons Worcestershire sauce

2 canned chipotle peppers in adobo sauce, chopped

¼ cup packed dark brown sugar

2 tablespoons clover honey

2 tablespoons molasses

Kosher salt and freshly ground black pepper

1. Heat the oil over medium-high heat in a heavy-bottomed medium saucepan. Add the onion and cook until soft, 3 to 4 minutes. Add the garlic and cook for 1 minute. Add the spices and cook for 1 minute. Add the ketchup and 1 cup water, bring to a boil, and simmer for 5 minutes.

2. Add the mustard, vinegar, Worcestershire, chipotles, brown sugar, honey, and molasses. Simmer, stirring occasionally, for 20 minutes to thicken.

3. Transfer the mixture to a food processor and purée until smooth. Season with salt and black pepper to taste. Pour the sauce into a bowl and let cool to room temperature. The sauce will keep, tightly covered, in the refrigerator for up to 1 week or in the freezer for up to 6 months.

VARIATION

Bourbon BBQ Sauce

Add ¼ cup bourbon (a good-quality one, but not your best one—keep that for sipping) to the pan after the onion-garlic mixture is softened. Cook until completely reduced, then proceed as directed above. Store, tightly covered, in the refrigerator for up to 5 days or in the freezer for up to 6 months.

Marinara Sauce

This is my favorite quick marinara sauce that I use for spaghetti and meatballs, on my pizza Margherita, and as a base for countless other dishes. Using top-quality San Marzano tomatoes is really important in achieving a balanced sauce. I like adding basil at the end.

MAKES 4 CUPS

2 tablespoons extra-virgin olive oil

1 large Spanish onion, finely diced

5 garlic cloves, mashed to a paste with ¼ teaspoon kosher salt

¼ teaspoon Calabrian chile flakes

2 tablespoons tomato paste

2 (28-ounce cans) whole peeled tomatoes, undrained

¼ cup chopped fresh flat-leaf parsley

1 tablespoon finely chopped fresh oregano

Kosher salt and freshly ground black pepper

¼ cup chopped fresh basil leaves (optional)

1. Heat the oil in a large Dutch oven over high heat until shimmering. Add the onion and cook until soft, about 4 minutes. Add the garlic and chile flakes and cook for 1 minute.

continued >

2. Add the tomato paste and cook, stirring constantly, until deepened in color, about 2 minutes. Add the tomatoes and their juices and cook until the tomatoes begin to break down, using a potato masher to help crush them, about 15 minutes. Add the parsley and oregano and cook until the mixture thickens, about 15 minutes. Season with salt and pepper.

3. Stir in the basil (if using) and taste for seasoning. Use immediately, or let cool to room temperature and store, tightly covered, in the refrigerator for 3 days or in the freezer for up to 6 months.

Roasted Peppers & Chiles

I use roasted peppers and chiles a lot, and I mean *a lot*, a lot. They pack so much flavor—from spicy to earthy—in such a small package. I slice and fold them into relishes, as well as purée them and stir into sauces and condiments.

Bell peppers or poblano peppers

Serrano, Fresno, habanero, or jalapeño chiles

Canola oil

Kosher salt and freshly ground black pepper

1. Preheat the oven to 425°F.

2. Brush the peppers and/or chiles with a few teaspoons of oil and season with salt and black pepper. Arrange the peppers and/or chiles on a sheet pan and roast, turning a few times, until the skins are charred and the flesh is soft, about 20 minutes for peppers and 12 minutes for smaller chiles.

3. Transfer the peppers and/or chiles to a bowl, cover the bowl tightly with foil or plastic wrap, and let steam for 15 minutes. Remove the skins and seeds and use the flesh according to the recipe. Store, tightly covered, in the refrigerator for up to 5 days.

Roasted Garlic

When it's the sweeter, more mellow flavor of garlic I'm after—as opposed to the assertive taste of quickly sautéed garlic or the sharp taste of raw garlic—this is how I get it. On set, I have to use higher heat and less time than I call for here in order to quickly roast the garlic within the given time restrictions, but I far prefer to roast it for a little longer at a lower heat when I have the time.

MAKES 4 HEADS

4 heads garlic

½ cup extra-virgin olive oil

Kosher salt and freshly ground black pepper

1. Preheat the oven to 400°F.

2. Using a serrated knife, slice off the top quarter of the garlic heads, exposing as many cloves as possible. Arrange the garlic heads, cut-side up, in an 8- or 9-inch square baking dish (make sure the garlic heads sit flat).

3. Drizzle the oil over each head and season with salt and pepper. Cover the dish tightly with foil and roast until lightly golden brown and soft, about 1 hour. Let cool slightly.

4. From the bottom up, squeeze each head to push out the garlic cloves (peel skins from any completely enclosed cloves). Transfer the garlic and cooking oil to an airtight container. Store in the refrigerator for up to 2 weeks.

Avocado Relish

Sometimes I call it guacamole, sometimes I call it avocado relish. You can just call it delicious. I prefer my version with some texture, not completely smooth; the key to that is not to overmix it. I have been making this recipe since I was nineteen.

MAKES ABOUT 4 CUPS

4 Hass avocados, cut into large dice

¼ cup finely diced red onion

Juice of 2 limes

1 or 2 jalapeño or serrano chiles, fresh or roasted (see left)

¼ cup chopped fresh cilantro leaves

Kosher salt and freshly ground black pepper

Combine the avocado, onion, lime juice, chiles, and cilantro in a large bowl. Using a fork, coarsely mash the ingredients together. Season with salt and pepper to taste.

EGGS

Yup, I'm gonna say it: When in doubt, put an egg on it! It's trendy (if one can call this most simple of ingredients trendy) but true. There is something about a poached or fried or soft-cooked egg that wows the judges every time. The key, though, is that an egg has to be perfectly prepared, and the common denominator for all methods is the yolk. It has to be *just* right! So, if you are going to add an egg, learn how to make it perfectly by following these recipes.

Poached Eggs

A perfectly poached egg—with its warm, creamy yolk surrounded by a pure soft white—is a beautiful thing. This is one time where you really want to make sure your eggs are super fresh—the fresh ones always hold their shape better when poaching. Whatever your eggs' age, a splash of vinegar will help them set.

SERVES 4

2 teaspoons distilled white or white wine vinegar

Kosher salt

4 large eggs

Freshly ground black pepper

1. Line a plate with paper towels or a clean kitchen towel. Fill a high-sided medium pot with 3 inches of water. Add the vinegar, season with salt, and bring to a simmer. (Look for just a few bubbles; it should never boil.) Gently crack an egg into a ramekin and then slowly slide the egg into the center of the pot, letting the water swirl around it and allowing the white to envelop the yolk. Repeat with 3 more eggs.

2. Cook until the whites are set but the yolks are still runny, about 4 minutes. Once the eggs are perfectly poached, remove them from the water with a slotted spoon and let drain on the paper towels. Season with salt and pepper. Serve immediately.

Perfect Scrambled Eggs

Creamy scrambled eggs can't be rushed, so keep it low and slow—and don't skimp on the butter.

SERVES 4 TO 6

12 large eggs

4 tablespoons cold unsalted butter, cut into small pieces

¼ cup crème fraîche

Kosher salt and freshly ground black pepper

ADDITIONAL FLAVORINGS (OPTIONAL)

¼ cup thinly sliced scallions

2 tablespoons finely chopped fresh chives

4 ounces Bûcheron goat cheese, cut into pieces

1. Crack the eggs into a large bowl and whisk until light, frothy, and uniform in color. Strain the eggs through a fine-mesh sieve into a separate bowl.

2. Combine the butter and crème fraîche in a large nonstick sauté pan. Pour the eggs into the pan, set over low heat, and mix gently with a heat-resistant silicone spatula or a wooden spoon until soft curds form, about 6 minutes. Remove from the heat (the eggs will still be somewhat wet). Season with salt and pepper and stir in any additional flavorings you'd like. Let stand for 1 minute more to allow the heat of the pan to finish cooking the eggs. Serve immediately.

Fried Eggs & Over-Easy Eggs

The only difference between fried eggs and over-easy eggs is that the over-easy is, well, turned over, while the fried is not. There's always a risk of breaking the yolk with over-easy, though, so my tip is, instead of flipping the egg, cover the pan for the last few seconds of cooking until the white is set but the yolk is still runny. No flipping = no broken yolk.

1 tablespoon unsalted butter

1 large egg

Kosher salt and freshly ground black pepper

Melt the butter in a nonstick pan over high heat. Crack the egg into the pan, reduce the heat to low, and cook until the white is set and the yolk begins to thicken but has not become hard, 2 minutes. Season the top with salt and pepper. Cover the pan and cook for another 15 seconds for a runny yolk. Slide onto a plate, or alongside whatever you are serving it with.

Soft-Boiled Eggs

I don't really eat a lot of soft-boiled eggs or use them in my cooking, but I have had to make them on *Beat Bobby Flay* for ramen soup and, most notably, for Scotch eggs (see page 143). The sign of a perfect soft-boiled egg is the jammy center when you break into it. This is a foolproof method for hitting that mark every single time.

6 large eggs

Fill a large bowl with ice and water. Bring a medium pot of water to a simmer over medium heat. Using a slotted spoon, carefully lower the eggs in and cook for exactly 6 minutes. Remove the eggs one by one with the slotted spoon and plunge into the ice bath. Let the eggs sit until cool, about 5 minutes, before carefully peeling.

DUELING TEXTURES

Balance is one of the most important factors in good cooking. You're always looking for a balance of seasoning, acidity, and, just as important, contrasting textures. Flavor is often cited as the most important factor when it comes to delicious food; however, when it comes to the final decision, texture usually wins. Think about fried chicken: It could be perfectly seasoned, but if it isn't crunchy, it's just disappointing. A bowl of creamy, cheesy grits is delicious, but top it with crispy oven-roasted bacon and that dish flies off the charts. These recipes are some of my favorite ways to add crispy, crunchy layers of texture to just about any meal.

Bobby's Spice Rub

Yes, a spice rub adds flavor, but applied properly and seared in a cast-iron skillet or on a hot grill, it also creates an amazing crust on steaks, burgers, ribs, chicken, and even fish. I use this often on *Beat Bobby Flay*, for example in Spice-Crusted Shrimp with Cheesy Grits & Pickled Chiles (page 57) and Spice-Crusted Lamb Gyros with Tangerine-Harissa Sauce & Pomegranate-Pickled Shallots (page 123), to name just two.

MAKES ABOUT ⅔ CUP

⅓ cup sweet Spanish paprika

2 tablespoons ancho chile powder

2 teaspoons ground coriander

2 teaspoons ground cumin

2 teaspoons mustard powder

2 teaspoons dried oregano

1½ teaspoons kosher salt

1½ teaspoons freshly ground black pepper

Whisk the paprika, ancho chile powder, coriander, cumin, mustard powder, oregano, salt, and pepper in a small bowl until combined. Store in a tightly sealed container in the pantry for up to 6 months.

Crispy Rice

If there is one single dish that is responsible for me winning on *Beat Bobby Flay*, it is this one—not served on its own, obviously, but alongside braises and Asian-inspired dishes. If the judges were tied on their decision, this coconut rice with its crispy bottom was the deciding factor. This recipe is specifically for coconut rice, but the flavor possibilities don't end there—you can use plain rice cooked in water, or cooked in chicken or shrimp stock, depending on what works best with your dish.

SERVES 4 TO 6

1 (13.5-ounce) can unsweetened full-fat coconut milk, stirred well

2 teaspoons kosher salt

¼ teaspoon freshly ground black pepper

2 cups Carolina long-grain rice

½ cup thinly sliced scallions, plus more for garnish

¼ cup canola oil

1. Combine the coconut milk, 1½ cups water, the salt, and pepper in a medium saucepan and bring to a boil over high heat. Stir in the rice and return to a boil. Reduce the heat to medium-low, cover the pot, and cook until the liquid is absorbed and the rice is tender, about 18 minutes. Remove the pan from the heat and let sit, covered, for 5 minutes.

2. Uncover the rice and fluff with a fork. Spread the rice in an even layer over a large sheet pan and let cool completely, about 30 minutes. The rice can be made up to 24 hours in advance; store it on the sheet pan, covered with plastic wrap, in the refrigerator. (In fact, you will get better results if you make the rice the night before.)

3. Combine the rice and scallions in a large bowl. Heat the oil in a large cast-iron or nonstick skillet over high heat until shimmering. Add the rice and, using a heavy-duty metal spatula, immediately press the rice down into the pan until the top is flat. Cook, without stirring, until the bottom becomes golden brown and crispy, about 5 minutes (start checking at 4 minutes, making sure not to burn it).

continued >

4. Turn the rice over and press down firmly on the top again. Cook until the bottom is golden brown and crispy, about 5 minutes more. Transfer to a platter, sprinkle with more scallions, and serve.

✖ **NOTE:** On the show, I would have to make the rice (which always takes 18 minutes), spread it on a sheet pan, and pop it in the blast chiller for 10 minutes before crisping it in the pan. If you have the foresight and time to make the rice the night before, or if you have leftover rice from a night of takeout, the results will be even better, because the rice really needs to be cool and the grains separated to get the most crispiness. It will not work with warm rice.

Anchovy Bread Crumbs

This is one of my favorite ways to add texture and salty flavor to pastas and risotto. Gotta love that umami/texture double punch.

MAKES 1 CUP

⅓ **cup extra-virgin olive oil**

5 oil-packed anchovy fillets, chopped

3 garlic cloves, mashed to a paste with ¼ teaspoon kosher salt

1 cup panko bread crumbs

Finely grated zest of 1 lemon

Freshly ground black pepper

1. Heat the oil in a medium skillet over high heat until shimmering. Add the anchovies and cook until dissolved, about 2 minutes. Add the garlic and cook for 1 minute more.

2. Add the panko and spread into an even layer. Cook until golden brown, about 3 minutes. Flip the crumbs, press them into an even layer again, and cook until the bottom is golden brown, about 3 minutes longer. Add the lemon zest and season with pepper and more salt, if desired.

3. Spread on a large plate or sheet pan and let cool. Store, tightly covered, in a cool, dry place for 1 day, or in the refrigerator for up to 3 days. Recrisp in a dry skillet over low heat before using.

Crispy Chicken Skin

Crispy, crackling chicken skin is another win-grabbing addition. NEVER waste the skin of chicken—instead, crisp it up on the stovetop for some salty, savory, crisp bites of deliciousness. You can also slowly render chicken skins over low heat to make your own schmaltz, which can then be added to matzoh balls (see Alex Reznik's Matzoh Ball Soup, page 168), used to fry onions for French onion soup, or even used to fry chicken—chicken-fried chicken, what could be better?

Canola oil

Chicken skin

Kosher salt

Line a plate with paper towels. Pour 2 inches of oil into a medium saucepan and heat over medium heat until shimmering. Working in batches, add the chicken skin and cook, occasionally stirring with a slotted spoon, until golden brown and crispy, 4 to 7 minutes. Remove and drain on the paper towels. Season with salt.

Oven–Roasted Crispy Bacon

You can add bacon to almost anything and earn bonus points, a tactic I have been known to utilize on *Beat Bobby Flay*. The key to perfectly cooked, flat, crispy bacon is cooking it on a sheet pan in the oven. Less mess *and* less messing with. If you're a bacon purist, you can leave it as is, but to make it "extra," sprinkle it with brown sugar (see Variation) or brush with one of the glazes that follow.

✖ **NOTE:** Brown sugar needs to melt and caramelize in the oven, but the other glaze variations should be applied only after the bacon is cooked or else it will burn.

MAKES 12 SLICES

12 thick-cut or thin-cut slices bacon

1. Preheat the oven to 425°F.

2. Arrange the bacon on a sheet pan, leaving ¼ inch between each slice. Bake for 10 minutes for thin-cut bacon or 16 minutes for thick-cut.

VARIATION

Brown Sugar–Glazed Bacon

Remove the bacon from the oven 5 minutes before it's done and sprinkle evenly with 7 tablespoons light brown sugar. Return the bacon to the oven and bake for 5 minutes more.

Glazes

Once the bacon is cooked, carefully tilt the pan and drain as much fat as possible into a bowl. Blot the top of the bacon with paper towels and then brush the tops liberally with ½ cup clover honey, maple syrup, sorghum syrup, or, for even more flavor, one of these quick glaze recipes.

Honey-Mustard Horseradish Glaze

2 tablespoons Dijon mustard

2 tablespoons whole-grain mustard

2 tablespoons prepared horseradish, drained

¼ cup clover honey

Kosher salt and freshly ground black pepper

Whisk together the mustards, horseradish, and honey in a small bowl until smooth. Season with salt and pepper to taste.

Maple-Mustard Red Chile Glaze

2 tablespoons Dijon mustard

2 tablespoons whole-grain mustard

2 chipotle chiles in adobo, puréed until smooth

¼ cup pure maple syrup

Kosher salt and freshly ground black pepper

Whisk together the mustards, chipotle chiles, and maple syrup in a small bowl until smooth. Season with salt and pepper to taste.

Crispy Shallots

Crispy shallots, savory and slightly sweet, are used a lot in Southeast Asian cooking, and they are delicious. I love topping everything with them, and they are great for snacking, too. You can store them in a tightly sealed container in your pantry. Simply recrisp them in a 325°F oven on a sheet pan for a few minutes before using.

MAKES ABOUT 4 CUPS

½ cup rice flour

½ cup plus 2 tablespoons ice water

Kosher salt and freshly ground black pepper

Canola oil, for frying

4 large shallots, thinly sliced into rounds

1. Whisk together the rice flour and ice water in a medium bowl until smooth. Season with salt and pepper.

2. Line a plate with paper towels. Heat about 2 inches of oil in a large saucepan or deep sauté pan over medium heat until shimmering. Working in batches, dip the shallots in the batter and let the excess run off. Fry until golden brown and crispy, 7 to 9 minutes. Drain the shallots on the paper towels. Store in a container with a tight-fitting lid at room temperature for up to 5 days.

Toasted Coconut

Coconut is my jam. I love topping both desserts and curries with toasted coconut for a crispy hit of warm, nutty flavor. Keep an eye on it when it's in the oven, and remember to stir it at least once while cooking, as it can burn quickly.

1 cup sweetened or unsweetened shredded or flaked coconut

1. Preheat the oven to 325°F.

2. Spread the coconut on a sheet pan in an even layer and bake, stirring a few times, until lightly golden brown and crispy, about 12 minutes.

3. Transfer the sheet pan to a wire rack and let sit until the coconut is completely cooled. The coconut can be stored, tightly covered, in the pantry for up to 1 month.

Candied Nuts

I often use nut brittles as garnish for dessert battles. Sometimes I add a touch of chile powder, cinnamon, or another complementary spice to the brittle, so consider the recipe below as a jumping-off point. It's a basic ratio of nuts, butter, and sugar and can be doubled or tripled easily. It works well with any nuts; some of my favorites are almonds, Marcona almonds, pecans, and pine nuts.

MAKES ABOUT 1¼ CUPS

1 tablespoon unsalted butter

¼ cup pure cane sugar

1 cup whole nuts

1. Line a sheet pan with a silicone baking mat or parchment paper lightly misted with cooking spray.

2. Melt the butter in a medium nonstick sauté pan over high heat. Stir in the sugar and cook until it melts, 5 minutes. Add the nuts and cook, stirring occasionally, until caramelized, about 5 minutes.

3. Transfer the nuts to the prepared pan in an even layer, carefully separating them with a fork if needed. Let cool completely. The nuts will keep at room temperature, tightly covered, for up to 5 days.

Toasted Nuts

Whether I am adding them to a cookie or cake batter, folding them into rice, or garnishing a curry or braised dish, nuts have to be toasted first to bring out their flavor and give them an extra crunch. I always toast nuts whole and chop them once they've cooled. Here is the best way to do it.

1 cup whole nuts, such as walnuts, pecans, hazelnuts, and cashews

1. Preheat the oven to 325°F.

2. Spread the nuts on a sheet pan in an even layer and bake for 4 minutes. Stir, spread back into an even layer, and toast for 4 minutes longer. Store in a container with a tight-fitting lid at room temperature for up to 5 days or in the freezer for up to 3 months.

ONE-TWO ACID PUNCH

If you pay close attention to what the judges and the cohosts say on the show, you are definitely aware of how often the term "acid" comes up. That's because acid is one of the most important components that make up a winning dish. Much like salt, acid competes with bitter flavor compounds in foods, reducing our perception of the bitter notes while brightening other flavors. Chefs often season dishes not just with salt and pepper but also with acid before serving, using a squeeze of lemon or lime, a splash of vinegar, a dollop of yogurt or crème fraîche, or a few tangy pickled onions to achieve just the right finish. Sometimes you want to taste the acid itself, such as when you squeeze lemon over a piece of fish. Other times the effect is more subtle, as acid can balance a dish and tease out other flavors without calling attention to itself. While I often add the acidic note to a dish via a single ingredient, there are a few components to dishes—like my favorite pickled red onions—that have recipes of their own.

Pickled Red Onions or Shallots

I have a large jar of homemade pickled red onions in my refrigerator at all times. They're the perfect way to add "flair" to a dish, and I love topping pizza, avocado relish, fish tacos, and nachos with them. Truth be told, sometimes I just eat them on their own. Grenadine adds an additional touch of sweetness while amplifying the onions' vibrant magenta color.

MAKES ABOUT 2 CUPS

3 cups red wine vinegar

1 cup fresh lime juice

¼ cup pure cane sugar

¼ cup grenadine

1 tablespoon kosher salt

2 large red onions, halved and thinly sliced, or 8 large shallots, thinly sliced crosswise

1. Combine the vinegar, lime juice, sugar, grenadine, salt, and 1 cup water in a large saucepan. Bring to a boil over high heat and cook, whisking a few times, until the sugar has dissolved, about 5 minutes. Remove from the heat and let cool for 5 minutes.

2. Put the onions or shallots in a nonreactive container with a lid and pour the brine over the top. Let cool. Cover and refrigerate for at least 1 hour and up to 48 hours before serving. They will keep in the refrigerator for up to 3 months.

VARIATION

Saffron-Pickled Shallots

Replace the red wine vinegar and lime juice with white wine vinegar and add a small pinch of saffron to the pickling liquid.

Pickled Chiles

These pickled chiles are a thousand times fresher than any canned variety. Float them on a spicy Bloody Mary, scatter them across a plate of nachos, or layer them on a cheeseburger—you'll find plenty of ways to sneak them into any meal.

MAKES ABOUT 1½ CUPS

2 cups red wine vinegar

3 tablespoons pure cane sugar

1 teaspoon kosher salt

8 large fresh chiles, such as Fresnos, jalapeños, serranos, or habaneros, thinly sliced

1. Combine the vinegar, the sugar, salt, and ½ cup water in a medium saucepan and bring to a boil over high heat. Cook until the sugar and salt are dissolved, about 5 minutes. Remove from the heat and let cool for 5 minutes.

2. Put the chiles in a nonreactive container with a lid and pour the brine over them. Let sit for at least 30 minutes for a quick pickle or let cool, cover tightly, and refrigerate for at least 1 day and up to 72 hours.

Homemade Hot Sauce

There are tons of great artisanal hot sauces on the market these days, not to mention commercially produced ones like Frank's RedHot and Tabasco, so by all means use your favorite if you have one. But if you're up for it, try making your own—it's easy to do, and you can tailor its heat and flavor to your liking.

MAKES ABOUT 4 CUPS

1 pound fresh chiles, such as Fresno, jalapeño, serrano, or habanero (or a combination of any or all)

2 tablespoons canola oil

Kosher salt and freshly ground black pepper

1½ cups white wine vinegar, cider vinegar, or rice vinegar

Clover honey (optional)

1. Preheat the oven to 425°F.

2. Arrange the chiles on a sheet pan, add the oil, sprinkle with salt and pepper, and toss to coat. Roast, stirring once, until golden brown and blistered, about 12 minutes.

3. Remove the chiles to a bowl, cover tightly with foil or plastic wrap, and let steam for 15 minutes. Remove the skins and seeds from the chiles and discard.

4. Combine the roasted chiles (or fresh chiles, if using fresh), vinegar, and ½ teaspoon salt in a blender and blend until smooth. Taste the sauce and, if it is too hot or acrid for your taste, add a drizzle of honey to balance the flavor. The hot sauce can be stored, tightly covered, in the refrigerator for up to 6 months.

ACKNOWLEDGMENTS

Usually in each book I've written, I have a significant list of people whom I'm thankful for in the context of bringing that book to life. In this case, after careful deliberation, I've decided there is just an overwhelming number of people who need to be acknowledged. Out of pure fear of accidentally leaving some people out, I've decided to give a group thank-you to all who have had a hand in bringing *Beat Bobby Flay* to life—in the arena, on the screen, and throughout these pages.

So to all of the chefs, cohosts, production teams, culinary squads, Food Network execs, publishing peeps, and, of course, the B-Team, my friends and members of my family: Thank you for getting on this ride with me. I've never had so much fun with a spatula in my hand. Calabrian chiles, anyone???

Bobby Flay

INDEX

Published in the United States by Clarkson Potter/Publishers,
an imprint of Random House, a division of Penguin Random
House LLC, New York.

www.clarksonpotter.com

CLARKSON POTTER is a trademark and POTTER
with colophon is a registered trademark of
Penguin Random House LLC.

Photographs on pages 2, 3, 7, 10, 82, 96, 102, 112, 142, 156, 172,
184, 190, 208, and 242 from the *Beat Bobby Flay set* provided
courtesy of Food Network.

Library of Congress Cataloging-in-Publication Data
Names: Flay, Bobby, author. | Banyas, Stephanie, author. |
Jackson, Sally, author.
Title: Beat Bobby Flay : conquer the kitchen with 100+ battle-
tested recipes / Bobby Flay with Stephanie Banyas and Sally
Jackson.
Identifiers: LCCN 2020050751 (print) | LCCN 2020050752
(ebook) |
ISBN 9780593232385 (hardcover) | ISBN 9780593232392
(ebook)

Subjects: LCSH: Cooking. | LCGFT: Cookbooks.
Classification: LCC TX714.F627 2021 (print) | LCC TX714
(ebook) |
DDC 641.5—dc23
LC record available at https://lccn.loc.gov/2020050751
LC ebook record available at https://lccn.loc.
gov/2020050752

ISBN 978-0-593-23238-5
Ebook 978-0-593-23239-2

Printed in China

Photographer: Ed Anderson
Food Stylist: Santos Loo
Assistant Food Stylists: Susan Vu, Jun Tan, and Dagne Aiken
Prop Stylist: Valerie Aikman-Smith
Prop Assistant: Rick Corcoran
Editors: Jennifer Sit and Lydia O'Brien
Designer: Jan Derevjanik
Production Editor: Joyce Wong
Production Manager: Kim Tyner
Composition: Merri Ann Morrell and Zoe Tokushige
Copyeditor: Kate Slate
Indexer: Elizabeth T. Parson

10 9 8 7 6 5 4 3 2 1

First Edition